Two for Holding
A SINGLE FATHER COLLEGE HOCKEY ROMANCE

LASAIRIONA MCMASTER

DRAMA LLAMA PUBLISHING

Copyright © 2021 by Lasairiona McMaster

The moral right of Lasairiona McMaster to be identified as the author of this work has been asserted in accordance with the copyright, designs, and patents act of 1988.

All rights reserved.

No part of this book may be reproduced in any form or by any electronic or mechanical means, including information storage and retrieval systems, without written permission from the author, except for the use of brief quotations in a book review. Your support for the Author's rights is appreciated.

All the characters in this book are fictitious and any resemblance to actual persons living or dead, are purely coincidental.

Dedication

For every parent out there – you're not alone.
None of us know what the fuck we're doing and we all question ourselves.
To be honest, sometimes I also question my child's childing.
For Lewis – I'm kidding. Mostly.

CHAPTER 1
Sabrina

Since when did Target sell vibrators? It really was becoming a one-stop-shop. After her second call of the day from her parents, Sabrina stood weighing up two adult toys like she was deciding whether to buy crunchy or smooth peanut butter. Since crunchy PB was for heathens, however, committing to a battery operated bed partner was proving to be more difficult. She was tempted to try the Vibrating Feather, but the Vibrating Arc looked like it would be more fun, so she grabbed the multicolored box and tossed it into the cart next to the pack of razor-blades.

Something special happened when you walked through the sliding doors of a Target store. It was as though you were transported to another world just by crossing the threshold. A world where everything you never knew you needed lay under one roof. To get to the magical world of all-the-things, you first had to pass by the gauntlet of a Starbucks counter, restrooms, and fresh hot popcorn.

Corporations knew you needed to empty your bladder before you embarked on an Olympic sport level shopping trip. Get them in the door, and don't let them leave.

On the other hand, maybe the universe knew you needed to keep your hands occupied with chocolate Frappuccinos and the most delicious snack known to humankind: salty, buttery popcorn. Walking around with both hands free, you'd end up selling your left kidney to pay for the $1,600 cart you'd inevitably end up with at the checkout.

One hand on the handle of the cart, she steered around the not-quite-big-enough space, while the other hand cradled a venti, double chocolatey chip crème Frappuccino. She was doing a service to her bank account, and her left kidney – she was, after all, rather attached to it. At least that's what she told herself as she steered the cart around the sunglasses, sun hats, and purses section.

She'd have to factor some kind of penance-walk into her week for having such a ginormous indulgence. But for now, she sucked a stubborn chocolate chip out of the straw, coughing when it hit the back of her throat, and made her way into the clothing section.

Her Target time was sacred, methodical, and even though she'd been around the aisles countless times before, she still walked each and every one, each and every time. Who knew what shiny new treasures they'd put out since the last time she'd visited? Sure, it was only three days ago, but a lot could change in three days.

She reached out and traced her fingers along the shoulder of a gray sweater hanging at the front of a display. Why did clothes never look quite the same off the rack? You fell in insta-love with something hanging on a faceless mannequin, but when you tried it on in front of those judgy AF dressing room mirrors, it was all kinds of wrong.

Not feeling a clothing-spree vibe from today's trip to Valhalla, she set off to find snacks, a screeching noise grinding her to a halt. Unhooking the broken clothes hanger caught in the wheel of her cart, she pushed forward.

By the time she got to the cereal aisle, Sabrina had a mismatch of items in her cart. She picked up a floppy hat to add to her growing collection and kids' sunscreen – because despite her golden brown skin, she still burned to a crisp, even in the Minnesota winter sun.

She had grabbed three pairs of socks, already un-pairing them in her head, because she never wore a matching pair.

The cereal aisle brought out her inner kid, always torn between what she wanted to eat and what she *should* eat. The lure of Cinnamon Toast Crunch was winning out as she scanned the shelves. A soft *pop*, followed by the unmistakable tinkling of spilling cereal onto the linoleum floor made her spin to find the source of the noise.

A little girl, no more than three years old, sat cross-legged with a bag of Lucky Charms on her lap. The box was cast aside, torn open, shards of colored cardboard strewn across the aisle. Cereal and marshmallow shapes littered her Princess Anna costume and surrounded her like a rainbow of brightly colored sugar. Her plastic crown had slipped off-center and clung to her mop of dark ringlets.

The aisle was otherwise empty. Where were her parents?

"Hi." Sabrina closed the eight-foot gap between them and crouched low. "Does your mommy know you're here?"

The little girl's head canted and her eyebrows stitched together in a confused frown. She shoveled another handful of cereal into her already chewing mouth before offering a saliva-covered pile of reconstituting marshmallows to Sabrina.

Giggling, she shook her head, while untangling the little girl's crown and putting it right. "No thank you, but we should probably find your parents. I'm pretty sure they're going to be worried about you."

"Jude!" A dark-haired man sprinted toward them from the end of the aisle. He raked his hand through his stylish hair before scraping a palm across his stricken face. "I..." He bent over, hands on his knees before straightening and rubbing his chest. He crouched next to the little girl. "We've talked about you wandering off, baby girl."

The little girl giggled, shoving a handful of cereal at her older brother's face.

"Not funny, Ju-Ju." He re-straightened her crown.

Sabrina's ovaries clenched. Unsure of how to extricate herself from the situation, she opted for the back-away-quietly-and-hope-no-one-notices approach.

It was all going so well until the traitorous toasted oat pieces crunched underfoot.

The man's head jerked up as though he'd only just realized someone else was there, and he did a double take. So did she. Oh god. She'd know those cornflower blue eyes and shirt-straining six-pack anywhere. Russell Stewart from her French class.

Her stomach lurched, threatening to upheave the now curdling Frappuccino from its sloshing grasp. Embarrassment clawed at her chest, forcing her breaths to come in short, shallow pants.

She'd done a stellar job of avoiding him since their unfortunate encounter in the men's restroom when he'd rescued her with a wad of toilet paper from another stall earlier in the semester. She swallowed hard and wiped a clammy palm along her thigh. Maybe he didn't remember her. Maybe things like that happened to him all the time and she wouldn't stand out among the droves of women who threw themselves at his deliciousness.

She swallowed again.

She forced her eyes back to the little princess. So he spent his Saturday mornings hanging out with Anna of Arendelle. Interesting. It still didn't cover her embarrassment at having met him in the men's room, but it soothed her wound just a tad.

Say something. You're just staring at him! Speak!

"R-Russell?" Whose voice had come out of her mouth? And why did it sound so raspy?

The worry and fear painted over his face as he'd run toward them dissipated, replaced by a mask of calm indifference. But his eyes... they weren't just indifferent, they were cold. As icy as Elsa's freakin' castle atop The North Mountain.

Sabrina was heart-on-her sleeve fire. Every emotion that rippled through her, she wore like a badge of honor. She was passionate and outspoken, and as strikingly handsome as Russell Stewart was with his chiseled jaw and pale blue eyes, she had no idea how to handle... ice. She shivered.

Despite being on the hockey team, Russell Stewart kept to himself. He was often missing from parties and group activities, shrouded in an air of mystery. Seeing him interacting with his little sister, the panic, fear, overtly raw emotion that had distorted his otherwise stoic face, squeezed her heart.

"I'll just..." She pointed a thumb over her shoulder and turned to leave, hugging the box of Cinnamon Toast Crunch against her chest.

Cereal crunched underfoot, but she didn't stop, she kept walking, pulse thundering in her ears.

She liked to people-watch. It didn't hurt when the people she watched looked as delectable as Russ did. They'd barely spoken two words to each other in their whole first year in class together, so he couldn't hate her, could he?

"Let's get you cleaned up, princess."

A smattering of Lucky Charms fell to the floor as Jude stood. The sound of a hand sweeping against fabric, for some reason, made Sabrina smile.

"Hey! Uh... I don't know your name, but you forgot your cart."

Her cart, right. She could pretend it wasn't hers so she

wouldn't have to look at his unfairly attractive face again. She could pretend she hadn't heard him.

"No, don't. Jude!"

Before she could act, a tiny hand slipped into her palm and tugged her arm. When Sabrina turned, the little girl pointed at her cart and yanked her toward it.

Russell raised an eyebrow and gave a shrug. He stepped toward Jude, arms outstretched. "C'mere, punkin."

Jude looked up at Sabrina, then back to Russell, before dropping Sabrina's hand and flinging herself at Russell's leg. It was the cutest thing she'd ever witnessed, but it seemed Russ had missed the glint of sheer joy and love in the little girl's eyes. *His* eyes were on her cart, or more accurately, on something *in* her cart.

Wonder Woman socks, Tampons, surely he'd seen those before, unless he'd lived a sheltered life... What in her soon-to-be purchases was so exciting it was holding him rapt?

Her stomach coasted off the edge of a cliff and dropped in freefall.

His eyes were pinned to the vibrator box. He tipped his head as though he was trying to either read the box or figure out where it went and how it worked.

Beads of sweat broke out over every inch of Sabrina's body as Russ's curiosity morphed into something else right in front of her eyes. She didn't know him well enough to know what the look meant, but despite the Ice King radiating chilly fuck-off-and-leave-me-alone vibes, something warm flickered in his gaze.

She cleared her throat and his gaze flicked from the cart to her face.

Strike that, something hot.

And if she didn't take her cart and leave, she'd need to strip off and jump into one of the freezers in the frozen section to survive.

He jerked his chin at her basket, face deadpan. "Have fun."

Unable to look him in the eye, she grabbed the handle of the cart and fled.

Russell Stewart had seen her buying a vibrator, in Target. After seeing her in the men's room at school. It was official: she'd have to change schools, leave the state, and change her name. Maybe she'd move to Canada.

"More, Daddy!"

Sabrina stumbled over her feet, attempting to spin the cart in front of her for support so she didn't crash onto her face.

Daddy?

What? No. He couldn't be the little girl's father, right? How had she been in class with this man for over a year and not known he had a child? She pulled her top lip between her teeth. It wasn't that unusual – there was plenty she didn't know about people in her class. But a kid?

She cast a furtive glance over her shoulder. Russ's forehead was leaning against Jude's.

"No more cereal, bug. You won't eat your lunch. We need to go find someone to get me a broom so I can sweep up this mess of yours. Then we gotta get some groceries, grab you a birthday present, *then* we gotta go see Mimi."

The little girl's face lit up like Time Square at the mention of Mimi.

"Deal?"

The little girl nodded.

Smiling to herself, Sabrina rounded the corner into the next aisle. This side of Russ was nothing short of adorable, but it left her with questions she had no business wondering about.

Was Russ in a relationship? Who was the girl's mother? Didn't Russ room on campus with one of the other hockey players? Who had the little girl when he was at school, her Mom? Mimi?

As she picked up her groceries, the question that kept coming up was whether or not Russ would give another thought to the fact he'd just busted her purchasing a vibrator.

Turned out, Target's wonders had nothing on the mystery that was Russell Stewart.

CHAPTER 2
Russell

Russell's heart still raced as he swooped Jude up and attempted to coax her tiny, thrashing body back into the seat of their cart.

Did kids somehow grow extra limbs when it came to things like dressing them, bathing them, and trying to cram their tiny frames into a cart? It sure as hell felt like it.

"No! No, no, no, Daddy!"

He rubbed at the stubborn knot in his chest. How did parents cope with the burden of responsibility hanging over them for eighteen years?

Would it get easier? Or would his current fears simply morph into the next ones?

His stomach clenched. Considering his experience of the first two years of her life, it was the latter. Running off in a Target superstore was one thing, but boyfriends? He needed to figure out a way to keep her young so he wouldn't have to give her future boyfriends a beat down.

"No, Daddy! No!"

"Baby girl, I need you to sit in here, okay? This is what happens when you run off and give daddy a heart attack."

The little girl folded her arms and scowled. He kissed her cheek and the duo set off to find a staff member to ask for a dustpan and brush to clean up the cereal carnage his two-year-old-terror had left behind.

He turned into the next aisle, and there she was... again.

Previously referred to in his brain as Sexy-in-the-Stall, she would now be known as Vibrator Girl. As he approached the Target employee he created a persona for the new and unsuspecting superhero standing staring blankly at the label of a can of soup.

Nothing quite said 'superhero' like the ability to hand out orgasms on command. He chuckled, covering it with a cough behind his hand when she turned and caught his gaze.

"Excuse me." He approached the older lady stacking the shelves with a warm smile. "I'm sorry but my daughter burst open a box of cereal in the next aisle." Jabbing a thumb over his shoulder toward the cereal, he gave an awkward laugh before cramming his hands in his pockets and rocking back on his heels. "I was wondering if you could get me something to clean it up with, please."

Her gaze flitted between the still-scowling two year old gripping the handle of the cart, and Russell. The woman's pursed lips puckered as though she was fighting a smile and mirth danced in her eyes. She gave a slow and somber nod. "Absolutely. But I'm sorry to say, the person who caused the mess must be the one to tidy it up."

Jude's eyebrows relaxed from their deep frown and shot up her forehead. Eyes wide, her jaw dropped open.

He chuckled. "I'm sure Princess Anna wouldn't mind picking up after herself, right Punkin?"

The little girl shook her head and the Target employee smiled. "Don't sweat it. I'll take care of it."

Russ waved a hand at her. "No, please. At least let me help

clean up? I need to grab the empty box so I can pay for her... uh... snack, anyway."

She lowered her voice. "It's all good. It can be our little secret, right Princess Anna?" She winked at Jude before tapping the side of her nose and leaving, humming *Do You Want to Build a Snowman* from the Disney movie *Frozen*.

Raking a hand through his hair he shook his head. "That won't always happen, little one. You should always be prepared to clean up your own messes." He tapped her on the nose.

A snort sounded from Vibrator Girl, still holding the can of soup. "I'll say." She turned to him, eyes wide, and a hand clamped over her mouth.

Fighting the smile making his lips twitch, he raised an eyebrow. Was she blushing? She was freakin' adorable.

"Oh god. That wasn't supposed to be out loud."

Instead of answering, he pushed the cart toward the end of the aisle. He needed to get out of her orbit before he did something stupid, like kiss those perfectly plump, Cupid's bow shaped lips.

She was rounding the corner into the next aisle, so he skipped it, despite needing chips and dip. He didn't want to spend the rest of his shopping trip bumping into the woman who probably thought he was the world's worst father for having lost his two-year-old daughter in the belly of Target, even for a millisecond.

Shame crept along his skin, making his cheeks warm. Never again would he listen to the pleas of the tiny terrorist surveying her confinement as though trying to mastermind a prison break.

Sitting secured in the cart was officially required Target procedure and she'd just have to deal with it.

"Hiiiii!" Her little arm shot out, hand waving back and forth.

Expecting the merciful Target employee who cleaned up after his wayward daughter, he turned. Nope. Not his Target angel after all.

Vibrator Girl groaned, before her visible disappointment at seeing him morphed into a shy smile. She curtseyed to Jude. "Your Majesty."

Jude giggled.

With an incline of her head and a perfectly cool and passive face she added, "Sir Warm-and-Fuzzy."

This woman.

Before he could react, her eyes narrowed at him, she turned, grabbed her cart, and left.

Despite her radiant beauty, the woman's glare-y judgment was killing his shopping vibe. He'd love to hear her name just one parent who hadn't chased their kid through the aisle of a store.

He'd come back at another time… when there was one less sassy, orgasmic superhero to sour his mood in every freakin' aisle.

"Come on, Miss Mischief. Let's blow this popsicle stand and go see Mimi."

"Yay!" Jude's face lit up and she clapped. "Mimi! Mimi!"

He stuttered to a stop almost as fast as he started moving.

Shit.

He at least needed to grab toilet paper. He grimaced. He'd assured his roommate, and best friend, Linc, that he wouldn't forget to grab it when he was out.

Surely he'd be safe from Vibrator Girl in the toilet paper aisle.

"Gotta grab some TP first, baby girl. Can't have Uncle Linc being big mad at Daddy, and stranded on his porcelain throne now, can we?"

"Unca Ink!" She clapped again.

Russ managed to get in and out of the toilet paper aisle

without a Vibrator Girl sighting. He grabbed a family sized bag of Lays, a jar of creamy spinach dip, a multipack of Veggie Straws, and a gallon of orange juice on his way to the self-checkout.

In the parking lot, he sprinted toward the Chevy Impala his parents bought for him when he first found out he was going to be a father. Part of him always thought it was a guilt gift for the fact they got divorced during his SATs, but since he had a baby on the way he couldn't let pride come between him and a safe ride for his kid.

When the cart picked up speed, he lifted his feet off the ground, leaning over the handlebar. Jude shrieked with glee, throwing her head back, dark curls bobbing in the breeze.

"Again!" Her demands started as soon as the cart stopped when they got to the trunk of his car.

"Sorry, Ju-Ju. We can't spend the day causing cart chaos in the Target parking lot."

"Hiiiii!" She waved at someone to his left and his stomach dropped as he turned to see Vibrator Girl loading bags into the trunk of the car two spaces down.

She curtseyed again, this time with a flourish of her arms, sending Jude into a new fit of laughter, but a frown tugged the woman's brows together when she looked at him.

What was this woman's deal? Was she a helicopter mom who judged other parents by her own standards?

Did she have the perfect angel at home waiting for her to return with her carrot sticks and organic hummus?

Wasn't all hummus organic?

First she found his kid eating a bag of Lucky Charms alone in the cereal aisle, then she saw him recklessly free-wheeling his cart through the parking lot with his toddler on board.

He mentally face-palmed.

Would she somehow pop up when he didn't have her in bed by 7PM on the dot, too?

Huh. There wasn't a single tub of hummus to be found in her cart – organic or any other kind for that matter.

Irritation forced a growl-adjacent noise from his chest as he tossed his purchases into the trunk. He was a damn good parent, and he wasn't letting a woman with a cart full of junk food and a permanent frown on her face judge his relationship with the most important woman in his life.

"Uh-oh!" Jude smacked her palm against her head.

He'd been so caught up in his internal monologue that he'd missed the dull clink of a tiara hitting the deck a few feet from where Vibrator Girl stood.

"It's okay, Princess. I got it." V.G. stepped toward the fallen crown.

Russell surged forward. "It's good. We're good. I got it."

Jumping back as though he'd electrocuted her with his words, she mumbled something under her breath and turned back to her car. She paused, gave one final, low curtsy at Jude and wished her a pleasant day with her Prince Charming before bounding into her car and driving away.

Unfortunately, his embarrassment didn't drive away with her.

Why was he so bothered by her frowns and pursed lips? Why did he care what she thought of his parenting skills?

It's not like they were even friends. Other than seeing her a few times in class since their encounter in the men's bathroom, their paths never crossed.

What did her opinion of him matter?

He couldn't answer as he strapped Jude into her rear-facing car seat and closed the door.

What was it about the woman that was getting him so bent out of shape?

His dick twitched in his pants.

It knew the answer, but Russell wasn't prepared to listen to it. What the hell did he care what she thought about him, anyway? And what did it have to do with his dick? Shit. *Did* he have a crush on Vibrator Girl?

Something sharp jabbed his ribs and he bolted upright. Blinking in the dim space, he tried to remember who and where he was. The smell of sweet jasmine and mint mixed with the musty smell of old books assaulted his nasal passages. He rubbed his eyes before rolling his neck and groaning.

Ugh. He'd obviously been asleep long enough for his neck to go stiff.

He reached for his ribs. Someone had poked him, right?

Movement to his left made him start.

Was he dreaming? Or was Vibrator Girl crouched next to his table in the library? If he was dreaming, his subconscious was a cruel bastard.

She looked glorious.

Beams of early morning, golden sunlight from the window high above the library bookshelves lit her up like an angel. Her black, wavy hair hung in front of her face. It took everything he had not to reach out, tangle his fingers in it, and pull her in for a kiss.

He reminded himself he didn't have time for distractions, even if they were beautiful, sassy, women who spent their time glaring at him.

Definitely not a dream.

If it was a dream, she'd have a wide smile on her face and be gazing at him adoringly. She'd also likely be very, very naked.

In reality, however, her brows pinched together and her chocolate, almost black eyes glinted with irritation.

"He lives." Her snarky hissed words were the only sounds

in the all but deserted library. She waved before standing upright. "Actually, I knew that already. Wanna know how I knew that already?"

His brain fought to process her quick-fire speech. Heavy, tired muscles and stinging eyes were doing their level best to drag him back under into the land of nod.

"I'm going to take that grunt as a yes. I knew you were already alive because of the snoring."

What the fuck? He didn't snore.

Did he?

He opened his mouth to speak, but his brain remained on the struggle bus. And even if he had something pithy to retort, she wasn't stopping to let him.

"That shelf-shaking, thunderous, obnoxious noise coming out of someone so peaceful looking was quite the juxtaposition."

Was this chick a theater major, or what? Talk about being dramatic.

"I'm all for grown-up naps and all that, but some of us have work to do. Call me old fashioned, but I came to the library for... y'know... quiet." She turned to leave, before pausing and pointing at the desk. "You might wanna clean that puddle up, too."

He brushed a hand across his chin despite knowing he didn't drool. What the hell was this woman's problem with him?

She sat two desks away, facing him. Pulling a green shiny packet from her pencil case she tore the colored foil and pulled out a chocolate covered marshmallow. His stomach growled in approval of her early morning snack choice.

Would she be any more inclined to share her snack with him if she knew Russell's name was on the packet? Okay, fine, so he wasn't Russell Stover, but he *was* starving, and contemplating offering her twenty bucks for one of her treats.

Pushing back from his desk he closed the space between them, pulled out a chair, and dropped onto it.

She paused from sucking the sticky residue off her thumb and met his gaze with another frown.

Her mouth made a popping noise as she pulled her thumb out, and her tongue snaked around the tip. His dick twitched, clearly not getting the message that this woman just wasn't into him.

"Can I help you, Mr. Warm-and-Fuzzy?"

The corner of his mouth twitched, lips tugging into a lazy smile. "If I recall, it was *Sir* Warm-and-Fuzzy. And yes, yes you may help me, Vibrator Girl."

She coughed, presumably inhaling a chunk of marshmallow because her face turned red and she gulped from her water bottle as she smacked on her chest with an open palm. "V-Vibrator Girl?"

"Not all superheroes wear capes." He shrugged, then jerked his chin at the open packet on the desk. "What's it gonna take for you to give me one of your Stover mallows?"

She giggled, but didn't sound amused. "I see how this works." She folded her arms.

Uh-oh. Arm folding was never good.

"Ice Prince till your stomach rumbles, then you wanna be friends with me to commandeer my snacks?" She waved a dismissive hand. "Be gone, King of Cold."

He chuckled. Was this woman for real? He was coming to her in his hour of need – despite her thinking him a shit father – to ask for sustenance. She was dismissing him, yet had the audacity to call *him* cold?

"Name your price. There's a twenty in my wallet with your name on it."

"For what it's worth..." She tore a chunk of the second chocolate coated marshmallow with her forefinger and thumb, popped it in her mouth, and moaned, before licking the chocolate off her finger. "Daddy Russell is much nicer than..." She gestured at him.

He snorted and leaned back, crossing his ankles, and hands behind his head. "You wanna call me Daddy?"

Her half-squeak half-hiccup and the wide-eyed look of horror painted across her usually scowling face was worth it.

"I mean, it's not my kink, but if it'll get me one of those marshmallows, you can call me whatever the hell you want."

Narrowing her stare, she leaned forward, forearms on the table.

"What?" He shifted under the weight of her heavy gaze.

"I just find it hilarious that you want me to share my snacks after being a douche canoe to me."

"Huh? When was I a douche to you? I gave you toilet paper in the men's restroom – that's, like, the complete opposite of being a douche." Confusion and irritation swelled in his chest. He was a great many things, but surely he'd remember being a douche canoe to a beautiful woman.

"The other day in Target." Her shrug suggested indifference, but the sadness in her eyes gave him pause.

"You mean the day you witnessed one of my epic fail parenting moments and got all Judge Judy with your glaring?"

It was her turn to look confused. "I... what? I wasn't judging you. You're adorable with your daughter, and she's precious."

He dragged a hand through his hair. "Then why all the scowling?"

Throwing her head back, a bright laugh erupted from her. "Oh, Sir Warm-and-Fuzzy, t'was not *I* who was scowling."

Was she right? Linc often called him a scowly bastard so there was every chance she was right. Groaning, he shook his head and covered his face. "I'm sorry. The guys say I have the male equivalent of Resting Bitch Face. And I guess..."

Ugh. What was it about this woman that made him want to bare his soul?

Maybe if he said it in French he wouldn't feel like such an idiot.

"J'étais embarrassé."

"Mais pourqoui?"

"Because I lost my kid in Target, Vibrator Girl." He smiled at her wince. "That's not exactly something to be proud of. And you witnessed it in all its panicked glory."

She popped another chunk of fluffy, chocolatey coated goodness into her mouth before leaning to the side. From deep in her backpack, she produced another triple pack of Russell Stover marshmallows.

He bit down a groan. Was she going to tease him all over again? If he had to watch her eating chocolate covered marshmallows he was going to blow his load in his pants. She wasn't going to share. He was going to have to endure watching her tongue darting out to lick chocolate and sticky marshmallow from her lips while his stomach growled in protest.

Brandishing it at him like a sword, she sighed. "While Vibrator Girl is a solid superhero name, my name is Sabrina, and I'm sorry if you think I had RBF too. I'm menstrual." She slid the package of treats across the table to him.

"I guess that explains the bottomless supply of marshmallows." Russell wasted no time diving in, cramming an entire pumpkin-shaped treat in his mouth.

"Wait, what? No. These aren't period-provisions. This is my every day supply." She gave a wicked grin. "I have an unhealthy obsession with these chocolate covered marshmallows. Just wait for the post-Halloween clearance next week. It's one of my favorite times of the year."

"Valentines sales the other?"

She grinned, almost blinding him with her beautiful smile. "And Easter."

"I didn't think India celebrated Easter." Warmth spread in his chest as her smile grew.

"We don't. My family, I mean. There's a substantial Christian population in India who celebrate it just fine. But I feel like just 'cause I don't celebrate it, doesn't mean I should miss out on discount candy." She winked at him.

"True statement." He crammed another treat into his mouth, chewed and swallowed.

Groaning, she reached for the last one in his packet. "If I'd known what a heathen you are, I wouldn't have shared at all. Cramming that shit in there like it's a crappy Hershey's bar that you need to swallow fast so it doesn't stick in your throat. Dude, this is a Stover-freakin-mallow. Savor that shit."

He liked Hershey chocolate just fine, but the reverence with which she talked about a piece of candy made him wish she'd talk about him like that... Or, about anything, everything, whatever the hell she wanted to talk about, just to hear her voice.

She swooped up his last pumpkin and brought it to her lips, pausing.

His dick stirred again and he fought down a groan as she closed her eyes and inhaled before dragging her tongue along the curve of her lips.

Fuck.

What he'd give to be a goddamn marshmallow about now.

He was going to need to go back to the dorm and blow off some steam under a cold shower to the memory of her mouth wrapped around the pumpkin pinched between her fingers.

No matter how many times he silently reminded the growing bulge in his pants he had no time for girls, it wouldn't listen.

He'd never been more aroused at the sight of a woman with something other than his cock in her mouth.

Clearing his throat he sat up straighter, leaned across the

table and plucked what was left of the snack from her fingers. "I think..." His voice broke. He swallowed and tried again. "I think I can take it from here."

There was no way his dick was letting him forget the image in a hurry and he couldn't pick his kid up from Mom's house sporting a permanent hard on.

Jude.

His heart squeezed and his shoulders sagged.

Between school, hockey, and being a full time dad, he really didn't have time to date. No matter how stunning she looked, or how tempting her mouth was while wrapped around... well, anything.

He pursed his lips and studied her as she watched him right back.

If he couldn't date the stunning woman sitting in front of him, the least he could do was set her up with someone who'd treat her well.

While he wasn't dating, Linc was, and Will had been asking around to see if anyone knew of someone they could set him up with.

Russell had found her. "Can I get your number?"

CHAPTER 3
Sabrina

"Wait, what?" Quinn poked her head up from behind the book she was reading. They'd finished lunch in the cafeteria and had gone back to their dorm room for an hour between classes. "He took your snack, your cell number, and you're going on a date with a *different* hockey player?"

Sabrina closed her eyes and rolled her lips between her teeth. "Mmhmm."

She didn't get it either.

"But I thought Russell Stewart set your panties on fire."

He did. He was also an enigma.

And apparently a huge tease.

Sabrina might not have had much experience with boys, and sure, Quinn did often say that she wouldn't know flirting if it walked up and smacked her in the face, but he *was* flirting.

She was sure of it.

Behind the guarded, prickly exterior, she'd seen heat in his eyes.

Hadn't she?

Not only that, but more than once she'd noticed him shift in his seat or tug at his pant leg.

Maybe it wasn't because of her. It could have simply been a case of morning wood. He had just woken up from a nap after all.

Or maybe it was her who'd been asleep in the library.

Maybe she'd dreamt the hottest player on the college hockey team watched her eating a chocolate covered marshmallow like he wanted her to suck on his—

"Earth to Bre!" Quinn clicked her fingers. "I said I thought Russell Stewart made your lady parts dance."

Her cheeks burned. He did. And they were. She pressed her thighs together in a futile bid to keep the want at bay. "You say that like you know anything about hockey."

"Ah, ah, ah! Don't deflect. I know enough to know those Pirates are all fine AF. I've seen them in their suits around campus." Quinn fanned herself with her splayed open book.

"Right? Talent *and* sex appeal? It's just not fair. What about the rest of us?"

"You're plenty sexy." Quinn winked at her. "But I still don't get why you're going on a date with this Lincoln dude when you are crushin' on Russell."

Sabrina flopped onto her bed with a soft plop and a long groan. "I panicked, okay? I was on the phone to Mama, and the phone rang right after I hung up so I thought she called back."

Quinn rolled her eyes.

Sabrina pointed an accusing finger at her. "I saw that eye roll. Yes, again. Grandma is getting sicker, my sister is having complications with her pregnancy, and—"

Quinn held up a hand. "Did they ask how you're doing?"

"Well, no, but—"

"Nope. We've heard how Grandma is doing, and how the chosen sister is doing. They *never* ask how you're doing, Bre. I don't like it. It's not fair. And right now, I really wanna hear more about how you're going on a date with the wrong Pirate."

Sabrina couldn't even argue. No matter how many times a day they called, they never asked how she was. Only how her grades were, how her finances were, and if her room was clean before bestowing yet another guilt trip about how she should be home to help out her ailing family members.

She shook her head. "Fine. This guy Will called and said he got my number from Russ. So cue my confusion. He asked if I was single, and interested in going to dinner with his friend." She groaned again, but raised herself up onto her elbows, blowing her hair out of her face.

"His friend, right? I stupidly assumed he meant Russell. But surely Russell would have called me himself since I gave him my motherfucking number." She held up her hand. "I know, I know. It should have triggered alarm bells. And my confusion grew, sure. But when he said it would be a free meal in my favorite restaurant my traitorous stomach answered before my brain could catch up."

Quinn tucked a bookmark between the pages and closed the book before leaning closer. "And after you committed to going?"

Shame burned Sabrina from the inside. "He asked if I wanted to know who I was going on a date with."

"So, basically the captain of the hockey team thinks you're a hoe who'll date anyone for a decent meal?"

"Yup." She popped the P. "That about sums it up. Cheaper than a hooker. That's me."

"And you're going on a date with someone you don't like, because someone you do like took your number but didn't use it?"

"What can I say? I'm a complicated woman."

"You need adult supervision."

Sabrina rolled her eyes. "Like this is news."

Sliding the stall lock in place, Sabrina rested her head on the back of the flimsy restroom door. What the hell was she thinking?

Not only had she agreed to go on a date with a man she wasn't into, but said date had no idea he was even going on a date at all.

Embarrassment coated her like a wetsuit.

Sure, he was delicious, in a Greek god kind of way, but Lincoln Scott just wasn't lighting her up like the Fourth of July the way his teammate did.

She cursed her people-pleasing self. She really needed to learn to say no. She didn't want to be in a restaurant with the tall blonde who looked like he could crush her like a bug without even trying.

And yet, here she was.

Sucking in a deep breath, she steeled her spine. All she needed to do was get through dinner. The food never failed to impress, and she knew enough about hockey to pass herself in conversation with the top goal scorer in the league, right?

He seemed like a nice guy, a little traumatized at the fact he was on a date with a stranger, sure, but who wouldn't be when they expected to be dining with a bunch of their besties?

She'd go back out, eat, help her date plot revenge for his friends setting him up with a stranger without his knowledge, then go home to drown her sorrows in a bottle of wine with her BFF.

Her phone chimed in her purse.

Quinn: How's the date?

> Sabrina: Why'd you let me do this?

Quinn: That good, huh?

> Sabrina: Worse. He didn't even know he was going on a date.

Quinn: Ouch.

Quinn: Wine's in the freezer. See you in an hour.

> Sabrina: This is why you're my ride or die.

Quinn: That, and I know too much for you to get rid of me ;-)

Any remaining tension left her shoulders, and she rolled her neck. So what if Russell fucking Stewart didn't want her? She'd find someone who did.

Someone better.

Someone who wasn't a confusing asshat.

Someone who was nicer, way more fun, and hotter.

Definitely hotter. Her nipples tingled, calling her out right there in the bathroom stall. Who the hell was she kidding?

The only man hotter than Russell fucking Stewart was Matthew Daddario in Shadow Hunters. He was the only reason she joined Quinn watching her favorite show on repeat as much as she did. And unless he was planning on divorcing his wife, in favor of Sabrina, she was shit out of luck. A girl could dream, right?

She made her way out of the stall and back to the table. God knows what Lincoln must have thought of her going to the bathroom yet again, but she'd rather have him believing she had a wicked case of the shits than know she was crushing on his friend.

Taking her seat, she sipped on her Dr Pepper.

"You okay?" His head tipped to the side, his brows pinched and his usually smiling mouth lay in a grim, flat line. "I'm sorry. I know I haven't been great company tonight. But if you're planning to make your escape out the bathroom window, could you please let me know if there is anything I can do to talk you out of it before you take the leap?"

She shook her head. His concern for her was sweet. So was his obvious concern for his reputation with the team. "I can't imagine many girls flee from having dinner with you, Lincoln."

"There's a first time for everything. They'll roast me if my first date in ages – who they set me up with no less – flees the scene through the bathroom window."

"It'd give them something to talk about, I guess. They sound like a good group of friends." Warmth expanded in her chest. Quinn was the same. That tried-and-true friend who simultaneously had your back and embarrassed the shit out of you till you wanted to move to a new country and change your name.

He nodded and sipped his beer. "They are. But enough about me. Tell me about yourself."

The server brought their entrees, and Sabrina scooped a heaping fork of steaming, vegetarian curry into her mouth, not caring that it would likely scald the roof of her mouth.

"We don't have to do the getting to know you thing, you know. I'm not your type, and you…"

He arched an eyebrow. "What about me?"

"You're not mine either." She shrugged and shoveled another forkful of food into her mouth.

"I see. Well. Give me a moment to sooth my wounded ego and I'll be right back with you."

She snorted. "I think your ego can take the occasional ding, Lincoln."

A chuckle shook his body. "Humor me. Tell me something about yourself. Contrary to popular opinion, not all athletes are self-absorbed ego maniacs. We may as well make the best of this not-my-type date. You can never have too many friends, right? What are you studying?"

Her heart tripped over the question and spluttered in her chest. Answering it would lead to a discussion about Russell who was in her class. She swallowed hard. Could she keep her I-want-to-do-dirty-sinful-things-to-your-friend feelings from her face?

"C'mon. That one's easy to answer."

She could see how those blue eyes and easy smile could have the ladies throwing their underwear at the guy across the table from her. "My family is from the Punjab, but I was born here in the US, in Seattle actually. And I'm studying French."

Three... two...

He took a bite of his curry and washed it down with a sip of beer.

One...

"My roommate studies French, too. Russ. Russell Stewart?"

And there it is.

A flicker of heat spread across her chest, up her neck, and into her cheeks like a wildfire ravaging a forest.

"Yeah, uh, I've seen him around." So much for keeping her crush under wraps. Was there a blimp overhead with a banner that read *Sabrina Sharma is hot for Russell Stewart*?

Linc narrowed his eyes, but she didn't follow up or fill the silence.

Could he hear her heart thumping?

She sure as hell wasn't going to meet his piercing stare. Instead she opted to push the food around her plate and hope he couldn't read 'Girl.'

"What about hobbies?"

Relief curled around her like a warm blanket and she swallowed past the puck-sized chunk of anxiety lodged in her throat. "I love musicals."

"Like... acting in them?"

"Watching, mostly. I haven't been in a drama group since high school. Maybe when I'm done with college I'll join a community production of something. I miss it."

"I could give you his number if you want."

Huffing out air like he'd sucker punched her, she shoved a small mound of food across her plate, casting her eyes to anything that wasn't him. "Whose number?"

Right, like she didn't know precisely who he was talking about.

His smirk mirrored her inner monologue. "Okay, I see how it is. We aren't there yet in our fledgling friendship. Sure, sure. So here's what we're going to do. How about I give you *my* number, then you can call me if you ever need to get hold of... someone else. How does that sound?"

Gnawing on the inside of her cheek she nodded. She handed him her phone. "That works."

"Did you text Lincoln?"

"No, Quinn, I didn't. We've been drinking wine all evening, did you *see* me text him?"

"Eesh. Your period makes you mean, Bre."

Sabrina pulled the comforter up to her chin.

"You should thank him for a nice time. He probably feels like shit."

"It's not my job to make him feel better, Q."

They were supposed to be attempting sleep. Lying in their beds, lights off. But Sabrina's brain wouldn't shut the hell up enough for her to settle. Quinn's bed squeaked as she moved. "This is true. But you're going to text him because that's just who you are. You always make people feel better, you can't help yourself. Night, girlfriend."

Staring at the ceiling she contemplated texting him. She didn't want to wake him up, or be a pain, but he wouldn't have given her his number if he didn't want her to use it, right?

With a sigh, she picked up her phone from the nightstand and unlocked it. She opened a message and typed Linc in the 'to' bar, but no contact appeared in the box.

What the hell?

Pulling up the list of contacts she started scrolling.

What had he saved himself under?

Passing the Ls, there was no sign of him anywhere. S for Scott? Nothing. N for not-my-type? Still nothing. Maybe he saved himself as Top Scorer, or Player of the Year?

Her breath caught when she got to the Rs. Russell Stewart.

He didn't.

She clicked his name and in the note section Lincoln had written: "His bark is worse than his bite. You'll thank me later."

She grabbed her lip between her teeth to smother the smile on her face. Despite loving the stage, she was clearly a truly terrible actress. She'd need to work on telling her face not to be so obvious.

When she pressed the message icon, three dots appeared in the text box. Her stomach clenched and her pulse kicked up.

Was he typing to her?

Fuck.

What would she say to him?

What was he saying to her?

Dear Sabrina, I'm sorry for sending you out on a date with my best friend. Be mine. Ktxbai, your Russell.

If only.

The dots stopped.

Her heart sank.
After a beat, the dots started again.
Her heart rate quickened.
She was utterly pathetic.
Say something.
She sighed.
Say... anything.

> Russell Stewart: So, how'd your date with Linc go?

That was it?

Not quite the declaration of undying love she was hoping for, but the Ice King had opened channels of communication. She could work with that.

CHAPTER 4
Russell

"Everything hurts and I'm dying." Finn dropped his head onto the table in Applebee's with a dramatic thud. A few of the team had dragged themselves out to eat after hockey practice and they'd all but collapsed into the booth upon their arrival.

"Could you die a bit quieter please? I have a headache." Will had already finished his first bottle of water and was working through a second while they waited for their server to come and take their order.

Russell rubbed the bridge of his nose. His entire body felt like lead. Coach had driven the whole team into the ice at practice. They barely made it out alive.

"Think Coach is having marital issues? Maybe he's in the dog house and by default so are we. Dude needs to get laid before he kills us all." He kneaded at the muscles in his neck with a groan.

He wasn't due at Mom's until the following day to see Jude after his morning session of classes, but he was reconsidering. He could pick up a few bags of ice, fill up Mom's tub, and sleep in it. Maybe by morning his muscles wouldn't hurt so much.

"What can I get you guys to drink?" A familiar, chipper voice had his head snapping around way too quickly and he groaned again.

Sabrina raised her eyebrows before smacking the end of her pen off the notepad she was holding.

Did she think he was groaning because she was there? She did, didn't she? That's exactly what her face said.

Fuck.

"Water, please." Will held up his empty bottle and gave it a shake.

"Make that two." Austin held up two fingers.

"Three please, Sabrina." Linc raised his hand.

"I'll take a water and a Coke, please." Finn was always keen to stand out from the crowd.

Russell and Sabrina had texted back and forth a bit after her date with Lincoln a few days prior, but there had been radio silence since. She'd said their date was nice, but she suspected his heart was caught up elsewhere.

She neglected to mention anything about her own heart.

He dropped his gaze to her chest, taking in the swell of her tits and the cut of her shirt before flicking it back to her now scowling face. Busted.

Lincoln coughed into his fist.

"What?"

Sabrina giggled. "What can I get you to drink, Sir Warm-and-Fuzzy?"

"Oh!" He'd been too distracted by the boobs to order a drink. Great. "Uhh. Water?"

"Are you asking me?"

Someone chuckled. Faithless fuck.

Get it together, Stewart!

"Water," he repeated with a firm nod. "Please."

Finn jammed his chin into the V space between his thumb and forefinger and tapped on his cheek as though trying to figure out what was unfolding in front of him.

"Any appetizers for the table?" Her hair was tied up in a ponytail, showing off her eyes, high cheekbones, and the sensitive spot on her neck where it joined her shoulder.

Shit. Was he drooling?

Was it rude to want to trail your tongue along the column of your server's throat? To nibble on her ear lobe just to hear her whimper and feel her tremble under your touch?

Stop. It.

A bead of sweat trickled down the back of his neck. Thankfully he'd just spent the evening running his legs off and his entire body was sweating. No one would suspect the beauty standing in front of him as the cause of his bodily reactions. Hopefully.

"What do you recommend?" Will, like the rest of the group, knew the menu inside out and back to front. But they often asked their server to pick something so they didn't have to adult and make the decision themselves.

Which begged the question how Russ had never noticed her before.

"Not asking me to do the TikTok dance." She gasped, hand flying to her mouth as if it could cram the sentence back in. She seemed to have a habit of saying things that should probably have been kept in her brain.

Five heads snapped up to look at her.

"What?" Russ wasn't doing the TikTok thing. He had no idea what she was talking about.

Finn clapped his hands. "Oh hell yeah." He pointed at her. "You and me, sister, we're gonna do that dance."

She sighed and dropped the hand holding the notebook to her thigh. "In your dreams, Funny Boy. Not happening. I'll bring you food and drinks. I'll endure noise, and bad singing –

within reason, but I will *not* be dancing the *Fancy Like* dance with you, Pirate." She spat the last word like it tasted dirty in her mouth.

Russell's eyes dropped to her lips.

Did she taste like sarcasm and sunshine?

He'd been sporting a semi from the moment he heard her voice, but he was verging on becoming uncomfortable if he stared much more.

She'd obviously cast a spell on him, because he couldn't drag his gaze from her face.

"We'll see. I want a Bourbon Street steak and an Oreo shake, please." Finn closed his menu and handed it to her.

She groaned. "So, is that a no on the appetizers then?"

Finn shook his head. "No, we want apps, but I'm in the mood for a Bourbon Street steak and an Oreo shake." He hummed as she wrote his order down. "Some whipped cream, on the top, too."

She held up a hand. "Stop singing at me, or I'll spit in your shake."

Finn nudged Russell. "I like her."

Squeezing down a wholly unnecessary and inappropriately possessive growl, Russell nudged him back. "Leave the woman alone, Finn. I'll take the... uh..."

"I'll have the strawberry balsamic chicken salad." Will stretched his menu over to Sabrina.

"The fuck? Are you sick?" Finn reached across the table and touched the back of his hand to Will's forehead. "A fucking salad?"

Lincoln handed his menu to Sabrina. "We'll take the pretzels and cheese dip, and breadsticks with Alfredo sauce for the table. And I'll have the classic bacon cheeseburger fully loaded, with onion rings."

Finn offered a fist bump to Lincoln. "Thank fuck for that. We'll make up for the greenery on Mo's plate."

Austin ordered a steak and when Russell finally got to speak he'd forgotten what he wanted.

What was it about this woman?

She cleared her throat. "This is where you tell me what I can bring you to eat, Ice King."

Apparently his dick spoke fluent sarcasm. It twitched every time she took a shot at him.

Will chuckled, Linc hid a grin behind his fist, and even Austin was smiling.

"I really like her." Finn pointed at Sabrina.

"Finn, I swear to god. I'm going to beat you to death with a breadstick if you don't shut the fuck up and let me order my food."

Finn swept his hand as if to say, "Go right ahead."

"I'll have a full rack with fries."

"I bet you will." Finn cracked up at his own joke.

Sabrina blushed, clutched the menus to her chest, and nodded. "I'll get this started for you guys." She hurried away from the table, without a backward glance.

Russ jabbed a finger at Finn. "You fucker. I'm going to kill you with my bare hands."

"I heard athletes had big appetites but I gotta admit... I didn't expect you guys to finish all of that food." Sabrina reached across the table, her tits mesmerizing Russell as she leaned.

Finn smirked, but quickly leaned back when Russ jabbed him in the ribs with his elbow. Austin raised an eyebrow, but said nothing.

When she straightened up, arms full of empty dishes, Finn belched. "I still have a little room."

Russell covered his face with a groan and kicked his friend.

"Ow! What now? Oh. Yeah. Sorry. Excuse me."

Sabrina shook her head. "It's okay, I have brothers. I'm used to boy behavior." She shrugged. "Can I bring anything else?"

"We're going to explode" and "no thank you" groans rumbled around the table. "Just the check please." Austin drained the last of his drink.

"Sure." She flashed a small smile and hesitated before shaking her head and leaving.

"Sooooooo...?" Finn jerked his head forward and raised his eyebrows.

"So what?" Playing dumb wouldn't work with his friends, but it was worth a shot.

Finn rolled his eyes and tutted. "Dude. Who is she? What are your intentions with her? And if you don't want her, can I have her?"

Russell surged forward to murder Finn in the middle of Applebee's and Linc slapped an open hand against his chest.

"Ah-ha. So you *do* like her. Noted."

Sabrina appeared, check in hand. "Everything okay here?" Her brows knotted together. "Boys, if you're going to kill each other, please try not to get blood everywhere. That shit's super hard to clean up. Who's taking this?" She waved the check. A table nearby burst into a rousing – if not tone deaf – rendition of *Happy Birthday*.

Will accepted it, but each of the men at the table got their wallets out.

"Teamwork, I like it." She collected the cards and left. Russell took the opportunity to stare, once again, at her perfect ass.

How the fuck had he ever let Lincoln take her out on a date?

"I have no idea how you willingly set her up with me, man." Linc echoed his thoughts.

Shit. Were his thoughts written in Sharpie across his forehead or something?

Finn whistled. "*That*'s the chick Will asked to go on a blind date with Linc?"

Russ grunted.

Guilt pooled low in his stomach. He didn't have time for distractions, that much was true. But the idea of anyone, especially his best friend, touching a single silky hair on her head made him clench his fists beside his thighs.

Will chuckled. "Classic deflection. Fails every time. You shoulda known better than to set your best friend up with a woman who makes you want to punch your teammates."

Sabrina returned with five checks and five pens. "Thanks guys, it's been a pleasure." Her gaze lingered on Russell for just a beat longer than everyone else before she backed away a step, then another, before pivoting and walking away.

"Alright, let's get out of here." Linc stood up from the table. When Russ tried to stand, Linc's palm curled over his shoulder. "Except you. You need to stay here."

"He's right." Austin pulled his coat off the back of the seat and slipped it on. "Don't fuck it up." For a sex guru, he sure was a man of few words.

Don't fuck it up. Right. Like that was going to be easy when she already thought he didn't want her by virtue of the fact he sent her out on a date with his best friend.

He raked a hand through his hair and nodded. "Yeah." He glanced at the door to the kitchen that Sabrina had disappeared through. "Okay." He picked up all five receipts. "You assholes better have left her a good tip or I'm putting fleas in your jockstraps."

"Daaaaaang. That's cold, Stewie." Finn offered his fist and Russell met it with his own. "Go get the girl, man."

The guys left, and Russ waited leaning against a pillar for Sabrina to reappear. "Hey."

"Shit! Russell, you scared the crap out of me. Have you been here this whole time?" She had her purse and keys in her hand. Her hair was loose, framing her face.

He nodded. "Yeah, I was just waiting to give you these." He handed her the receipts which she handed to a passing coworker. "And to ask when your shift was over, but I guess..." He gestured at her. "It's over?"

The tip of her tongue snuck out to wet her lips. "Yeah, I'm just heading home. Is something wrong?"

"What? No. Why would you think something was wrong?"

Blowing her hair out of her face, she rocked back on her heels. "I dunno. I just..."

Rip off the BandAid, Russ. Get to the point.

"I'm sorry I sent you out on a date with Lincoln." He jammed his hand in his pocket to stop himself from reaching out and dragging the pad of his thumb across her lips. "I knew he was interested in someone else and I still set you up anyway. It was dumb and I'm sorry."

She regarded him with narrow eyes for a moment. "Do you like cheesecake?"

"Do you know anyone who *doesn't* like cheesecake? If you do, you need to unfriend them. And report them to law enforcement. They're clearly psychopaths and murderers."

Her laugh was light and airy. She walked behind the counter, rummaged around for something, and emerged with a broad smile. "Follow me, Pirate."

CHAPTER 5
Sabrina

Despite the chill in the crisp, fall evening air, Sabrina felt like she was standing next to a blazing fire.

His name was Russell Stewart and he was sitting on a bench around the corner from the restaurant looking at her expectantly. "I feel cheated. This is a bench, not cheesecake." The corner of his mouth twitched before lifting into a smile.

She opened the bag she grabbed from work and pulled out a plastic container with a piece of salted caramel cheesecake inside. "Keep up the sarcasm, Sir Warm-and-Fuzzy, and I'll be eating both pieces of cheesecake." She winked at him.

He accepted it, and the plastic fork, with a wide grin. "What flavor's yours? I'm not opening this till I know yours isn't better."

Giggling, she plopped onto the bench next to him, her skin hypersensitive to his thigh being in such close proximity. He smelled masculine and fresh. He'd obviously come straight from practice: his hair was still slick, his cheeks flushed, probably from the hot restaurant, and every cell in her body wanted to lean into his neck and just sniff him.

Would he even notice? He'd probably notice, right?

"Sabrina?"

Her name falling from his lips had her smothering a moan. If asked, she'd say her pebbled nipples were because of the cold, but the way he said her name made her want to listen to it over and over again.

"Sabrina?" He was still waiting for her to answer.

Shit. "Mm?"

"Are you a vampire?"

"A... what?"

"Or maybe a werewolf? You've got a box of cheesecake on your knee, but you're staring at my neck like you want to tear my jugular out with your teeth. I could have sworn you just licked your lips." The corner of his mouth tugged into a lazy, knowing smile.

She popped open the cheesecake container and laughed. Was that her laugh? Why did it sound like a baby seal?

"Not a vampire, though I *do* love vampires. And to answer your first question, my cheesecake is the same flavor as yours." Her voice was husky and quiet.

She speared a piece with her plastic fork, scooping it up as it crumbled, and raised it to her mouth. "Sometimes my boss lets us take it so it doesn't go bad." She popped the creamy dessert between her lips, moaning when the salted caramel exploded on her tongue.

"You need a minute?" His grin was sinful.

Her cheeks heated and she shook her head. "I'm good."

He had some nerve suggesting she was the werewolf. If the wolf in *Twilight* had smiled anything like Russell, everyone in the entire world would have been Team Wolf.

No question.

Edward who?

Damn.

It might not have been politically correct to identify as a

piece of cheesecake, but she wanted him to lick her the way he was caressing that dessert with his tongue.

Fuck.

She squeezed her thighs together but couldn't stop the heat licking low in her belly. His eyes darkened, gaze smoldering. Never in her life had she wanted to strip naked in the middle of fall or any other season for that matter, and demand a man do... things... to her.

But watching him devour a slice of salted caramel cheesecake had her battling her rational thoughts of A – not get frostbitten nipples and B – not getting arrested for indecent exposure.

She wanted to throw caution, and her clothes, to the wind, and let Russell Stewart savage her like the dark and broody God of all things scorching that he was.

"Ask it." His deep timbre pierced the charged atmosphere, startling her.

She inhaled some crumbs, leaned forward and smacked her chest a few times as she barked out a cough.

Great. Nothing quite says "sexy" like coughing graham cracker crust crumbs all over your non-date-date.

When she stopped coughing she took a sip of water from the bottle in her bag and wiped her mouth with the back of her hand. "Ask what?"

He didn't meet her gaze. "You want to know about Jude, right? Where her mom is, why we aren't together. Yadda, yadda, yadda." His voice was flat.

Had the fact he was a single father ruined opportunities for him in the past? Her heart pinched at the thought. "What? No!"

Everyone had "baggage", it wasn't a good enough reason to hold back. It certainly wasn't a good enough reason to overlook a chance with a great guy like Russell.

Okay, fine, so she didn't know whether he was a great guy

or not, just that he was hot as hell, but still. She was pretty sure he wasn't a serial killer. She'd seen him with his daughter and witnessed the adorableness in all its glory.

Anyone would be crazy not to take a chance on being with him simply because he was a single father to a toddler.

If anything, the fact he was a hockey player would count against him more in her book. It was the campus's worst kept secret that those boys were players both on and off the ice. Two car doors slammed shut across the parking lot and two couples made their way into a bar.

She slid closer to him on the bench in a thinly veiled attempt at stealing his heat through his clothes. Shivering, she put her hand on his thigh. "None of that is my business if you don't want me to know about it."

"She's gone." He jabbed at a piece of cheesecake on the tray resting in his palm but still wouldn't meet her gaze. His down-turned lips and curled forward shoulders screamed grief and pain.

The night breeze brought a wave of goosebumps up her arms. Was this what heartbreak felt like? That beautiful baby girl had lost her mother? How overwhelmingly sad.

A sob lodged itself in her throat, curdling with the cheesecake. She felt his loss, bone-deep.

"I'm so sorry, Russell." She gave what she hoped was a reassuring squeeze of his leg fighting the twitch of her arms. They wanted to wrap themselves around him and hug him till his sadness went away.

"It's okay. I've adjusted. We both have."

"Do you...? I mean..." Dropping her fork onto her leg she gestured, searching for the words.

He tilted his head. "Do I...?"

"Do you have a good support system? Do your parents help you?" She wasn't intending on being rude or offensive, so she hurried to elaborate in case he picked her up wrong. "I mean, you probably already have it more than covered. You have a whole team of brothers to step up too. But if you ever need anything, at all, I'm only too happy to help."

He bristled, and his jaw ticked. "We're good."

She'd offended him. His words hit her like a glass of ice water falling in her lap. "Of course. I didn't mean... I just..." Pushing out air, she forced herself to pause. "I was just trying to help. I'm sorry. I didn't mean anything by it. She's delightful. And smart. I like a girl who knows what she wants and pursues it relentlessly."

When his forehead wrinkled, she kept going. "I can't tell you how many times I've wanted to plant my princess-costume-clad ass on the floor in Target and eat cereal straight from the box."

His chuckle breathed warmth back into her chilling bones.

"She's... something. That's for sure." A broad smile split his face and emotion swam in his eyes as he rubbed the back of his neck. "She's my whole world."

"I can tell." She pressed her chest. Her blooming heart was attempting to break free from its rib-prison and her ovaries were crying at how endearing he was over his precious little girl. Her heart pinched. Was that what unconditional love looked like?

A heavy silence fell between them as he finished his cheesecake, but she couldn't peel her eyes from his lips long enough to take another bite.

When his head jerked up, he pursed his lips. "What?"

She shook her head. "Nothing."

He narrowed his eyes and pointed his fork at her. "That's not nothing face. What is it?"

Heart racing, palms sweating, and ass frozen to the bench, she reached out, hesitated for a second and grabbed a fistful of his shirt.

Ignoring the anxiety welling in the pit of her stomach she

pulled him to her. He followed without resistance. Surely he had to know what her intentions were, so the fact he hadn't thwapped her off was good, right?

She was going with good.

Anticipation spread goosebumps up her arms as her lips moved toward his.

There was no turning back.

Loosening her grip on the front of his t-shirt, she slid her hand to cradle his chin. A couple of day's growth brushed against the palm of her hand before her fingers wove their way into the hair at the nape of his neck.

Did he just growl?

He smelled like sandalwood with a faint hint of eucalyptus. On her intake of breath, he sprang forward, the plastic tub on his lap falling to the ground with a dull clink. Strong hand cupping her jaw, he captured her mouth like he owned it. Sparks flitted across her skin as his tongue demanded entry into her mouth. She melted into his grip and parted her lips.

Somehow she managed to move her cheesecake out of the way before her body arched toward him of its own volition, and her fingernails scratched his scalp.

Was he breathing for her?

Her heart hammered so hard, it couldn't possibly still be working.

She shivered as he nipped at her bottom lip before dotting kisses along her jaw and dragging his tongue down the side of her neck.

Clawing at his scalp, she dragged his mouth back to hers. He tasted of salted caramel and confidence. Her body was a dead car battery and his kiss was the jumper cables, shocking her right to her very soul.

Did that noise come from her?

She would've been embarrassed if she could think of anything beyond the pulsing ache between her thighs and using all her energy to stay focused on not climbing into his lap and grinding against his crotch.

That wasn't cool, right? First kiss dry humping wasn't on the approved list of socially acceptable activities.

Someone should tell that to my fucking clit.

Every nerve ending was on fire, every sensation heightened. It was no longer cold. With every lock of their lips, her body tingled with the hottest heat that ever hotted.

The only noise in the still night was their heaving breaths and hungry clashing of tongues. And if she never smelled anything other than Russell "all-man" Stewart for the rest of her days, she wouldn't be mad about it.

A strong arm curled around her ass and slid her into his lap. Knees on either side of his thighs, she gripped his face with both hands.

Apparently, first date grinding was okay by him and she was there for it.

He hadn't simply jumpstarted her engine, he'd shifted into high gear and they were racing down the speedway toward the checkered flag. Kneading her ass with his fingers, he pulled her down against his sweats. She gasped as his hard length rubbed against the apex of her thighs.

Fuck.

He was big.

She added "big dick" to the list of things he had going for him as she ground against it, growing more and more frustrated at the layers of clothes between them, though reveling in the friction the material provided against her soaking wet panties.

The faint taste of copper permeated her mouth. Someone was bleeding. Had she bitten his lip or had he bitten hers? Did it matter? She didn't give a shit, and either he hadn't noticed or just didn't care.

Somewhere close by, a horn blared and a car door slammed.

She started, a jolt of pain searing through her face as her nose crashed into his and their foreheads knocked together. She shot back, landing on her ass on the cold sidewalk.

"Shit." Her chest heaved and her pulse raced as she rubbed at the tender spot above her eye.

They stared at each other for a minute, maybe twenty. For all she knew, it could have been an entire day, time was officially an abstract construct as they scorched each other with their gazes. Neither moved nor spoke.

Her hand ventured to her swollen lips. They tingled as though he was still seizing them with his mouth.

"Bre. Bre! You forgot your—oh, shit. Are you okay?" Gregg, her coworker and one of her very favorite people in all the world, sprinted from the door of the restaurant to where she was frozen in place. He crouched next to her on the ground at Russell's feet.

"I saw you sitting on the bench when I took the trash out back. You forgot your jacket." He offered her the coat. "Are you okay?" His voice was slow and his gaze flickered back and forth between her and Russell.

"I should get going." Russell brushed the back of his neck and stood.

Why couldn't she move? What the hell had she just done?

Embarrassment coated her body like sunscreen: pungent and sticky, and it would probably take two showers and a whole hell of a lot of scrubbing to get it off.

Gregg offered her a hand, but she stumbled again as she attempted to stand. Russell lurched forward and grabbed her arm before she hit the deck again.

"Numb feet." *Stop talking, idiot!*

Heat scorched her cheeks. Dusting off her butt, she dared

meet his stare, but his intense eyes were unreadable. "I should get going."

She nodded but now that she wanted words to form, none came. Had he broken her tongue while he was sucking on it? Did it not work anymore? Where the fuck were her words?

"Will you be okay getting home?"

Nodding again, she idly brushed the pad of her thumb along her bottom lip. Smiling, he stepped back from her, stumbling over the curb but righting himself with the grace of a gazelle. No ass planting for Mr. Stewart. Just her.

"Find your joy." Gregg tossed his classic goodbye catchphrase at Russ as he left, adding a salute as well. Did Russell Stewart make everyone crazy? "Looked like he found plenty of joy down your throat, girlfriend."

Russell paused, as though he'd heard Gregg's poor attempt at whispering, but he didn't turn back.

Her heart hadn't yet slowed and her shirt was cold and damp against her back. A shudder rattled through her. Her home state of Washington was never this cold. Damp, grey, wet, but never as dry and skin-stinging, bone-deep cold as Minnesota, even in the fall.

Speaking of wet, she'd have absolutely had sex with him right there on the bench. Watching his retreating form, she wondered if he would have, too.

When he was out of sight, Gregg gripped her elbow and tugged her so she was face on. "What in the steamy smolder just happened? I mean, it was hot as hell, whatever it was. Did you see his eyes? And that jaw."

He fanned himself. "Hot damn. Dark and brooding doesn't work for everyone, but it definitely works for him. But I di-Gregg. Tell me everything."

She opened her mouth to speak and dragged her thumb along her still-swollen top lip. Again.

"From your lopsided ponytail and those puffy lips, I could

take a wild guess that you were mackin' on him, girl. Good for you, it's been a while, right?"

It had not only been a while, but she'd never been kissed like that.

She'd never been so consumed by a kiss; so possessed by need and desire, so driven to rip someone's clothes from their body to get closer to them.

Was that what it was supposed to be like? Or had Russell Stewart ruined her forevermore?

Judging by how fast he hauled ass from the scene, she wouldn't get a repeat performance. But she sure as shit had enough material for her spank bank to go to town with her battery operated boyfriend when she got home.

CHAPTER 6
Russell

The Snow Pirates had lost their last two games, so Coach Swift added extra practices to their already slammed schedule. Russell wasn't sure if the man was punishing the team, or himself, but either way, they were serving their penance.

And penance fucking sucked.

His muscles burned, his eyes stung from sweat and exhaustion, and he was pretty sure the funky smell permeating the rink was him.

"I'm dead on my mothafuckin' feet." Finn bent over at the waist, cupping his stick across his thighs. Sweat dripped from his face onto the ice as he sucked in deep, gasping breaths.

"I'm not sure I even have feet anymore." Linc squirted jets of water from his squeezy bottle into his wide-open mouth, then over his face.

"Ten more minutes, guys." Despite his peppy tone, their captain, Will, was as heavy on his legs as everyone else. He stood in a small circle with Johnny, Ryker, and Sébastien, working on quad passing. Without moving, Johnny and Ryker executed five passes between themselves, after the fifth pass, Johnny did a touch-pass give and go with Will, then another to Sébastien.

Johnny scowled, Seb yawned, and Ryker leaned forward on his stick as though it was the only thing keeping him upright.

Considering how every cell in Russell's body screamed for mercy, it probably was.

"Ten more minutes, guys." Finn mimicked his best friend's tone, standing upright and stretching his stick over his head, wiggling at the waist. "Wait. Stewie... isn't that..."

Russ tracked Finn's gaze across the rink. Sure enough, Sabrina stood next to the door to the tunnel, nose buried in her phone, and a pale blue, Snow Pirates beanie pulled low over her ears.

What was she doing there? She had to be there to see him, right? She didn't skate – at least not that he knew of.

Was she dating someone else on the team?

A ripple of something sticky and sour he couldn't identify passed through him as he scanned the group, but no one else was paying her attention. He had no right to be jealous, if that's even what the unsettling shot through his spine was. All they'd done was kiss. Did she have the impression it was something more?

Who in their right mind would be out of bed at 7AM on a Friday morning if they didn't have to be?

"Stew?" Linc elbowed him.

"Yeah?"

"What's your girl doing at practice?"

Scraping a gloved hand over his chin, Russ shrugged. "I dunno. And she's not my girl. I don't have girls." Was he irritated to find her in his space? Or was he glad to see her? He couldn't decide.

He shuddered, and sent up a quiet prayer that this woman wasn't a Category Five Clinger. That was all he needed.

"Sure she's not. It's perfectly normal for people to just visit the rink at the ass-crack-of-dawn when they don't play."

"Does she even skate?" Austin passed the puck to Finn, who passed it back with less enthusiasm.

Russ shrugged again. He didn't know much about her, other than he'd almost fucked her on a bench less than twelve hours ago. A grin pulled at his mouth at the memory.

As though she felt his gaze, her head snapped up and she gave a shy wave.

"Finders keepers!"

There was a collective groan from almost everyone on the ice at Coach's announcement of yet another drill.

"I'm literally going to die." Finn's whining would have been amusing if Russell's body wasn't making similar declarations.

"Y'know in Northern Ireland they put a Canadian loonie under the ice for good luck at the start of the season. Maybe we'll ice over your body and leave you there for all eternity." Austin smacked Finn on the shoulder before skating away to join the group.

"That's dark, man."

Will set out one puck in a designated area for every two players on the team and each duo battled for the puck until the thirty second timer sounded. Once the whistle blew, the players without a puck moved to the edges of the rink to take a knee and cheer on their friends.

The game continued until only two players remained standing. Will stood a few feet away from Johnny, eyes narrowed, jaw firm.

"He'd better fucking beat that asshole." Linc's words came out on a menacing growl, but it was loud enough to carry. A ripple of agreement passed through most of the team.

When the thirty seconds started, the guys who weren't battling for the puck cheered like it was game seven of the

Stanley Cup finals, rather than two men working a puck protection drill.

Twenty seconds.

A quick glance at Sabrina brought another smile to Russ's face. She was as absorbed in the skirmish of sticks as everyone else.

Ten seconds.

Competitiveness fizzed through his veins as his leader, and friend, fought for team pride. Both men heaved with effort, and anxiety twisted in his gut as Johnny smirked, edging ahead.

Five seconds.

Four.

Three.

Two.

A final grunt sounded from Will and he captured the puck as the whistle blew.

Roars of celebration erupted on the ice and he could have sworn Sabrina gave a subtle fist pump from the corner of his eye.

Unreasonable seeds of irritation took root in his stomach. She was obviously waiting for him, but he had no idea why. Sure, their kiss had been good. Better than good. Okay, if he was honest, he'd admit that kissing Sabrina had been the best kiss of his entire life, but he didn't have time for a relationship.

And after one not-even-a-real-date this chick stood at his hockey practice, in his space, cheering on his teammate.

That wasn't okay. In fact, it was more than a little creepy.

How did he always end up picking the crazy ones?

"Clear this shit away then hit the showers!" Coach's bellow made Sabrina jump, sending her phone slipping from her hand, but she caught it before it hit the deck.

"We got this, go see what she needs." Linc pushed him from behind.

"Get another one knocked up, Stewart?" Johnny snorted as he hit the tunnel out of thumping distance. Whatever that dude's issues were, ain't nobody had time for them. Russell had a clinger to un-cling.

As a rule, playing hockey worked out most of the life stresses held tight in his neck and shoulders. But seeing the girl he'd played tonsil tennis with the night before standing in front of him only made his muscles tense.

Skating toward her, he attempted to come up with a nice way of letting her down without getting her upset in front of his entire team.

"What are you doing here?"

She winced.

Yelling at her probably wouldn't be the way to avoid drama. He swallowed and cleared his throat. "Sorry, I just... I wasn't expecting to see you."

She glanced at her feet and plucked at the hair tie around her wrist.

Great. He was probably a minute or less from making her cry.

"Sorry." Her dark eyes met his. "I didn't mean to overstep. But..." She reached into her bag and pulled out a small, square object. "You left your wallet in Applebee's last night, and this is the only place I knew for sure I'd find you. I figured you'd need it today, and since I have class this morning, I thought I'd bring it to you."

He glared at the wallet as though it had somehow betrayed him. It was barely 7AM. Classes didn't start for at least another hour, maybe more.

She came in early just to give him his wallet?

That wasn't only bullshit he could smell, it was absolutely, positively eau de clinger, with a hint of jasmine. Damn, she smelled good.

She brandished it at him again before a frown knotted her

brow. "I didn't take anything if that's what you're worried about."

Chuckling, he accepted the wallet. "The only thing in there is an empty Dave and Busters card. It's Linc's favorite place to go."

"And your license, debit card, cash..."

"So you *did* look inside."

"Yeah, to see who it belonged to." She folded her arms. "Sorry if that wasn't the right thing to do."

She was apologizing for being a good citizen and doing something nice?

With a huff and a frown, she turned to leave.

"Sabrina?"

She paused, tossing a wary glance over her shoulder.

He slapped the wallet off his palm before waving it at her. "Nice catch."

Her features darkened, and she paused as though contemplating a reply before she shook her head and left. Regret pinched his insides as he watched her leave, but he didn't follow her.

Twenty minutes later, he was showered, changed, and hitting the parking lot to dump his kit bag in the car.

"Well?" Linc hip checked him with a light bump as they approached Russ's car.

"Well, what?" Russ unlocked the car.

Linc tossed his bag into the open trunk and arched an eyebrow. "That's how you're playing it? Do yourself a favor and just give it up, Russ."

Sighing, Russ dumped his bag in the trunk and slammed the lid. "I forgot my wallet and she brought it to me."

"At 7AM?"

Russ nodded.

"That's... nice."

Russ grunted.

"It *is* nice. So, why you mad about it, bro?"

"Don't you think it's kinda weird? No one's that nice for the sake of being nice."

Linc snorted. "If she arrived in your jersey, with a fresh batch of cookies to watch you play? Sure, she wants to have your babies and already has a wedding folder with your face stuck on every picture of the groom."

"That's oddly specific."

Linc ignored him. "But returning your wallet so you don't have to cross town to get it later? Or so you don't freak out and cancel all your cards – that's a real ball ache." He shrugged. "Nice."

When Russ didn't answer, Linc continued. "Not everyone's out to get you, man. And it's okay to like her, you know." He held up his hands in surrender. "I mean, if you wanted to."

Something stirred in the pit of his stomach right before it growled, demanding food. "Breakfast?"

"I got a prior engagement, man. Peace out!"

As he stared at Linc's retreating form, he wondered where Sabrina went after she left the rink. Linc was probably right. Something he rarely liked to admit, but perhaps she was simply being nice. The least he could do was buy her a coffee to say thanks.

Pulling his phone out, he slicked a hand through his still-wet hair.

> Russell: Coffee?

> Sabrina: Uh… Did you mean to send that to me?

It was his turn to cringe. He'd been sharp with her, sure, but had he really been that bad?

> Russell: I did. Let me buy you a coffee.

> Sabrina: But... why?

> Russell: Coffee is life.

He climbed in the car and buckled up.

> Sabrina: Tea is life, but I suppose I could lower myself to drink coffee with you. I just didn't get the impression you were happy to see me this morning.

> Russell: Then let me change that.

> Sabrina: Sugar Bean?

The tightness in his shoulders eased and he smiled.

> Russell: See you in ten.

At 7.30AM Russell walked into the Sugar Bean. He had exactly thirty minutes before he needed to jog to his first class of the day. Having stayed up almost the whole night to catch up on his assignments and working his ass off at practice, he needed to mainline some strong java if he was going to survive the morning of mandatory computer lab.

The desire to skip class and nap was strong.

Sabrina's smile was guarded as he approached her table.

"Hey."

"Hey. You don't have to do this." She toyed with the edges of a sugar packet on the table.

"What if I want to?"

"I'd probably call you a liar."

He winced. "That's fair. I'm sorry, Coach Swift is busting our balls right now and... never mind. Suffice to say buying you coffee is the least I could do for being a grump this morning. And since this beautiful girl I know kindly brought back my wallet, I can even pay for it and everything."

"In that case, I'll take a green tea, please."

With a nod, he walked to the counter, ordered and paid for their drinks, grabbing a breakfast croissant and parfait with granola before returning to the table.

"Oh, that's okay. I've already eaten."

Embarrassment coated every inch of his heating skin. "Uh. Cool. I'll just... uhm... eat them both then, I guess."

She giggled. "They're both for you anyway, aren't they?"

He nodded, scratching the back of his clammy neck.

"For the record, if we repeat this process and you do happen to think of me when you're grabbing food, you can keep the yogurt." She winked at him before blowing the top of the mug cradled in her hands and taking a sip.

"Duly noted." He devoured the croissant in two mouthfuls. "I gotta leave soon, I have a lab at eight."

When she didn't answer, he lifted his gaze from the parfait he was tearing open. Her eyes were wide.

"What?"

"Nothing."

"What?"

"I mean, I'm not one to judge..."

"But?"

"I guess I've never seen a post-training hockey player eat before."

He shoveled a heaped spoonful of yogurt and granola into his mouth. "What does that mean?"

"Are you even chewing before you swallow, or is it just going down whole?" Disbelief and amusement coated her words as she shook her head. "You don't have to worry about running out of time before class, you're basically snorting your breakfast. You'll make it with time to spare."

If he hadn't already swallowed, his mouthful of yogurt

would have sprayed all over her *Wicked* – the musical – shirt when he burst out laughing. "What can I say? I'm hungry."

"You mean hangry."

A pang of guilt jabbed his stomach, souring the food he'd eaten. She seemed normal, not at all clingy or overbearing. In fact, she was almost cool in her treatment of him, as though he was the one somehow irritating her. Considering he'd barked at her at the rink, could he blame her?

He jumped when his phone vibrated in his pocket.

Mom calling.

"What's wrong?" He'd barely pushed the accept button before he was talking.

"Grandma fell in the shower. She's in an ambulance en route to hospital. I don't know how bad it is yet. I know you have class this morning, and I wouldn't ask if it wasn't an emergency... I don't think the hospital is a good place for Jude to be."

Sabrina's brows pinched, and her eyes swam with concern. The coffee shop was quiet, Mom was not. There was no doubt she could hear every word.

"I'll talk to my professor. Be there ASAP."

"I know your lab is important this morning, sweetheart. I'm sorry."

"I'll handle it. No sweat." He hung up and turned the phone over in his hand a few times. "I gotta go."

Maybe Linc could watch Jude while he was in class. He was on thin ice with Professor Dyer. She not only hated hockey, but she seemingly hated him. For playing it or existing, he wasn't sure which. It wouldn't be easy to make up the lost time. In fact, she'd probably make it impossible or just fail him outright.

Fuck.

He punched out a message while shoveling another spoon of yogurt into his mouth.

> Russell: 9-1-1. Can you watch Jude for two hours?

> Linc: I'm not on campus, sorry. Will or Finn?

He grunted, tucking the phone back in his pocket. He'd have to live with the fallout with Dyer. His baby girl came first.

Warm fingers curled around his forearm. "Russell?"

His eyes drifted to hers, pausing on her lips as they travelled. What was it about how she said his name that made his pulse quicken?

She didn't move her hand and instead gave his arm a squeeze. "I don't have class until later. If you want, I can watch Jude until you're done with your lab."

Defensiveness ricocheted in his ribcage like a pinball in a machine.

He shook his head. He didn't need her help, he could handle it himself. "It's all good." Taking another gulp of his coffee, he turned, leaving a frowning Sabrina watching him go.

He reached for the door and glanced back. Sabrina's curled-up hand was pressed against her mouth and her down-turned eyes were dull. He didn't know her all that well. Could he trust her with the most important person in his life?

The corners of her lips lifted in a small, almost reluctant smile, and she tossed him a wave.

Lincoln's words came back to him. *Not everyone's out to get you, man.* Would it be so bad to let her hang out with Jude for a little while? Was it really worth the confrontation with Dyer when a potential solution to his problem sat fifteen feet away?

"It would only be for two hours, max." The words were out before his brain could overrule him.

She was already standing, grabbing her bag, and draining what was left of her tea. "Sure thing." She nodded. "I don't mind at all; happy to help. I don't have a car with me though, could you drop me there? Is it far? I could walk if it's too much trouble."

This woman.

"I got you." He'd be a few minutes late to the computer lab, but he'd rather take shit for being late than the ball ache of missing it altogether.

CHAPTER 7
Sabrina

"Who is this?" Russell's mother did little to hide her surprise.

Luckily, Jude had no such reservations. The little girl ran at her full throttle, splatted onto her leg, and wrapped her arms around tight. "Hiiiiiiiiiiiiiiiii!"

The little girl's excitement enveloped Sabrina, warm and full in her heart. A faint smile played on Russ's oh-so-kissable lips. She jerked her head, partly to clear her mind of the image of grinding against his crotch and partly to check if it was okay to pick Jude up. He gave a sharp nod before she opened her arms and the child mimicked her.

"Your Majesty! What a great honor it is to see you again."

Jude laughed as Sabrina picked her up and spun her in a circle.

"This is Sabrina, Mom. She's going to sit with Jude while I'm in class."

His mother narrowed her gaze and pursed her lips, face wrinkling as though she'd sucked on a lemon. "I need to get to the hospital." She hesitated before reaching for her purse on the counter.

A look passed between her and Russell and her frown deepened. She was very clearly not okay leaving her granddaughter with the strange woman in her living space.

Sabrina gave her a warm and what she hoped was a reassuring smile. "I have nieces and nephews."

The furrows between his mom's brows deepened.

I have nieces and nephews? What the hell kind of thing is that to say to someone? Why didn't you just lead with: I have higher brain function and can wipe my own ass?

Mrs. Stewart opened her mouth to speak, but Russell cut her off. "Mom, we need to leave."

She picked up her purse, walked toward Sabrina who was still holding Jude, cradled the little girl's face in her palm, and kissed her forehead. "Mimi will be back in a little bit, okay munchkin?"

"Bye!" Jude's entire body vibrated as she waved goodbye to her grandmother.

Russ was frowning. It was clear this family didn't leave Jude alone with people who weren't also family. He shifted his weight from foot to foot and his shoulders were scrunched against his ears.

"Does she have any allergies?"

He shook his head. "None."

Sabrina stepped toward him and brushed his bicep. "We'll be okay, Russell." Her voice was soft. "I got this. Go." Her confidence wavered under his intense blue-eyes, but she nodded to reassure them both that she had things under control. He hesitated, screwing up his face like he was waging an internal battle.

She sucked in a deep breath to flush out the annoyance creeping through her veins. He didn't know she was good with kids. He didn't know she could switch between princess and Avenger like a badass. Or that boxed mac and cheese was her specialty. He didn't know she was a fully qualified master negotiator of tiny terrorists.

This wasn't about her. This was about him. He was simply a scared father, leaving the most cherished piece of his life with a stranger.

"I promise I've got her."

He glanced at Jude, gave her a kiss and swept her hair from her face. "Love you, Punkin."

Could this man be any hotter?

Sabrina's ovaries were set to detonate if he didn't leave.

Holding up two fingers, he backed towards the door. "Two hours."

She nodded. "You have my number. I can send pictures, you can video-call from the bathroom, whatever you need."

He snorted. "I'm not some helicopter parent."

She followed him to the door and closed it behind him. She had suspected some kind of scene or reluctance on Jude's part to be alone with the stranger she'd met in the cereal aisle, but the iron-clad grip the little girl had around her neck as she snuggled suggested otherwise.

"Alright, little one, it's just you and me. What do you want to do today, hey?"

"Princess!"

"Yep, you are a princess. Princess Merida today if I'm not mistaken."

Jude wiggled until she put her on the ground. Gripping her by the index finger, she tugged and yanked until Sabrina caved and followed her down the hall.

"You princess!"

There was no way she could cram her adult frame into a tiny princess costume, but maybe she could grab a Hulk fist or Captain America's shield and pair it with a stylish tiara.

Russell shared a room with Lincoln in the dorms, but Jude stayed with his mom off campus. He probably split his time between the two. Unless he had a brother she didn't know about, the door to Russell's bedroom was open. Curiosity had her head craning back to try to catch a glimpse of Sir Grump-a-Lot's lair, but Jude's tug was insistent.

Jude's room wasn't at all how she expected to find it. There wasn't a single splash of pink anywhere in sight. A cubby-type-space had been painted navy blue. "Hero Up" was spelled out in white, wooden letters above framed pictures of superheroes. Six adult costumes hung from the wall on little white hooks, next to the same costumes in Jude's size. Matching action figures stood on top of a storage unit with fabric storage cubes nestled inside.

A huge paint-splatter effect rug lay in the middle of the room with the Avengers A printed over top of the bright splashes of paint. A superhero collage was painted on the wall above the little girl's bed which had matching superhero linens.

Next to the bed hung another six hooks with princess costumes, next to them stood a bucket filled with wands, plastic shoes, crowns and purses.

Jude directed Sabrina to the superhero costumes and tugged on the sleeve of the one hanging on the end.

Sabrina crouched next to her. "Whose costume is this?"

A smile lit up her perfect little face. "Daddy!"

Not quite the answer she needed. While Sabrina recognized the major superheroes like Captain America, she had no idea whose costume she was standing next to. Pulling out her phone she did a quick Google search. "You want me to be Captain Marvel?"

Her curls bobbed with a nod.

"Let's do it."

Grabbing the costume, she made her way to the bathroom to get changed, leaving the door open so she could see Jude playing in her room. The bathroom linked to Jude's room on one side, and Russell's room on the other. An inappropriate ache crept through her body as she changed into the costume.

Did it smell of him?

Bunching the fabric under her nose, she inhaled.

Her pulse quickened as his scent accosted her entire being. He dressed up as Captain Marvel to play with his child. Aside from being a severe grumpasaurus, this guy was everything.

With a little help from the two year old, she even got the zipper up. He'd stretched out the shoulders, but it didn't fall down on her. Good enough. Costume in place, and a last, lingering gaze at the unmade bed in Russ's room, she tore herself away to play with the impatient little girl shaking a coloring book at her.

Before long, both Jude and Sabrina were covered in marker, and despite a lack of glitter at the table, they both sparkled any time the light caught their skin. Had the pens been rolled in glitter? Was it already on the table before they started? Where the hell had all the glitter come from?

Jude slinked off her chair and ran into the kitchen. A moment later she returned with a sippy cup. "A-jus!"

"You want apple juice, Your Majesty?"

The little girl nodded with a giggle.

"No problem, why don't you sit back up at the table, and I'll bring you some juice."

Breakfast dishes littered the sink, and a half-eaten slice of toast with a healthy smattering of grape jelly lay discarded on the counter. Her heart squeezed. She'd been on the receiving end of a call just like the one Mrs. Stewart must have received earlier in the morning.

Her own grandma was sickly back in India, and the first call to say she needed to be taken to the hospital had been a heart-stopper. The distance made it all the more painful. She closed her eyes and pictured a similar scene in the very spot she was standing.

Would it be weird to wash the dishes?

She punched out a text to Quinn before filling the sippy cup half-full of water from the fridge and topping it up with apple juice. Lid in place, she gave it a shake to mix and turned to find Jude, arm outstretched and waiting.

> Quinn: No matter what my answer to that question is, you're going to wash those dishes. It's who you are, you can't help yourself. It's also why we love you so.

> Quinn: You're a good person.

> Quinn: And we both know you won't sleep tonight if you don't wash the damn dishes.

She set Jude up in the highchair with a snack of Cheerios and a cheese stick, and got to work. The kitchen was clean in no time, and soon after, a simmering pot of potato and Italian sausage soup bubbled on the stovetop.

> Sabrina: What if he's mad?

> Quinn: That you cleaned and made a meal for him and his mom while his grandma is in hospital?

> Sabrina: When you put it like that, I sound stupid.

> Quinn: There is no other way to put it. If he's mad about you feeding him, he's a dick.

> Quinn: Offer to replace the potatoes? I dunno. I have no idea why he would be anything but grateful.

> Quinn: This is where I tell you to spank your anxiety on the nose and tell it to STFU.

As Sabrina started to type a message asking if she should make something else, another message from Quinn appeared on the screen.

> Quinn: Step away from the kitchen.

She smiled at how well her best friend knew her and stirred the soup one last time before lowering the heat.

"Wanna watch a movie, princess?"

The little girl nodded and smacked the tray of the high chair.

Jude was chatty and animated until Sabrina logged in to her Disney+ account and selected the movie. When the opening scene of *Onward* appeared on the TV, she was silent. She snuggled into Sabrina's side as though she wasn't this random girl she just met, and stroked the back of her hand.

Sabrina had always believed she was born to be a mother. She spent her entire childhood bossing Tate Adams – the boy next door – into the role of her groom, husband, and father to their thirteen children. She had borrowed Mom's red dupatta to play dress up, draping it around herself as a bridal saree. Tate used to poke fun at her because brides wore white, not red. Looking back he probably should have been more concerned by the thirteen kids than her color choice of traditional Indian bridal gown.

She gulped and her vagina cringed.

As an adult, she'd reevaluated. And while she no longer dreamed of a sports team of kids, she wanted the whole nine yards: Big Indian Wedding with her extended family, fussing aunties, uncles, and cousins she hadn't seen for years, a doting husband, and lots of kids. A pang of jealousy that her older siblings and many of her cousins were already living her dream struck her in the heart.

Someday.

Halfway through the movie, Jude's yawns grew more frequent and her eyes drooped.

"Nap time?"

She nodded, her eyes watering as she yawned again.

"Alright little one, let's get you into bed."

Cradling the little girl close, Sabrina made her way through the open plan space and carefully plopped the already snoozing two year old into her bed. Stifling a yawn of her own, Sabrina plucked the crown off Jude's head and made sure there were no parts of her costume that could ride up or tangle around her neck.

A buzzing in her back pocket startled a small squeak from her, and she turned and fled the room, pulling the door closed behind her.

"Hey, Russell." She cleared her throat quietly. "Is everything okay?" She kept her voice a hushed whisper as she made her way back to the couch and logged out of Disney +.

His deep chuckle sent a shiver through her body, and she didn't miss the extra tingle in her core.

Down girl.

"Jude napping?"

"Yeah, she just went down."

"This one will probably be her short nap. She'll decide she's not actually tired and go down again later."

She smiled at how his affection for the blue-eyed princess radiated from every word.

"Uh…" A scratching sound came through the speaker, and she could almost see him rubbing the back of his neck, making that bitable bicep ripple.

Was it weird that she wanted to run her tongue along the corded muscles in his upper arm? What about this man made her lose her goddamn mind?

"Sabrina?"

"Uhm, what?"

He chuckled again. "Do you need a nap, too?"

"Mhmm." Her face burned.

"I said my grandma is going to be staying at the hospital for a while. Is there any chance you could stay with Jude for a bit longer? I need to go to Grandma's house and get things she needs, pick up something for Mom to eat, and take it all to the hospital. I know we have French this afternoon, but I was hoping…" He cleared his throat.

"I can totally stay with Jude. No sweat. I'll get someone to take notes for us so we don't miss out."

"Sounds good. Is she doing okay?"

She cringed. Would it kill the guy to say a damn thank you from time to time?

"She's a dream to hang with. Is there anything specific she eats for lunch? Or any routine I need to be aware of?"

"PB&J and apple slices, or whatever you find in the fridge. She's not fussy. Loves carrot sticks and cherry tomatoes – don't forget to—"

"I know, slice them so it doesn't get lodged in her esophagus and choke her to death."

"Wow."

"Too dark, sorry."

Footsteps shuffled behind her.

"A-jus!"

His laugh wrapped around her like hot cocoa. "How long did she last?"

"Twenty minutes."

"I'm hoping this is a phase and not the end of her two naps a day thing."

"Uhhhh."

"Lie to me, Bre. Tell me it's not the beginning of the end."

Her stomach flipped at him calling her Bre. Had she mentioned her nickname to him before? Had he heard someone else call her it? Either way, it did… things to her to hear him talk of her in a more intimate and familiar way. "Sure, and leprechauns are real."

He groaned. "Yeah. I figured. Anyway, I gotta jet." He hung up without waiting for her to reply.

She couldn't imagine him being deliberately rude, but his brusque manner rankled her. "Alright, princess. Let's get you some lunch."

CHAPTER 8
Russell

Other than the ticking clock in the living room, there wasn't a sound in the house when Russell closed the door behind him with a soft click. It was 1:30PM. If he were a betting man, he'd say his little princess was down for her real nap of the day.

But that didn't explain why there was no din from the TV, or quiet tapping of laptop keys, or a hushed voice as Sabrina chatted on the phone.

She wasn't in the kitchen, but the dishes had been washed, dried, and put away, and the smells from a large pot of some type of soup made his stomach growl. He replaced the lid with a quiet *ting* of metal against metal. He was absolutely circling back to that.

In Jude's room, Jude was passed out cold, but there was no sign of Sabrina. She wouldn't have laid down in his bed, would she?

His room was empty too, and more than a small wave of embarrassment hit him at how untidy he'd left his personal space. Hopefully she hadn't ventured in to snoop.

He found her in the living room, fast asleep on the couch, dressed as Captain Marvel.

Holy fuck.

His mouth dried up at the sight of her, and his dick stirred. He could rock a Marvel costume as well as anyone else, but the skin-tight material clung to her in all the right places. While the material had slipped off her shoulders, he certainly didn't fill out the chest area as well as she did.

Stop staring at the sleeping superhero, it's weird. And an invasion of her freakin' privacy.

He tore his eyes away, but the image was burned in his mind. Long, lean legs led to a perfectly round ass. His eyes traveled over her narrow waist, landing on what had to be a nice handful of cleavage. He hadn't quite appreciated her body while their tongues were dueling.

Stretched out on his sofa, quietly huffing out tiny snores, he couldn't help but admire how striking she was. A vibration in his pocket startled him out of his horny stupor, but he ignored the phone in favor of making her more comfortable.

He plucked off her shoes, tucked them under the couch, and, resisting the urge to stroke her peaceful face, he pulled his mom's lap blanket and covered her.

Two bowls of the most delicious potato soup he'd ever tasted later, he leaned back in the chair and kicked his heels up on a neighboring seat. His phone vibrated again.

Mom Calling.

"Hey. Everything okay?" He kept his voice quiet so as not to wake the sleeping women he was surrounded by.

"Everything's fine. You didn't reply to my text, that's all. Is Jude okay?" Her voice was laced with something, caution perhaps? Judgement? Whatever it was, his Spidey sense said it wasn't good.

"Jude's fine, she's asleep."

"And your lady friend?"

Was it the freakin' sixties?

"My *friend* is called Sabrina, Mom. And she cleaned the kitchen and made soup." A surge of protectiveness rippled through him. Mom was defensive of him and Jude, which was understandable after everything that had happened with Elise.

But whatever Jude's mother had done, neither he, nor Mom, knew enough about Sabrina to be passing judgments on Bre. Especially since she'd just made them lunch for a couple of days and saved them both from having to wash dishes after a long day of being at the hospital.

"That's... nice of her. Just be careful."

There was that word again. Nice. What Sabrina had done wasn't nice. It was compassionate, caring, and above and beyond. Nice was any one of the things she'd done for his family in the last few hours, but this was... more.

And what's more, if it had come from anyone else in the world, his mother would have not only agreed, but arranged for flowers, or chocolates, or some token of thanks. But because it came from an attractive woman he may or may not want to do dirty things to, her standards were different.

He opened his mouth to retort, slammed his jaw shut, clenched his teeth and ground out a reply. "I'm a grown man, Mom."

"Who made a mistake with a woman once before. I don't want to see you get hurt again."

"You can't live my life for me. If I'm going to make mistakes, they're mine to make. I know you want to protect me, I know you have the best of intentions but—"

"Are you dating her?" Her clipped tone suggested she wasn't in the mood for bullshit. But it also sent a jolt of indignation through him.

He wasn't in the mood for it, either.

It was none of her business who he was interested in.

"What if I am dating her?"

"I don't approve."

"I'm resenting the hell out of this conversation, Mom. Frankly, I don't care if you approve or not. You don't even *know* her."

"And you do? She's been in your life twenty minutes and we're already bickering over her. What does that tell you? I've told you time and again, sweetheart. It's not good for you, or Jude, to allow your genitalia to do the thinking for you."

She tutted. "You need to think with your *other* brain. You can't have women breezing in and out of Jude's life like some revolving door of one-night-stands. It's not proper or fair to Jude. She was so excited to see that girl today. What happens when she doesn't come around anymore?"

The assumption that he was somehow destined to fuck up every relationship he undertook because she deemed that he made a mistake with Elise sent his bones rattling. Something fiery coiled in the pit of his stomach.

He might have made a "mistake" dating Elise, but from that relationship he got the most important person in his entire universe. He didn't regret it for one second and he wouldn't wish for things to have happened any other way.

The fact she was referring to his daughter, her granddaughter whom she adored, as anything in the vicinity of "mistake" made him want to punch walls.

He sucked in a shaky breath and clenched his fist against his thigh. "Mom, I'm going to give you a free pass today because of everything that's going on with grandma. I know you have a somewhat jaded view on love after everything that happened between you and Dad. But not every relationship ends the same way yours did."

He flexed his hand. "Jude might have been unplanned and unexpected, sure, but she was not, nor will ever be referred to as a fucking mistake. She's the best thing to ever have happened to me and I wouldn't change her for all the world."

Mom sucked in a breath to reply but he hurried to continue.

"And while I'm at it, if I choose to pursue a relationship with Bre, or anyone else for that matter, that's my decision to make. I don't expect your support on the matter, but I do expect you to accept it." Suddenly the soup laid heavy in his gut.

"It would be confusing and upsetting for Jude when you break up, baby." Her voice was softer, as though it would somehow convince him of her rightness.

"Not everything is doomed to fail, Mom. And Jude is *my* daughter. *I* decide what's right for her. Not you."

"I'm only trying to keep you both safe."

"You can't protect me from everything, forever."

After an awkward, lengthy silence, Mom sighed. "So you're going to be seeing more of this girl then?"

"Her name is Sabrina, Mom. And I don't know. Maybe? But I sure as shit know I won't be influenced on whether or not I see her by your low opinion of my ability to make reasoned decisions."

A floorboard creaked behind him, suggesting he was no longer alone. Sabrina was listening. How much had she heard?

Dragging a palm along the curve of his neck, he cleared his throat. "I gotta go, Mom."

She sniffed. Was she crying?

"I'm just trying to do what's best for you, Russell."

"That was fine when I was a kid, Mom. But I'm a grown man now. I get to decide what's best for me." He didn't wait for a reply before he hung up and dropped his forehead to the table with a thump. "I'm sorry you had to hear that." His apologetic groan was somewhat muffled by the table, but he hoped she got the sentiment all the same.

"It's okay. She doesn't know me. I'm new in your life and she's trying to protect you. It's what parents do."

He lifted his head and turned over his shoulder. "Don't defend her. I need another minute of sitting in my self-righteousness before you bring the rationalization."

Her chortle was like a balm over an open wound. "I hear ya. Fuckin' parents, eh? Never know what the hell they're talking about." She winked.

"Now you're getting it."

"I see you found the soup... Hope it was okay for me to cook. I admit I got caught up in my anxiety over it. Cook or don't cook, cook more, what to cook, it was a whole thing, you know?"

Her nervous rambling was everything. The way her cheeks darkened, the way her hands moved animatedly as she spoke, the way her brain seemed to take just a moment longer than her mouth to catch up and realize she was rambling before she promptly snapped her mouth shut.

In any other woman, he'd find it irritating, but there was something endearing about Sabrina's babbling.

"I should probably..." She gestured a thumb over her shoulder.

His gut – and dick – yelled at him to kiss her. But the way she nibbled on her bottom lip and wouldn't quite meet his gaze suggested she wasn't as comfortable with him as he was with her.

Had his mother cock blocked him? Or was she not feeling the same things he was feeling? Was she—*gasp*—just not that into him?

His pride – and dick – shriveled like a grape in the sun.

Regardless of the reason, her vibe was off.

"Uh, sure. But you might want to change first." He grinned and gestured at her costume.

Her glance flickered to her body, to his face, and back to her body again. Eyes wide, she covered her chest with her palms, and groaned. "Oh shit."

"You look amazing. You have no reason to hide... that. And the soup was delicious. It might not last till Mom gets home."

Her smile was shy, and her gaze wary. But it was a smile nonetheless, and a smile was something he could work with.

"You're shitting me! What the hell are you doing here?" Finn handed Russell a beer and clinked his own against it. "Did hell freeze over and no one told me?"

Russ chuckled and shrugged. "I felt like kickin' back with my brothers."

"I'll drink to that." Lincoln clanked his bottle against Russ's.

They'd finally won a game, and Will had loosened their curfew so they could have one beer in the bar before heading home for the night. Russ wasn't going to stay at Mom's after their argument the previous night, and he didn't feel like staying in the dorms alone while Linc was out, so he went along with the crowd, despite not feeling it.

He scanned the bar as he sipped his drink. The jukebox played his favorite classic 80's rock, the beer was cold, and while he hadn't felt like joining the guys, the sight of Bre and her furtive glances was making it hard to remember why.

"You're staring." Lincoln's low voice was close to his ear.

"*She's* staring."

"You wouldn't know that if you weren't staring. You like her?"

Russell sipped on his drink to buy time from answering his best friend. "I don't have time to date."

"If you want it badly enough, you'll make it happen." Linc's forehead was wrinkled with deep furrows.

"Mom doesn't like her."

"Did she beat Jude? That's legit the only way your mom doesn't like her."

Russ sighed and took another drink. "She thinks... ugh." He picked at the label on his bottle. "She thinks I'm gonna fuck up and Jude will suffer."

After a long moment of staring hard at his drink, Lincoln finally spoke. "You know I love your mom, man. You know I do. But this... this isn't cool. You deserve to be happy. One bad relationship doesn't mean shit. You're not a fuck-up, Russ."

Some days he sure felt like one. Pressure squeezed the air from his body. He cleared his throat, but the slow suffocation continued.

Linc paused and took a drink before continuing. "And if you *do* want something with Sabrina, going in with that attitude will be prophetic. You'll be so convinced you're going to fuck up, that you'll fuck up."

Two women had sauntered up beside Russell and Linc flashing come-to-bed eyes at Lincoln.

As outgoing as he was, Linc was no threesome kind of guy.

"Ladies." Russell tipped his bottle at the pair.

"It's such a shame you're off the market, Russell. We could have a lot of fun tonight." One of the women ran a finger along his forearm.

Off the market? Since when?

He frowned. "What do you mean?"

"We thought you didn't date, but rumor has it you're dating someone in your French class."

If he denied it, they'd likely want him to take either or both of them to bed. A quick glance at Bre had his dick confirming there was only one woman in the bar he wanted anything to do with, and she wasn't standing in front of him.

If he admitted it, he was making a huge assumption for a woman who gave him a chilly brush off the previous night.

And committing to something he neither wanted, nor was ready for.

Not to mention, he didn't date.

Even if his dick was pointing at Sabrina like the needle of a compass.

As much as he was loath to admit it, Mom was right. Kind of. Only insofar as he shouldn't be dating. Jude, hockey, and school were his priorities.

He was a sophomore with a decent chance at the first round of the draft later in the school year. First round draft meant a world of opportunities opening up for both him and his baby girl.

His heart stuttered at the idea of leaving her to go play college in the national league. While he almost certainly had the skill to make it in the NHL, he wasn't sure he had what it took to leave his daughter to make it happen.

Either way, he didn't have time for women.

Even if said woman was attempting to shoot eye-lasers at the women lingering in his orbit.

If only his dick would listen and fall in line. Or fall at all.

He shifted in his seat, attempting to tug his pant leg.

"Nice." Linc rolled his eyes and shook his head. "Subtle, man. Real smooth."

Getting no interest from either Russell or Linc, the two women left to talk to their teammates further down the bar.

Beer bottle empty, unrelenting boner pressing against his thigh, and the woman he was absolutely, positively staying the hell away from six feet away, Russ stood to go to the bathroom.

If nothing else, perhaps he could have a quiet word with himself to try to convince at least his dick that having a crush on Captain Marvel wasn't the smartest idea he'd ever had.

CHAPTER 9
Sabrina

"Can you believe those girls?" Sabrina's words came out in a growl as she slammed her empty Cosmo glass onto the bar.

"What the heck did the glass ever do to you?" Quinn sipped the last of her drink. "You're staring."

"I can't take my eyes off the shameful display of... *that*." Her conservative, almost floor length skirt could have made six or seven of the skirts the bunnies were wearing.

"Are you being a dick about members of our gender, Miss Sharma?"

Guilt stewed in her stomach. Quinn was right. Just because she didn't wear short skirts didn't mean there was anything wrong with them. Why was she being such a dick about them? "Yes. No. Yes. Ugh. I don't care what they do with their bodies." Maybe Russell wasn't a relationship kind of guy, but he was a guy. What man wouldn't be tempted by a beautiful woman grinding against his lap like it was her right to? She groaned.

The bartender brought fresh cocktails and Quinn swooped her finger in a circle. It was her way of indicating to him to bring another when their glasses were empty. Thankfully, he was Quinn's cousin. To a bystander, however, she probably seemed like an entitled bitch. He made them strong, and based on the blonde running her finger along Russell's collar, Sabrina needed strong tonight.

Quinn picked up her glass of fresh Cosmopolitan and took a sip. "Mmm. Still the best in Minnesota, Monk."

He grinned at her praise. "Only the best for my favorite cousin, Q."

Quinn handed her the other glass. "Drink. And sure, I know you don't care what they do with their bodies. You care what they do with *his* body, right?" She ran her fingertip around the rim of her glass. "You're crushing hard on the hockey hottie. It's both adorable and concerning. I've never seen you this way about a guy before."

"Oh, you mean pathetic, jealous, can't form a coherent sentence when he's in the vicinity? Yeah, well. I've never known a guy like him before." Bitterness writhed like a serpent in her stomach. She knew he wasn't the relationship kind of guy, yet a yearning deep in her chest screamed that she wanted him to be.

Someone dropped a glass behind the bar causing her to start. A loud "fuck" was followed by a raucous cheer and woops from the hockey team.

"You've got it bad, girl. Drink up. Nothing cures jealousy better than a fruity cocktail. It's a scientific fact." She tipped her glass and swallowed half of the pink drink.

Sabrina took a sip of the tart, sweet nectar and shrugged. "Whatever. He can do who he wants. I don't care. He's an ungrateful douche."

Quinn laughed and finished her drink. Was she trying to set some kind of record? "Uh huh. I get it. Sure. Let's take the passive aggressive route and see where it gets you."

Sabrina glanced at Russell again and a shiver trickled down

her spine at the memory of his lips pressed against hers. She had no right to be jealous. He wasn't hers. They weren't a thing.

Hell, even his mom hated her. She wasn't sure what to do with that. Thanks to plenty of practice charming countless uncles and aunties she didn't quite know she was even related to at family dinners on trips to visit India, Moms loved her, it was one of her best party tricks.

As she turned to announce giving up on the evening and going home in a grump, someone shunted into her from behind. The pink liquid sloshed over the rim of her glass, coating her hand.

The sticky drink trickled down her arm as Quinn lunged for napkins and dabbed at her wet skin. Sabrina spun to face whoever had bumped into her.

Molly Morrison, journalist for the school paper, younger sister to captain of the hockey team, and all round badass – who had no idea Sabrina even existed – stood in front of her, alone. Where were her friends?

Molly's swaying and glassy eyes suggested she'd had more than her share to drink. "Sorry." Wisps of dark hair fell over her doll-like features as she struggled to remain upright. Her smudged eyeliner and red, puffy eyes screamed allergies – or boy trouble.

Unless she was allergic to hockey players, Bre's money was on the latter.

Over Molly's shoulder, Will and the rest of the team huddled in small groups chatting and laughing. Sabrina pushed her high school desire to be one of the cool kids aside and kicked her mother hen gene into drive. She was all about fixing other queen's crowns. She cringed. Except when she was being a jealous, judgy bitch to the women throwing themselves at Russell at least. This was her chance to redeem herself, even just a little, and Molly's crown definitely needed polishing.

She slid her arm through Molly's, linked elbows, and urged her forward. "Come to the bathroom with me?"

Molly's eyes narrowed and she pursed her lips. "Are you hitting on me? Gotta say, you get points for balls, Smalls. You get ball points." Her words slurred together.

Sabrina braced her arm against the woman who was now leaning heavily in the opposite direction. If she didn't get Molly moving fast, they'd both end up on their faces. "I'm straight. I just need to pee."

Clearly reading the situation, Quinn handed Sabrina her purse and her coat, but Sabrina couldn't risk letting Molly go to slip it on, or Molly would end up splatting on the floor. "It's okay, you get her home." Quinn's eyes flickered to something, or someone behind Sabrina and a shy smile played on her lips. "I'll stay for a while."

Sabrina squashed a smile of her own and tossed a backward glance. Russell hadn't reappeared from the bathroom. Was he in a dark corner making out with one of the girls who had thrown themselves at him? Shaking her head she turned back to Quinn, who was still smiling. Sabrina didn't know if it was a specific player on the hockey team her best friend was crushing on, or if it was simply some jock-orgy fantasy playing out in her head, but she'd let her enjoy the moment.

Guiding Molly through the bar, she hoped the frigid night air would help sober the girl up. Where were her friends? She was all for girl power and self-determination, but one of the perks of having besties was the right to veto the next drink and cut off your friend if she'd had too much.

It seemed Miss Morrison had passed "too much" a few exits ago and was in the "messy drunk" stage of the evening. Her brother stood at the bar with his back to them. Sabrina was going to get Molly out before he turns and realized how drunk she was. The last thing she needed was an overprotective big brother getting in her face for being irresponsible.

Sabrina shuddered. Mom and Dad had given her that lecture enough times for her to know Molly needed saving. And she was just the woman for the job.

She opened the door and a blast of cold air made the patrons standing around the entryway groan and grumble. "Sorry!" Throwing sympathetic smiles over her shoulder, she ushered Molly outside.

"Fuck!" A severe shudder passed through Molly's thin frame. "It's so fucking cold."

Sabrina couldn't disagree. Gooseflesh covered every inch of her exposed skin and her nose was already glacial. She led Molly to a nearby wall and pulled her coat off her arm. "Here, put this on."

"You don't have a coat."

"No, *you* don't have a coat, but I have more body fat than you so you can have my coat."

"You're nice." She swayed as she attempted to slide her arm into the hole of the jacket. On the fourth try, Sabrina gave up watching and helped the woman into her garment. "You're nice and men aren't. A tragic tale of friends and fuckers." Molly snorted. "Assholes. Every one of them. I'm sorry, person I don't know. But I think I'm gonna hurl. I'll try not to get it on your coat." She swayed and grabbed at a railing to steady herself.

Sabrina cringed. *Goodbye coat, it was nice while it lasted. You served me well.*

Doubled over, Molly hurled and hurled. How much vomit could such a small person produce?

Shivering, she crossed her arms and brushed her palms over her pebbled skin. Why had she given the drunk woman her coat again?

"Ugh. I'm never drinking again." Molly's wail was surprisingly coherent. Had she finished puking?

Nope. Round two.

For a brief moment, Sabrina considered pulling her phone out and reading on her Kindle app.

"Are you fucking crazy?" Russell's sharp, gravelly voice sent a bolt straight to her clit and her phone to the floor, bouncing off her toe along the way.

As she stood from picking up her phone, warmth wrapped around her entire body. Was he giving her his coat? She tried shirking it off her shoulder, but neither he, nor her frostbitten body would allow it. He pulled it around her and she slipped her arms into the oversized garment.

"I'll just be a minute." Molly held one finger up over her head as she leaned over the wall for round three. How much had the woman had to drink?

Warm, large hands rubbed up and down her arms as Russell stood in front of her. What could only be his 'dad scowl' was firmly in place. His brows pulled low over eyes that flickered with fury.

What the hell was this guy's deal?

One minute, he was ignoring her in the bar, and the next, he was eye-fucking her outside it?

If only he'd fuck-fuck me too.

Down girl.

"I asked if you were crazy. Why else would you be just hanging outside in this cold?"

"I..." She gestured at Molly. Had she fallen asleep over the wall? "I gave Molly my coat."

"Why?"

He folded his arms. She didn't miss the ripple in his biceps or how his shirt pulled across his chest at the movement.

Fuck. The man was radiating... anger, frustration, and pure sex.

Wasn't he cold?

Suddenly certain parts of her had thawed and were on fire.

"She has less clothes on than I do." She shrugged. "She was cold." Suddenly her argument sounded flimsy and weak.

"And you're not?"

"I—My skirt is way longer than hers."

"Do you spend your whole life taking care of everyone around you?" He spat it as though it tasted sour in his mouth, as though it was some horrible thing. It wasn't murder, or animal cruelty. It cost nothing to be kind.

She didn't trust her voice to remain steady, so she simply shrugged instead.

"And while you're taking care of everyone else, who takes care of you?"

She sucked in a breath to reply, but Molly snapped up from over the wall. "Ugh. Another fucking Pirate. Wonderful. Perfect. Just. Fucking. Peachy."

"Wait. What did I do?"

Molly scrunched her face up. "Assholes."

"Let's get you home." Sabrina might have been talking to Molly, but she also didn't want Russell to freeze to death. The world needed his glorious face in it, and she wasn't going to be the one responsible for the loss. Everyone would hate her if she was the reason Russell Stewart was no more.

She hooked arms with Molly and took two steps before Russ's strong arm grabbed her elbow.

"What are you doing?"

"Taking her home?"

"You're walking?"

"Well, I was, until this angry hockey player stopped me and now I'm standing in the cold arguing about walking."

Molly snorted. "This is hot. Continue."

"I'll take you both home."

Sabrina's stomach did that flippy thing that happens when you're cresting the top of a rollercoaster.

"No help from Pirates!" Molly waved a fist as she swayed and set off by herself.

"What's her deal?"

"I have no idea!" Sabrina chased after her and grabbed her by the arm. "Wanna talk about it?"

Molly pulled a hipflask out of her back pocket and took a slug. "Talk about what? The fact he's *dating*? The fact he's eye-fucking some half-dressed leggy blonde?"

Oh shit. Was she reciting back everything Sabrina had said to Quinn at the bar?

She shared a look with Russell. Clearly he was every bit as confused by Molly's declaration. He mouthed "Who?" and she answered with a shrug while Molly took a long pull from her flask.

"Molly, I don't think that's the smartest idea you've had."

"Neither's falling in love with a fucking hockey player." She slurred as she struggled to pull free from Sabrina's grasp.

Russell raised an eyebrow.

Fear clenched Sabrina's chest. Was Molly talking about Russell? Was she going to have to hate her lady-hero, or worse, fight her?

She'd had one taste of Russell, if fighting dirty and kicking Molly's ass was what it took to get another... She glanced at Russell.

Well, she'd consider it.

"You'll regret it in the morning." She ran a palm across the space between Molly's shoulders.

"I already regret it. Of all fucking men to fall for."

"I feel obliged to step in here and defend my hockey brothers. I dunno who you're hot for, but some of us aren't even assholes." He flashed a smile at Sabrina, who rolled her eyes.

Molly's chin quivered and her eyes brimmed with unshed tears.

She tipped the flask to her mouth and held it steady. Who on the team could have upset her to such an extent? Sure, Will was probably protective of his little sister to a degree, but she was a grown woman.

Unless it was more than simply a case of being attracted to someone on the same team as her brother. Unless it was more that she was attracted to someone closer to her brother... His best friend, for instance.

Oh fuck.

"Okay, I think you need to be cut off." Sabrina reached for the container.

"She looks like she'll cut you if *you* try to take that from her. Let her make her own mistake."

"My *mistake*, Russell, was falling for a fucking Pirate. Haven't you been listening?" She stumbled forward, dropping her now-empty flask to the ground with a clang giving Sabrina no opportunity to see whether Russell had reacted to the declaration or not. Did he already know Molly was hot for a hockey player?

"Where's your car? It's fucking freezing." Molly's teeth chattered so hard the words came out staccato.

"The first sensible thing either of you have said since I came outside." After picking up the flask, he linked his arm through one of Molly's, and Sabrina did the same on the other side.

"Have you been drinking, Russ?"

"Less than one. I'm good."

As they crossed the parking lot, Finn was climbing into his car. A blonde woman already sat in the passenger seat.

Double fuck.

Finn saluted Russell. "You guys okay?"

"We're fine." Venom coated Molly's words, but she had a

forced smile on her face that looked something between constipation and a grimace.

"It's all good. I got her." Russell seemed completely oblivious to the heavy atmosphere that hung over their space.

Finn hesitated for a minute, throwing a glance inside his car before nodding and climbing inside.

"Bastard."

"What the hell did O'Brien do to you?" Russell opened his car door and helped Molly inside, before opening the passenger door for Sabrina. She stared at him, eyebrows raised. "What? What's with that face?"

She gave a quick shake of her head. "I thought you were a smart man."

"Ouch. What did I do? I was nice and gave you my coat." He shivered dramatically as though proving a point.

"Russell?"

"Mm?"

"What color hair did Finn's date have?"

"I dunno? Blonde?"

She waited, but nothing registered on his face.

"And?"

He shivered again. It looked for real this time. "And what?"

He was obviously going to need spoon-fed.

"And what color hair did Molly say the woman draped over her crush had?"

"Blonde? I'm not following. Lots of people have blonde hair. Maybe they really do have more fun." He shrugged.

Irritation rattled through her at the sheer obtuseness standing in front of her. She face-palmed and groaned. "For the love of—"

"Wait."

Here it comes. She tugged idly at her coal-black hair, did he really think blondes were more fun?

"You don't think Molly..." He glanced through the back window. Molly was out cold. Her face smushed against the window, a trickle of drool emerging from the corner of her mouth.

He turned his head toward the direction Finn was driving before rubbing the back of his neck. "No way."

Sabrina raised her eyebrows.

"O'Brien?"

Sabrina nodded.

"Okay, but why is that such a big de—Oh fuck."

There it is.

"She's in love with her brother's best friend? Shit."

His dangling jaw would have been hilarious if his lips weren't turning blue. He pointed a finger at her. "We're not done with this. But if I stay out here much longer, I'm gonna lose a ball. Or worse."

She snorted and hopped into the car while he rounded the hood and slammed the door, once he was inside.

He fiddled with the dials on the dash, and hot air blew from the vents. Slapping his palms together, he shivered, before rubbing them together a few times and blowing between his clasped thumbs.

She sank deeper into his coat.

He side-eyed her as he started the car and drove toward Molly's apartment. "I thought you studied French. But I'm starting to think you're a secret agent or something."

"What the hell? Why?" Now she'd stopped shivering, she could truly enjoy his scent being wrapped around her once again.

"You figured out which Pirate Molly wanted just from the mention of blonde hair. That's next level observant right there. I'm impressed."

"I think you'll find a lot of women would have connected the dots."

"There were more dots?"

Sabrina nodded. "I've never seen her in such a state, which means it's big. She's clearly been crying." She checked off the "dots" on her fingers.

He frowned. "She has?"

"Smudged mascara and red eyes."

He strained to look in the rear view mirror, but it was too dark to see anything. "Huh. And big means... brother's best friend. Fuck. That is big. Too big." He shook his head. "This isn't good." His face was hard-set, lips in a grim line and jaw tight.

"But Will's a nice guy, right? I'm sure it'll be fine."

If Russell shook his head much more, it might spring free from his shoulders and rattle around the car. "Not fine."

"Wh—?"

"I mean, Will's a great guy, a good leader, but his number one rule is and always has been, stay the fuck away from Molly. I guess either Finn doesn't know Molly likes him, or he knows and doesn't care that she likes him. Or maybe he's saving them both by going a different direction. I dunno." He hissed air between his teeth. "I should not know this information."

"You can't tell him!"

"Which him? Will or Finn? Either way it doesn't matter." Russell stopped the car outside Molly's apartment building. "I won't. Of course I won't! I just..." He glanced in the rearview again. "It must be so hard for her."

Sabrina's heart melted in her chest like a popsicle on the Fourth of July. This caring, protective man who never fucking said thank you would be her undoing.

CHAPTER 10
Russell

Russell turned a barely-conscious Molly over to her roommate Cleo. Molly was going to have the mother of all headaches in the morning. With any luck, she wouldn't remember talking to them.

He had enough on his plate without a revved up Molly Morrison nipping at his heels to keep his mouth shut.

Back in the car, Sabrina's head lolled against the window. Had she fallen asleep, too? He didn't know where she lived, and she looked too peaceful to wake up.

He opened the door and eased himself into the driver's seat with as little noise as he could manage. His coat dwarfed her, but she somehow still rocked it like she was on a runway in Milan. Milan was where everyone walked the runway, right?

"I'm not sleeping. And if I was, your creepy staring would have woken me up."

He clutched his chest. "You wound me. I'm not creepy."

She waggled a finger at him. "But you don't deny you were staring."

"Can't blame me, Bre. You're gorgeous."

Her eyes dropped to her tangled fingers in her lap, but a

smile tugged at the corner of her lips. "I don't live far from here. I can walk."

"The hell you will." It came out sharper than he intended and her head snapped up, dark eyes glaring at him.

"You know you're not the boss of me, right?"

"I do know that, and I know there's every chance you'll get home just fine. But there's no point in being stubborn for stubborn's sake. Let me take you home, Bubbles."

"B-Bubbles?"

He shrugged. "Sounded good in my head at the time." *And my daughter is obsessed with the Power Puff Girls.* "I like nicknames."

"Is that why you call me Bre?"

He turned to her as a group of rowdy frat boys made their way past the car. "I probably should have asked if that was okay before going ahead with that one, huh?"

She smiled. "I don't hate it."

"I'll take it."

"I live over there." She pointed to the apartment building across the street.

"Can I walk you up?"

"Do I have a choice?"

He chuckled. She was such a contradiction of shy and sassy. It shouldn't have worked, but it did. "Always. No means no." He shrugged. "Doesn't mean I won't sit here and creepy stare at your ass till you get through the door of your building."

And stare I will.

She pouted. He smirked.

She crossed her arms. So did he.

"What's it gonna be... Bubbles?"

Her lips twitched before a loud sigh escaped her. "Fine. But I'm keeping the coat till we get inside. I like how it smells." Her eyes widened. "I mean, it's cold out there and you don't even need to go outside. You're choosing to, so you go without. Or something." She picked up speed with each word until she stopped as though she'd slammed into a solid wall. She groaned and got out of the car, letting the door close with a thump.

She liked how he smelled? It was a start.

He liked way more about her than how she smelled.

"Welcome to the Jungle." Sabrina turned the key in the lock and shunted the door open with her butt.

"Great song." Russell nodded his approval before a whiff of weed smacked him in the face.

She smiled. "Guns N' Roses fan?"

"Classic... most things fan. All-time favorite band is The Beatles though – in case you didn't figure that out from Jude's name." He clamped his mouth shut. He hadn't meant to say that or *anything* about himself really.

Broody and mysterious were his things.

No one had him down as a Chatty Cathy, and no one expected small talk from him. Just how he liked it.

Something about the woman standing wrapped in his coat made him want to share pieces of himself. Maybe she'd care that he didn't like the number forty three, or that he didn't like egg yolks unless they were scrambled or otherwise unidentifiable as egg yolks.

"I like the Beatles."

"Hm?" Had she kept speaking while he'd stared at her like a teenager on a first date?

She giggled. "I said, I like the Beatles."

"Can I walk you to your door?"

Her face contorted. She was going to say no.

Something inside him drove him to insist. "Please? Just... let me walk you upstairs?"

After a beat of what seemed to be indecision, her features softened and she relented. "Sure."

"Why?"

"What? What do you mean why? Didn't you want to walk me up?"

"I did, but are you letting me walk you up because it's what you want, or because you think it'll make me happy?"

She narrowed an eye and pursed her lips. "Can't it be both?" She took his hand and tugged him across the threshold. "Elevator or stairs?"

"Stairs."

She nibbled on her top lip and regarded him for a moment before seemingly deciding he was capable of climbing however many flights of stairs stood between them and her apartment.

With a nod, she turned, her hand slipping from his, but he caught it, laced their fingers together and opened the door leading to the stairwell. "The light's broken in the hall for the first three flights."

"I'll protect you from any monsters lurking in the dark."

Her palm was warm, soft, and small in his. Her fingers, slender and delicate, like that of a musician or artist, folded into his as if by habit.

As they rounded the first flight of stairs, he held back. Dark, unruly waves fell down her back. His jacket had slipped off her shoulder, taking with it her shirt, exposing the golden skin of her neck and shoulder.

Lust pooled in his stomach. Could he have another taste of this intoxicating woman without falling too far? He licked his lips, dick twitching at the memory of her melted against him on the bench.

Fuck it.

She stepped up onto the first step of the next flight of stairs, but he stopped her with an opened hand on her stomach, pushing her toward the wall.

On a squeak and a gasp she didn't resist the motion and collided with the wall with a soft "oof."

"Russell." Her whisper was a plea wrapped in caution.

In the darkness, her hand found his chest, landing over his racing heart. She walked her fingers along his collar bone. Despite being clothed, they burned a trail on his skin as they climbed higher. The searing intensified when they reached the edge of his shirt and skimmed along his neck.

Sliding his hand from her stomach to her waist, he closed the distance between them and captured her mouth with his.

He brushed his nose against hers and slid his hand under her coat, trailing his fingertips along the hem of her shirt. Every fiber of his being drove him forward, urging him to take her and make her his, but he pulled back, a tightness in his chest making it hard to breathe.

Her body was soft under his touch. All he had to do was lower his mouth less than half an inch and he could breathe again.

"You're giving me mixed signals." Her voice was airy.

"What do you mean?"

"Well, you're all..." She cleared her throat. "For lack of a better word, hard."

"Isn't hard good?"

She brushed her thigh against his dick, forcing a moan from deep inside of him. "Some hard is good." Her hands flattened against his lower back and slid up the length of his spine, pressing her fingers into his skin. "But aaaaaall of these muscles are hard, too."

Rolling his head back, her fingers curled into his scalp and a sound caught in the back of his throat.

"You're tense. If you don't want this, that's fine. But I do feel a need to remind you that you started it."

How could she think he didn't want her?

She was perfect.

From her beautiful smile, to her compassion, and everything in between. She was sunshine and funnel cake. She was the perfect Peggy Carter to his Steve Rogers.

He was the problem. He knew it. Mom knew it. It was only a matter of time before she'd know it too.

He wasn't enough for the mother of his goddamn daughter to stick around. How could he be enough for this ball of energy and light standing in front of him?

He dropped his forehead against hers. A warm palm slipped under his shirt and ran the length of his torso, sending a shiver through his muscles.

"I can hear you overthinking this, Russell."

"I like how you say my name."

She curled her fingers, and dragged her nails down one of his pecs. "I like how you say mine."

This woman.

When she got to the band of his pants, she reset her hand at his neck, and scratched another path down his chest.

A low growl rattled in his chest and his dick strained against his pants.

She brushed her lips against his, and words and anxiety collided in his throat. "Russell?"

"Hm?"

She grazed his jaw with the very tip of her tongue as she squeezed his cock. "Stop thinking."

Curling a hand around her chin, he tipped it so he could seize her mouth. Their tongues collided in a messy, hungry duel. She tasted of cranberry juice and sugar.

Maybe tasting her would be enough.

A beautiful woman was standing in front of him, urging him to act. It wasn't as though he was asking her to marry him.

He could taste her and leave without consequence, right?

He dragged his tongue down the column of her neck, nipping the sensitive spot at the bottom, not missing the way her muscles softened under his touch or the sigh that floated from her.

His lips followed the curve of her shirt's neckline, dipping ever so slightly between her tits. He cupped one and gave a gentle squeeze, enjoying the hum of satisfaction and the way her back arched into his other hand. Dropping to his knees, he picked up the bottom of her long skirt.

"What are you doing?" She grabbed at him in the darkness, catching the fabric on the shoulder of his shirt and his hair. She pulled, but he was a man on a mission.

"Tasting you." His hands skimmed the outside of her thighs.

"Oh." Her velvet skin was soft under his palms and her moan reverberated around the stairwell.

She was so responsive to even the gentlest of touches.

"You're going to want to concentrate on being quiet, Bubbles. I don't need people on the second floor calling the cops."

Her breath caught as he ran his fingers along the edge of her panties. Shunting her leg over his shoulder, he tugged her underwear to the side and dragged his tongue along her pussy. Her thigh tensed against the side of his head and if he wasn't mistaken, she'd all but stopped breathing.

Repeating the motion, slower, he dragged his tongue between her slick folds, applying pressure to her clit. Whether by reflex or intention, her hips jerked, and her fingers threaded through his hair.

He was well and truly fucked.

He'd barely tasted her and he was already a goner. There would be no taste and leave. There would be no more fighting his urges to make her his. There was just him, on his knees, and ready to worship her like the queen she was.

A door slammed somewhere above and she gasped, clutching his head against her. He grinned and slipped his fingers inside, curling them against her G-spot. The involuntary shudders and twitches that passed through her body as his tongue brushed against her clit did little to deter him from his mission.

He didn't care if whoever slammed the door happened upon them. His only mission was to make the woman he had pinned against the wall come over his face.

Her nails clawed into his scalp with a sting of painful pleasure as the languid strokes of his tongue had her entire body vibrating. Her shallow pants and squeaks remained quiet, but her chest heaved.

Grinning again, he nuzzled his nose over the sensitive spot before pressing against her G-spot and lapping at her swollen bundle of nerves. Her muscles tightened. She was close, grinding against his face like she couldn't get enough.

If he could breathe, he wasn't doing it right.

And he could breathe. She was holding back.

He needed to fix that.

Growling, he burrowed his mouth deep between her folds with a renewed commitment to make her come undone on his tongue.

"R-Russell." Her breathing had quickened, her body shook, her squeaks had elevated to moans, and she pressed him against the apex of her thighs as she rode his tongue.

He sucked her clit into his mouth and flicked it with his tongue, enjoying her inner walls clenching around his fingers. "I'm not stopping till you come for me, Bubbles. Elsa that shit and just let it the fuck go." Dragging his tongue lazily around her clit, he hummed.

Her hands slackened from his head as her muscles tightened and the quivering of her thigh over his shoulder intensified.

What started as a gentle ripple shaking through her body, built until a muffled screech erupted from her twitching body and the echoing sounds of skin slapping against concrete must have been her hand against the wall.

Pride and satisfaction crashed into him, almost distracting him from the pulsing ache in his pants.

Almost.

His tongue slowed to a leisurely stroke as her muscles softened and she caught her breath. Tiny shivers passed through her with each stroke.

"T-too... s-sensitive."

Blowing cool air over her slick and swollen skin, he chuckled at her gasp.

She grabbed him by his ear and hair and tugged him up her body. Her chest rose and fell in repeated quick succession. "If we climb another flight of stairs does that mean we level up the sexy times?"

"I'm not fucking you in the stairwell, Bre."

When her body sagged away from him, he stilled and wrapped his arms around her, burying his face in her neck. "Don't get me wrong. I want to fuck you." He leaned against her so she could feel the hard-on bulging in his pants. "But not here." His phone vibrated in his back pocket. "And not now. That's probably Linc. I have early morning practice and I'm already out past curfew."

She grabbed both of his cheeks and planted her lips against his. Like a spark to dry kindling, his body lit up, responding to her touch and needy kiss.

Breaking away, she gripped his hand and led the way upstairs. His heart pounded in his ears as they made their way up three more flights.

When they got to her door, he pushed her back against it, bracing his hands on either side of her face, boxing her in, and kissed her, hard. Her teeth gripped his bottom lip as a noise rattled in the back of his throat.

The door behind her opened and she fell back. Almost in

slow motion, she went into freefall, landing on her ass, hands outstretched on the floor beside her.

Her roommate surged forward in a blur of red hair. "Oh my God, Bre! Are you okay? I'm so sorry. I thought I heard something."

Her glower burned into him as though challenging him to laugh. He pursed his lips to contain his amusement.

She pointed a finger at him. "Don't you dare."

He dragged his finger and thumb across his lips like a zipper.

Her roommate helped her to her feet, and Bre dusted off her butt before giving her left elbow a rub. Had she hurt herself? Then it wouldn't be funny.

"Are you okay?"

Her roommate jumped back, as though she'd just realized someone else was there. Bre nodded, but rubbed her arm again.

"Put some ice on your arm. And your... eh... rear." He rubbed the back of his neck, his face suddenly warm, and uncertainty poking at his chest. "Catch you 'round, Bubbles." He gave an awkward wave. "This isn't over."

CHAPTER 11
Sabrina

"I still can't believe you... you..." It was rare Chatty Quinny lacked words. Usually the skill was in getting her to shut up. She waved her hand like a stop sign about an inch from Sabrina's face. "In the *stairwell*!"

Fanning her cheeks, she shook her head. "Who are you and what have you done with my wholesome, Indian-American girl next door, best friend? Sabrina Sharma does not just let a guy Eat. Her. Out. In. *Public*! Were you abducted by aliens?"

"Do you even need me for this conversation?" Sabrina laughed, but Quinn wasn't wrong.

She blew on her steaming cup of tea, face burning. She couldn't quite believe it herself. Russell's magnetism had pulled her into his orbit, and every time they were together, it felt like an electrical charge crackled between them.

And sparks definitely flew every time they touched. Gooseflesh spread up her arms and the heat in her cheeks intensified.

"You're reliving it in your head right now, aren't you? Don't even try to deny it, Bre. I can see it in your face. I'm less impressed at the skills of his tongue and more fascinated that he didn't bust a gut laughing when you fell on your ass. Again. That was another uber dramatic fall. He must like you."

Sabrina shook her head. It was already 11 on the morning after The Tongue Incident, and she hadn't heard from him. Granted, he had to sleep, get up early for practice, and probably do mere mortal things like bathe, eat, and brush his teeth.

She wouldn't see him until later in the day for French class. Her stomach tightened. Would he pretend she didn't exist? He had no reason to avoid her so it was totally fine. She was fine. They were fine.

Hell, there wasn't even a "they" to be fine.

Telling herself to get it together, she took a sip of her drink. "It's just a bit of fun. He doesn't do serious."

"And other lies we tell ourselves, by Sabrina Sharma." Quinn raised her mug in a toast.

Sabrina swept her gaze over the small dining space, not wanting to meet her friend's accusatory stare. Warmth swelled in her chest at just how much care they took in their modest little home. Living with Quinn was easy; they both had a thing for everything being where it was supposed to be, and neither could stand living in a messy space.

It was a match made in roommate heaven.

"Did I see new groceries in the refrigerator? Let me know how much I owe and I'll Venmo you."

Quinn's eyebrows shot high on her forehead. "You're kidding me, right? You get all hot and dirty in the hallway with a hockey hottie and we're talking about grocery money?" She groaned and thudded the table with her forehead.

Sabrina took another gulp of tea. Maybe if she burned her tongue off, she wouldn't have to repeat her X-rated escapades out loud to her best friend for the third time.

Her phone vibrated on the table next to her arm and her breath caught in her throat at the sight of Russell's name.

"Mhmmmm. Sure. Nothing serious." Quinn snorted.

"W-what?" The word died in her throat as she plucked the phone from the wooden surface.

> Russell: Morning. Just checking on your ass.
>
> Russell: I mean, and your arm, too. But mostly your ass. You keep falling on it.
>
> Russell: I guess that's just the effect I have on women, eh? Falling at my feet at every turn. ;-)

> Sabrina: Ugh. Don't be a pig.
>
> Sabrina: If I say my ass is bruised and hurty will you come kiss it better?

As soon as she hit the send button, her stomach went into free-fall. What the hell was she thinking? What the hell would *he* think?

Fuck.

Fucking fuckety fuck.

> Sabrina: I mean...

Should she play dumb?

Pretend she thought it was someone else?

Pretend Quinn sent the reply?

"What the hell did you do? Your face is a kaleidoscope of emotions right now and I can't keep up." Quinn's voice was dripping with amusement, but sounded far away.

Was this what a panic attack felt like?

> Sabrina: Oh my God.
>
> Sabrina: I didn't mean...

Her brain was fritzing. Like someone had pulled the cord to start the mower, but it was just making farty zerbert sounds and not actually starting.

The phone rang in her hand and she shrieked and dropped it with a clink against her mug. The liquid in the bottom of the cup sloshed as she snatched the offending phone back up and cradled it against her chest.

She'd been spared third degree tea burns *and* losing her caffeine, win-win. If she had only been so lucky when it came to her acute case of word vomit.

"Points for an interesting method, but hugging your phone doesn't make people go away, nor does it answer the call. Talk to the boy."

Sabrina wanted to smack the smug smile off her bestie's face. But instead, she peeked at the screen, hit the green button, and held her breath.

"You did too mean it, Bubbles."

Quinn clasped her hands over her heart and mouthed, "Aww."

"And if you want me to come kiss your ass better, all you have to do is ask."

Sabrina still hadn't breathed.

"Bre?" The humor in his voice dropped and concern blunted the single word.

"I'm here." Her squeak came out breathless.

"Breathe, Bubbles."

"Why do you keep calling me that?" She traced circles on the table in front of her, trying to ground herself and slow her racing heart.

"Don't you like it?"

"I've never had someone give me a nickname like that before. I'm not sure how I feel about it. I don't know what it means."

Quinn frowned. Sabrina covered the speaker and whispered, "Who's Bubbles?"

Russell chuckled.

Quinn covered her eyes with her palm and shook her head. She grabbed a pen and notebook from the counter and scribbled "Powerpuff girls???" in large letters.

"I have a little girl who watches cartoons. She loves the Powerpuff girls. I know she's the blonde one, and Buttercup is the brunette, but you remind me more of Bubbles, that's all."

"And how exactly did I do that?"

Quinn rolled her eyes and scribbled on the pad again.

Pure-hearted. Kind. Sweet. Energetic.

"Maybe we'll watch it together sometime, and you can see for yourself."

She's kinda whiny, tho. Which tracks, you're kinda whiny too, Bre-Bre.

Quinn cradled the notepad against her chest and squeezed her entire face into a smush.

He cleared his throat. "That's uh, actually not the only reason I called."

Uh-oh.

"What's up?" Her mouth dried. Oh shit, oh shit, oh shit. Was this where he was going to tell her he was done with putting pieces of his body near pieces of her body?

Her clit would be devastated.

Say it isn't so.

"Jude is losing her mind. She keeps getting mad at the TV and demanding something, but we don't know what. We've gone through a process of elimination, and I can't find whatever she's big mad about, which of course just makes her madder."

That was it? He wanted to know what she'd watched with his daughter?

Stand down, clit-alert.

The ball of tension in her chest eased loose.

"Was there anything you watched with her that you can think of? If not, I need to assume she hates the TV all of a sudden and throw it away or something."

She blurted out a laugh. "I signed into my Disney+ account and we watched *Onward*."

"*Onward*? What's that?"

"It's a cute Pixar film about two brothers."

"Huh. Cool. Looks like I'm going shopping. I'll check it out, thanks."

She loved how he'd do anything to make his little girl happy. Her insides swooned.

"I was thinking..."

"Did it hurt?" She gasped and shoved her fist over her mouth. Her knee-jerk reaction would be the death of her. Youngest of five children, her sarcasm button was jammed on at all times.

His guffaw soothed her embarrassment and she relaxed a little. "Depends on the day and what I'm thinking about. This thought however, did not hurt."

She smiled. "Continue."

Quinn leaned forward on her elbows, fists tucked under her chin, making dreamy eyes like what she was watching was the most romantic thing she'd seen since Anna Farris's grand gesture for Chris Evans in *What's Your Number?*

Oh man, she hadn't seen that movie in so long.

"Bre?"

Shit. He was still talking.

"Yeah? I asked if you wanted to come over and watch a movie some time."

Quinn was nodding frantically across the table.

"Oh, y-yes, I'd like that."

"Cool. I won't even force a Marvel movie on you."

She could hear the smile on his face but must have stayed silent for a beat longer than reasonably expected.

"Sabrina?"

"Yeah?"

"You *have* seen the Marvel movies, right?"

"If I say no, will it mean you won't do that thing with your tongue again?"

Quinn collapsed into a heap of giggles on the table top, and Russell laughed so hard, it took a while before he spoke again.

"I'll absolutely do that thing with my tongue again."

A shot of desire struck low in her core.

"But I might inflict a Marvel movie on you after all. I'm surprised you haven't seen any of them. So many girls love them for no other reason than The Chris Factor."

Quinn had composed herself enough to nod and fan herself again.

"You're gonna need to elaborate."

"The Chris Factor?" He paused as though simply repeating himself would be enough to transmit the missing information into her brain. "Chris Pratt, Chris Hemsworth, and Chris Evans."

"Oh! I know that one. I loved him in *What's Your Number?*"

Russ groaned. "We'll fix this. Not tonight. I have a game. But, this... we need to fix this."

It was as though she'd personally affronted him by not having seen a single Marvel superhero movie. What was the big deal? Was she really missing out?

Quinn had written another note on the pad. *I've licked Captain America. He's mine. You can't have him.* She shrugged and whispered, "I don't make the rules."

"What time do you get off work?"

She dropped a fork onto the table she was cleaning with a squeak. It was her Wednesday night shift at Applebee's, and Russell was definitely not on the rota. What the hell was he doing here?

Russell chuckled. "Sorry." He leaned over and picked up the fork, sliding it onto the pile of plates in her hand. "I didn't mean to startle you."

"What are you doing here?" She blinked, attempting to slow her runaway heart to normal, and remind her libido that she was in her place of employment and couldn't dry hump a hockey player where he stood.

What the hell was her problem?

She was a strong, smart, self-sufficient woman, studying another language in a good college, and working a side hustle to pay her way. Okay, so her parents paid for her tuition, but Sabrina had drawn the line at accepting their help for her accommodation. She didn't want them going into any more debt than they'd already accrued for her older siblings just so she could get a good education. She loved kids, animals, old people... She killed bullies and mean people with kindness, and she wanted to change the world for the better someday.

Sure, she hadn't quite figured out how, but she wanted to. That had to count for something.

Never before had she been so reduced to a puddle of need and want by a man's mere presence before.

He was a drug, and she was willingly addicted.

"I came to ask what time you're getting off work." He smiled, giving a half-shrug as though he thought that much was clear.

"In about an hour."

He checked his watch. "Movie?"

She nibbled on her lip. "We have homework for class tomorrow."

Arching an eyebrow, he scoffed. "And you haven't done it already."

Heat radiating up the back of her neck, she nodded.

"If you don't want to, that's cool." He spread his arms and took a step back.

"I do."

"Then what?"

Her eyes dropped to the floor. "What if I hate all your favorite movies?"

Someone called her name from the kitchen.

Pinching her chin between his finger and thumb, he lifted her head so their eyes met. "Then you don't like my favorite movies. Not everyone is going to like everything, and that's fine. Look, I'll be back in an hour, okay?"

She nodded, suddenly feeling foolish.

"Great." He booped her nose and left.

Ninety minutes later, she sat on one side of the couch, while he sat on the other. She wasn't sure whether she was nervous that his mom could arrive home at any time or because she was simply nervous being around him. Either way, her chest grew tight.

Her legs were tucked up under her butt, and an oversized bowl of popcorn with melted butter sat on the empty cushion between them. They'd agreed to watch the movie at his mom's house. She was out for the night, Jude was already in bed, fast asleep.

"You ready?"

She nodded.

"Do you want to choose? Or do you want me to choose?"

"You choose." She took a sip of water.

"Okay, but I warn you, if I choose, we're in for the long haul. We start at the beginning and work our way through every last movie until you're inducted into the Marvel-verse fandom."

"Sounds kinda... geeky."

He chuckled. "Geeks are hot. *Captain America: The First Avenger* it is!"

Throughout the movie she cast furtive glances at him. His eyes never deviated from the TV. From the moment the opening sequence began, he was rapt, almost reverting to an excited little boy right in front of her eyes.

"Wow." She stretched her hands over her head. "That was..."

"Not yet."

"What do you mean not yet? The credits started."

She didn't miss the eye roll of epic proportions. "Bonus scenes, mid and end way through the credits in most of the movies."

"You're so intense." When the credits had finally finished, she untucked her legs and wiggled her toes.

"What did you think?"

"I can see why Quinn licked him." She groaned at yet another overshare popping out of her mouth. "I liked it. I'm excited to see what comes next."

"Music to my ears." He turned to face her on the couch, crossing his legs crisscross applesauce. "If movies aren't your thing, what is?"

"Oh, I love movies. I'd just never seen Marvel before."

He leaned towards her, brushing a wisp of hair from her face, sending tiny shimmers of excitement through her. "What kind of movies?"

"I love musicals."

His face wrinkled as though she'd said she liked kale.

Ew. That was a hard pass, even for her vegetarian self.

She was convinced no one really liked kale, they just liked to punish themselves.

"What's... your... favorite?" The way his voice curled at the end of his question suggested no matter what she answered, he wouldn't get it.

"Never seen one, eh?"

"Maybe Mary Poppins or something as a kid."

She sighed and clapped her hands. "I *love* Mary Poppins. I suppose musicals just appeal to me culturally. Most mainstream Indian movies are musicals. I do like Broadway more, though. Probably thanks to growing up here. The King and I is my favorite. I love Godspell, too." The blank look on his face tugged a giggle from her. "I'm speaking Dutch to you, aren't I?"

"Nope. Arabic. I'm sure Dutch would overlap with French in some spots and I could pick up the occasional word. This? This is all-the-way foreign to me." He shifted closer to her.

She snorted. "I'll have to change that. Or at least get Jude on my side. Girl power and all that jazz."

"She's way into Marvel, too. Her birthday party next week is going to be superhero themed." He trailed the pad of his thumb over her lips and her pulse quickened. Her attention flickered between his eyes and his mouth.

Was he going to kiss her?

The thrumming through her body demanded he kiss her.

Loudly.

She needed it.

But she needed to stay calm, and not come off as some sex-obsessed maniac.

Nice girls do nice things.

As much as her pebbled nipples tried to convince her otherwise, she was sure this wasn't what her mother had in mind when she'd given out those lectures.

Never make the first move.

Don't seem too keen.

Don't sleep with a guy until you're married.

She shook her head, a vain attempt at dislodging her mother's words from her memory. She wasn't a prude, nor a virgin, but the idea of taking charge of her sexuality, or even instigating something... made her breath falter in her chest.

Not to mention, Jude could wake up at any moment and interrupt their privacy.

She forced her buzzing body to still and sucked in a deep breath.

His knowing smile suggested he could read her mind. Or at least hear her thudding heart.

Closing her eyes, she struggled for calm.

She was focused solely on the throbbing between her thighs. Her panties were damp and her jaw ached from clenching.

Something surged through her veins. Bravery? He made her feel brave.

When her eyelids flickered open, lust swam in the depths of his cornflower eyes. She leaned forward and he met her halfway, a shiver rippling through her as he cupped her face and pulled her closer.

The kiss started gently, laced with hesitation. No tongues, just lips and featherlight caresses. She traced her hand down the front of his shirt, enjoying the way his body curved, bringing her forward on his chest as he arched.

She shook her head and broke off the kiss. A frown pinched his forehead. Dragging her palms down his chest, she pressed him further backwards. After not returning the favor in the stairwell, she didn't want him to think she was all take and no give.

Without breaking eye contact, she tugged the band of his pants and undies, freeing his thick, semi-hard cock from confinement. Her pulse tripped over itself as her heartrate quickened. Gripping the shaft, she pumped a couple of times before teasing the tip with her tongue.

A low rumbling moan from Russ confirmed he most definitely didn't hate it. When his fingers curled into her hair, she took him deeper into her mouth, humming around him and cupping his balls.

His hips jolted off the couch, jerking his dick deeper into her throat. She fought a laugh. No matter how anxious she was about pleasing him, the warmth consuming her chest at him melting under her touch was unstoppable.

Her entire focus was on keeping her teeth away from his length as he fucked her mouth, grunting with every thrust. She squeezed his balls and he groaned. "Fuck. So close."

"Hey, I'm home!" The light flicked on as Russell's mom's voice travelled across the open plan living space.

Sabrina coughed. Inhaling a rather large dick into her airway wasn't the best idea when said dick's mother had just joined the room.

Shit.

Russ grabbed a throw cushion from the sofa next to him and covered his crotch while attempting to wiggle his pants back up. Sabrina wiped her mouth and smoothed out her clothes.

"It's okay." His whispered encouragement, coupled with the brittle smile on his face, were less than reassuring.

It was definitely not okay.

"Hey sweet—Oh!" The dramatic gasp from his mother made Sabrina's skin crawl. "I didn't realize… oh my!"

Sabrina sprung from the couch, knocking over the empty bottle of water. "Shit. Shoot. Sorry, I was just leaving."

"Clearly."

"Mom!"

"Well. What reaction would you like from me, Russell? It's hardly what I expected to come home to." She turned away so her back was to them and folded her arms.

Ouch. What the hell was this woman's problem? They were consenting adults. Jude was still asleep…

Shit. Jude *was* still asleep, right?

Rescuing the water bottle from the floor, she screwed on the top. Russ was on his feet, the outline of his still-hard penis visible through his sweats.

"You don't need to leave." Russell's voice was hard.

"It's okay. You have early practice tomorrow, right?"

He nodded, his nostrils flaring. "Stay."

She wrapped her arms around herself and rubbed her biceps. "I should definitely go."

He reached out and stroked her arm. She wanted to collapse into him and hide from the mortification engulfing her from the inside.

Pulling his hand away, she dropped it by his side, leaned in, and gave him a chaste peck on the mouth. "I'll see you tomorrow."

His frown deepened, but his hand met the curve of her spine as they walked to the door. After such a nice evening, leaving with a sour taste in her mouth felt ugly. Shame coated her skin and wedged in her throat. What would her parents think if they knew how she'd behaved? She wanted the ground to open and swallow her whole.

"I'm so sorry." Her low whisper came out a croak as she fought back tears.

His arms folded around her. "No. I don't accept that apology, Bubbles. You did nothing wrong. We did nothing wrong.

I'm sorry. I'm sorry she's so damn rude." He squeezed her once more before stepping back and grazing her cheek with his knuckles.

A whirlpool of emotion churned in his eyes, and his fists clenched at his sides. He offered her a smile, but they both knew it was weak. Blowing him a kiss, she turned on her heel and didn't look back.

CHAPTER 12
Sabrina

"This party is dumb." Sabrina drained the last of whatever potent mixture lay in the bottom of her red solo cup and scoured the kitchen for her next fruity victim.

"You've said everything sucks since—"

Sabrina smashed a hand over Quinn's mouth. "Don't say it." She shook her head frantically.

Was her head still moving after she instructed it to stop? That only happened when she was drunk, and she was most certainly not drunk. "I'm not drunk enough to mention it again."

"Still no word from him?"

It had been two days since the object of her affection's mother had come home to find Sabrina's lips wrapped around her darling son's rock hard cock. She hadn't heard a word from Russell, or his cock, since.

At first she'd been patient, stewing in her shame and embarrassment. Then she'd called her parents to distract her, pretending everything was normal, all the while dying inside.

What would they say if they ever found out? But the more time that passed, the more she was just plain pissed.

"Drink." Quinn thrust a cup at her, pink liquid sloshing over the brim.

"What is it?"

"Does it matter? Drink." Quinn touched the bottom of the cup and helped Sabrina tip it to her mouth. "You're insufferable. We both need you to drink."

Guilt surfed the pink drink all the way to her stomach.

It was a fair assessment.

Everything was irritating her. The lack of decent snacks at the house party... the obnoxiousness of the jocks loitering around with hot girls clinging onto their every word... the booming music... she shouldn't have come to the dumb party, and they both knew it.

"Sorry." She passed the cup back to Quinn. "I'm just going to go. I don't mean to be Debbie Downer."

Quinn rejected the cup and shook her head. "I'm not letting you leave like this. Who knows who you'll murder with that scowl on the way home? Look, there's a bunch of hot guys in a circle about twenty feet behind you playing spin the bottle. They're short on hot girls. Let's kiss that hockey player right out of your system."

Her friend tugged her across the room and plopped on the carpet with a "Hey" to everyone else in the circle.

It wasn't a smart idea.

But maybe kissing someone new would help her forget about the tall, dark, and panty-meltingly handsome hockey player she couldn't get out of her head.

What could possibly go wrong?

She had barely downed half her drink and plopped on the floor between Quinn and a slim, Asian dude with green glasses and an intriguing scar on his chin when things went wrong.

Russell fucking Stewart sauntered over to the group and

dropped onto the floor in their circle. There was no way he didn't see her, which meant he was ignoring her. Jackass.

He wore a Captain America shirt and a pair of navy sweats. Couldn't he have at least made some kind of effort?

Ugh. What was it about hot guys? They fell out of bed, at best ran some product through their hair, tossed on a pair of old sweats and still looked hot as fuck, when women spent thirteen hours getting ready just to leave their house.

Not her, but... other women. Women who knew how to apply make-up that didn't make them look like Coco the freakin' clown.

She drank another huge mouthful of liquor and it burned the whole way down.

Burned like the smoldering glare Russell was throwing her way.

What was his deal this time? Had mommy's good little boy decided Sabrina had corrupted him on the couch? Was he not allowed to play with her anymore?

She suppressed a snort.

Damn. Too far. Drinking made her mean.

Three couples had kissed so far. Quinn was currently making out with some geeky looking guy Sabrina had never seen before, but her attention kept dragging back to the angry hockey player scowling at her from across the circle.

She returned his frown with a frown of her own. The corner of his mouth twitched.

Was he laughing at her?

Was her anger somehow amusing to him?

Beautiful brooding bastard.

Taking another swallow, she paid attention to Quinn's spin. It landed on Sabrina. No biggie. They'd kissed before and they'd kiss again.

When she returned to her space in the circle, there was a heat to Russell's fury. For a moment she wondered what it would be like to get angry fucked by a hockey god whose tongue made her smother cries for deities from all pantheons she herself didn't believe in.

When she spun the bottle, she wasn't sure whether she wanted it to land on him or not land on him, but the growl with which he surged towards her as it stopped on him had her clit aching for his touch.

She shoved her palm in his face. "This doesn't mean I'm not angry at you."

He pushed her hand away. "This doesn't mean I'm not angry at you, either."

"What the fuck are you angry at me f—?"

His mouth captured hers mid-sentence and fireworks exploded as their tongues collided. She wasn't sure if it was the alcohol, rage, or proximity to the man molded from pure sex, but heat spread through her entire body as she grabbed the front of his shirt and gave him every bit as good as she got.

"That is so fucking hot." Quinn's whisper wasn't so much a whisper, jolting Russell and Sabrina apart. Quinn's cheeks flared as red as her hair, presumably when she realized the whole circle had heard her... Including the still-glaring Russell who sat back in his space.

Sabrina touched a careful fingertip to her swollen lips as Russell pulled out his phone and jabbed at the screen.

Her phone vibrated in her ass pocket. Fuck him. He could wait. She leaned back, casually lifting her drink and taking a sip. His eyes narrowed, more thumping of his screen and her ass vibrated again. She smiled at him, eyebrow arched.

Another vibration.

Another drink.

The vibrating stopped when Russ's roommate, Linc, stopped to talk to him. She tossed him a wave when he caught her eye, before pulling out her phone and shaking her head at the list of notifications from him on her screen.

> Russell: We aren't finished here.
>
> Russell: You know damn well what you did.
>
> Russell: Are you ignoring me?
>
> Russell: Real Mature.
>
> Russell: I can do this all night, Bubbles.

She snorted.

When he turned his attention back to her, her entire body ignited. She gulped, cautiously, half afraid she would swallow her tongue, choke, and die in the process.

Her lady parts were not ready to die without first having the full Russell Stewart experience.

Was he licking his lips?

Holy shit.

He was licking his lips.

She sent up a prayer to the gods she didn't believe in, adding a few more for good measure.

But the heat in her body only intensified.

Maybe praying to multiple gods was where she had faltered.

Maybe it really did have to be an either-or situation.

Maybe in this case, more was not better.

Maybe... shit. He was still staring.

She needed to go home and put herself out of her misery. Distance between her and he-who-glared, his equal parts ice-and-heat stare would both cool her down and clear her head.

Drinking the last of her drink, she turned to tell Quinn she was leaving – following it up with a text because her best friend's tongue was down another guy's throat, and she was 92% convinced she hadn't heard a damn thing.

She stood, waiting for just a moment for the full effect of the alcohol to hit her. Grinning, she gave herself a mental pat on the back for not falling on her face. Or, in fact, her ass.

Without a backwards glance, she strode to the door, slipped her coat over her shoulders, and stepped outside. She'd made a clean escape, so she slowed her pace.

"Are you crazy?"

She groaned, spinning to face the owner of the gruff voice.

"You ask that a lot."

"Let me take you home."

"Pfft." She wasn't sure any words had come out of her mouth, but her derisive snort-hiccup was pretty clear. "We're pissed at each other, remember?"

He charged two steps toward her, putting himself within arm's reach. "Damn fucking straight we're pissed at each other. You subjected my two-year-old daughter to a movie about two kids trying to bring their dead father back."

Once they'd filtered through her alcohol-induced-fog, his words splashed over her like ice water. She had in fact done that. She nodded slowly. "I did do that." Her voice came out a whisper and her jaw trembled. "I didn't think." *Shit. Poor Jude. She's already lost one parent, and I made her watch a movie about losing a father.*

"Of course you didn't think." His voice had gone from sexy, grumbly angry dad voice, to pained and loud. He jerked his thumb at his chest. "I am all she's got. And while it wasn't a second thought to you, we don't know how her little brain processed the fact that those boys had no father and brought him back from the fucking dead."

His body vibrated with rage, but she wasn't afraid of him. In fact, she wasn't even sure the anger he was spraying her direction was truly all meant for her.

"I'm sorry. You're right, I didn't even think about it." She stepped to him, hand outstretched, ready to touch the collar of his jacket, but she stopped.

Was it her place to comfort him?

Her body hummed yes, but her brain and the creases on Russell's forehead gave her pause.

He heaved out a breath and his body deflated. "Your turn."

"My turn?"

"Why are you pissed at me?"

"Oh. It doesn't matter."

"Agh!" He raked his hands through his hair. "Of course it matters. Obviously I upset you, too. Why don't you just confront the problem so we can move forward?"

He wanted to move forward? She could hardly tell what with all the yelling and arm flailing he was doing.

She tilted her head and scanned his face for any sign that the invitation to speak her mind was a trap. It wasn't something she was used to. As the youngest in the family, and a woman, she'd always known her place at home.

Don't talk when the grownups are talking.

Let the men speak first.

Sit quietly and don't make a scene.

It didn't matter what was wrong, her parents would undoubtedly take her siblings' side anyway. So she made herself small, quiet, retreated to her books and never rocked the boat.

All Russell seemed to do was rock the damn boat, and it worked for him. Sparks of energy flew from him as he spoke, as though saying the things that were bothering him, cleansed him somehow.

Maybe it could work that way for her, too. Maybe she'd feel better for getting it off her chest.

She squared her shoulders and took a deep breath. "You let me leave your house the other night after your mom..." She waved a hand. "Y'know. And I haven't heard from you since."

He paled. "I've been busy. I had practice, and school... I—"

She held up a hand, hurt pinching her insides like someone had put a line of clothes pegs on her heart. "Too busy to talk to me. I get it."

Of course he was too busy to talk to her. The world blurred at the edges and her head spun. Was the cold air making her drunker? Or had the alcohol just taken a while to affect her?

Either way, she was too close to the man who had no time for her, the man who never said thank you, the man whose mother hated her. She needed distance. Her breath stopped in her tightening chest.

His nostrils flared and his lips rested in a firm, straight line. Dude was pissed.

He probably thought she was some super-clinger or something dumb. So she needed a little assurance his mother hadn't cockblocked her all the way out of the picture. Was that really so bad?

From the deepening V between his eyebrows, she was taking that as a yes.

He stepped toward her.

She stepped back.

"Let me take you home."

She held up a hand. "Just..." She stepped back again. "Give me a minute to think away from your hotness."

His face broke into a bright smile. "You think I'm hot?"

She groaned. "Oh please. Every time you move, you scorch the earth."

Like he didn't know. How could anyone think he wasn't hot?

He chuckled, but spread his arms wide and took a step back.

She loved how he respected her boundaries, which only

made his beautiful face frustrate her all the more. She was angry at him, damn it.

Canting his head, he raised an eyebrow. "Is 'die of frostbite' at the top of your bucket list or something?"

Her feet stuttered as she stepped toward him. Without missing a beat, he swooped in and caught her.

What a jerk.

She sighed, frustration leaving her body on a shuddery breath. "You're making it really hard to be angry at you when you're being all..." She flapped an arm at him.

"Sexy?" He struck a pose, hand behind his head. "Adorable?" Another pose. "Chivalrous?" And another.

As she laughed, he grabbed her hand and led her across the street to his car.

She wagged a finger at him. "I'm not kissing you tonight."

He smirked. "You're too drunk for me to let you kiss me tonight, Bubbles."

"That's what I just said!"

The smirk that made her want to smack him or suck him stayed on his face the entire ride to her apartment. He circled the car and opened the door, leading her to the entrance of her apartment building.

He brushed a light kiss on her knuckles, then flashed his mega-watt smile that made her knees weak and somehow expelled every ounce of air from her lungs.

"Text me when you get home." Great, now she sounded like someone's mother.

He shoved his hands in his pockets before heading back to his car. She watched until he drove out of sight before stumbling her way up to her apartment and falling – still fully clothed – onto her bed.

It wasn't long before Russell texted, which was just as well because alcohol was making her eyes and muscles heavy.

> Russell: Home safely. Hydrate and take some Tylenol, Bubbles.

> Sabrina: You're not the boss of me.

> Sabrina: But I admit, that does sound like a smart idea.

She shimmied off her pants and dragged her shirt over her head before hunting in the bathroom cabinet for Tylenol.

> Russell: What are you doing tomorrow?

> Sabrina: I have a four hour shit tomorrow.

> Russell: You really need to take better care of that ass, Bre.

> Sabrina: What?

Her breath stopped as she re-read their messages.
Oh shit.

> Sabrina: SHIFT!!!!!! A four hour shift.

> Sabrina: Ducking autocorrect!

> Sabrina: Fucking. No one is EVER saying ducking. Not ever.

> Sabrina: I really wanted to kill you tonight.

> Russell: Wow. It's always the quiet ones.

> Sabrina: KISS. I really wanted to kiss you tonight.

> Russell: Mhmm. I really wanted to "kill" you tonight, too.

She snorted a bray of a laugh as she climbed under the comforter

> Sabrina: I quit. I'm going to bed. We can talk tomorrow.

> Russell: Sure. After your epic shit. Sweet dreams, Bubbles.

> Russell: And drink the water!

CHAPTER 13
Russell

"She just... gave it to Cleo?"

Cleo and Linc were officially a thing, whether Linc was ready to admit it or not. He was head-over-heels for the sassy Latina, walking around with love hearts and glitter and shit popping out of his head.

"Cleo said she just walked right into the Sugar Bean and asked her to give it to you. You and Sabrina... are you a thing?"

It was the morning after Linc handed him a gift bag for Jude, from Sabrina, and Russell was still every bit as pissed off as he had been at the time. Russell, lying on the floor of their dorm, hands tucked behind his head, growled. "I thought we were working on it, but I guess not since she gave the gift to Cleo and not me."

But did he want to be?

"So she's just being friendly? And not girlfriendly?" Linc's warm words did little to melt Russell's ice-hard irritation. "Did you piss her off?"

"What am I? Clairvoyant?"

"Have you asked her why she gave it to Cleo and not you?"

Russell focused his attention on amplifying his Fuck Off

Waves in the hopes Linc would drop it. Russ had dropped Sabrina at her apartment a few days prior, they'd texted a bit before bed, but he hadn't seen or messaged her since. She'd sent him a few texts and tried to call, but he was busy and hadn't answered her. Surely that couldn't be why she'd gone to Cleo? So he was busy, so what? It wasn't like it was a big deal.

Then Linc landed home with a superhero bag and it became apparent that it was, in fact, a very big deal, because she didn't even want to see him to pass along a gift.

Why did he care so much that she'd given the bag to Cleo and not him? He wasn't sure, but he cared more than he wanted to admit.

Linc ignored Russell's silence and kept up his inquisition. "So you didn't text her to ask?"

More silence.

"You guys haven't spoken since you dropped her home?" His frown was almost comical, as though he was doing a jigsaw puzzle and couldn't find the last piece to complete the picture. "You just ghosted each other?"

Russ scrunched up his face. "She texted me a couple times the next morning. And called, once, but I was busy and didn't call her back." He shrugged.

Linc sat up on the bed and slapped his pillow. "You *still* haven't texted her back?"

"No!" Russ was practically bellowing at his best friend. In truth, he had no idea why he was so frustrated. He growled again.

"I feel like you need to talk to the woman, man. You're... feral."

"I just don't know where I stand with her. One minute we're... y'know..."

"You fucked her?"

Russell's head connected with his palm with more force than he intended. "No." He groaned.

"So basically you left things after your mom interrupted?"

Russell nodded. "I took her drunk ass home. She was too drunk to have a serious conversation with. And she was kinda quiet." He paused, recalling the night. "She was a bit quieter than normal, I figured she was embarrassed because Mom burst in on... Anyway, at first I was too angry at Mom for what happened, for what she'd said. I thought when I'd cooled off I'd circle back to talk to Bre but I got busy."

"Did you communicate this to her? Give her a heads up that when you cooled off, you'd talk? Or that you got busy and you'd talk to her in a few days?"

It felt as though Lincoln was attempting to steer Russell somewhere, but he was so caught up in knots he had no idea where the conversation was leading.

"We were supposed to talk the next day."

"But?"

"But... we didn't? I just told you I didn't answer her. What do you want from me, man?" He raked his hands through his hair.

"Hey." He held up his hands, palms facing Russ. "I'm trying to help here, okay?"

Russell nodded and gestured for his friend to continue.

"Is there any reason she might think you didn't want to talk to her after you dropped her home that night?"

"Other than the days of not answering her texts?"

It was Linc's turn to groan. "Know what I don't get?"

"What's that?"

"Why the hell people think you're this suave ladies' man. You're like a fucking caveman."

"I don't *do* relationships, Linc. You know this."

"Does she?"

Maybe she just needed space. Maybe *she* didn't do relationships, or whatever they had become. *Or maybe your Fuck Off Waves were too strong and sent her running.* "Yeah,

I'm pretty sure—aw fuck." He covered his face with both palms.

"Russ?"

"Yeah?" His reply was muffled by his hands. He refused to move them. He didn't want to see Linc's smirk.

"Is it at all possible that the lovely Sabrina might not have wanted to bother you in case you thought her too dependent? Too needy? Or, I dunno, I mean, I'm grasping at straws here... in case she thought you got the impression she wanted more than you were willing to give her?"

Scrubbing a hand over his bristly jaw, Russ groaned again and leaned forward, resting his elbows on his knees and his head in his hands.

"Is it possible she's keeping her distance to protect her heart from the tall, dark, single father hockey player who has an overflowing plate and who doesn't date?"

"It's possible."

"Is it also possible the aforementioned hockey player thought she was a stage five clinger when all she did was return his wallet to the ice rink?"

"Also possible."

"What was that? I couldn't quite make that out since your head is buried in your oh-fuck-he's-right hands."

"Smug isn't a good look on you, Linc."

"Like it or not, Russ, your fuck off vibes can be pretty strong. The intimidating thing works for you, especially on the ice, and to keep the bunnies at a safe distance. But you gotta lower the drawbridge if you want to actually let someone in."

Russ pushed off and stood up. "I don't know that I want to let *someone* in, Linc. What about Jude?" He paced like a lion in a cage. Indecision churning in his stomach. And something he couldn't identify clawing at his chest.

"You mean, the kid *someone* dropped a gift off to a stranger for? Oh, I dunno, Russ. I feel like she might have a vague idea of just how important Jude is to you, what with all the trouble she went to so your favorite person had something for her birthday."

Lincoln wasn't wrong.

Sabrina not only made sure the most important person in his life had a gift for the most important day of the year, but she was also keeping her distance, giving him the space he needed too.

But what about what she needed?

Guilt gnawed at his gut. "I'm heading out."

"Atta boy!"

Bent over a table, reaching for silverware at the far end, Bre's perfect ass made his dick stir in his pants. He'd bet on her being at work, but now he'd made his way to Applebee's and stood three feet away from her, he wasn't quite sure what he wanted to say.

He set the gift bag on the table next to her elbow and waited for recognition. She straightened, glanced at the bag, then him, then back at the bag.

Her face fell, mouth slack, eyes sad. "You don't want my gift?" The pain wrapped around her words squeezed the air out of his body, and he shook his head.

"It's not that."

In hindsight, he probably should have considered that it might look like he was returning her gift.

She pursed her lips and gestured at the armfuls of dishes. "I'll be right back."

He nodded, chewing the inside of his cheek. What if Linc was wrong and she'd created space because she wasn't interested? And the gift to Jude was just a sweet gesture?

Get it together, damnit.

When she returned, she rubbed her palms on her thighs, a shy smile on her face. "I wasn't sure I'd see you again. When you didn't text..."

"Yeah. I'm sorry about that."

Someone hollered from the kitchen and Bre winced.

"Look, I know you're working, I know I shouldn't have just shown up here and..." He brushed a hand over his stubble. "I know I was a jerk and didn't message you when I said I would but I don't want to give Jude your gift."

When her eyebrows rose on her forehead and her eyes bugged wider, he hurried to continue.

"I want you to give it to her yourself. At her birthday party. Saturday morning, 10AM."

"Isn't it game day?"

"You're following hockey now?" His shoulders loosened. Hockey was safe territory. He knew hockey, he understood hockey.

She smirked. "It's a hockey campus, stud. Some girls follow the sport, not the ass."

"Speaking of ass... I hope you're taking care of yours." He winked at her and a smile tugged at her mouth.

The yell from the kitchen repeated.

"Saturday at 10AM?"

He pointed finger guns at her. "That's the one. Mom's place. See you there?" Hope punctuated every word. Could he be any more pathetic? And finger guns? Really? The woman was making him embarrass himself in public.

She giggled and pointed finger guns right back at him with a wide smile. "Yup, see you there."

No trace of mockery, just kindness in her eyes. His heart squeezed. *This fucking woman.* He nodded, warmth curling around his chest, and turned to leave.

"Russell?"

"I know you probably have everything figured out already. But is there anything you need me to bring? Should I come early to help set up?"

Shaking his head, he stepped back. "It's all good. We have it covered."

Her face fell for just long enough for him to register the disappointment, but she quickly replaced it with a soft smile.

You gotta lower the drawbridge if you want to let someone in.

He might not need help, but maybe he wanted it. Or maybe it was something he needed to give her, the opportunity to help.

Maybe it was time to crack the drawbridge.

"Uh... But if you wanted to come early to help keep the birthday girl out of our hair while Mom and I set things up... That would be okay too."

Her eyes brightened and her teeth pinched her bottom lip as she nodded.

Staring back at her with an equally wide smile, he waited for the irritation of accepting help from someone to settle low into his stomach. But even as he walked back to the car, there was no sign of it. In fact, relief seeped into his muscles at the idea of her being around to help out at Jude's party.

He was officially in new territory. He had no clue how to navigate not doing everything by himself. Mulling it over as he drove home, tendrils of doubt curled around his spine.

Either she'd show up, or she wouldn't.

Either she'd help, or she wouldn't.

Either she was reliable, or she wasn't.

And it was almost time to find out.

❄

The doorbell chimed at 8.31AM on Saturday morning.

Russell smiled. She was on time. A good start.

His anxiety loosened like a shoelace coming undone.

When he pulled the door open, she stood with a smile on her face, dressed in an oversized sweater and princess leggings, and holding a tray of hot drinks in one hand and bags in the other.

"Morning!" Her smile was contagious. She leaned forward, kissing his cheek. There was no trace of apprehension about being in a confined space with his mother anywhere on her face. "Did you sleep okay? Or were you running through lists of things in your brain all night long?"

Stretching, he yawned. "I slept. I'm exhausted. The extra practices, the group projects, the birthday party..."

Her smile flipped to a concerned frown. "It's a lot."

Taking the tray of hot drinks, he ushered her inside and closed the door.

She dropped her bags onto the island in the kitchen. "Thanks for letting me do this."

Something other than the fact she seemed to enjoy spending time with him and his daughter was going on. Her shoulders rolled forward, and dark circles lingered under her sad eyes.

"Everything okay?"

She nodded, but her fake smile wasn't fooling anyone. "It's my grandma. She's sick and deteriorating. My sister is heavily pregnant and having some health issues there, too. My family seems to think I need to drop my whole life and hurry home to tend to everyone else. Add in work, and school..."

"It's a lot." He echoed her own sentiment back at her. Only hers sounded way more than what he had on his plate.

Nibbling on her lip, she nodded again. "I just needed to

feel useful, I guess." Her rigid shrug held more than she was leading him to believe.

"It's okay to live your own life, you know." He reached out to stroke her cheek as her chin trembled.

Shit. Was she going to cry?

"Hiiiiiiiiiiiiiiiii!" Toddler bed-head in all its glory, Jude flung herself at Sabrina with a squeal.

Sabrina's entire demeanor changed in less than a second. She pulled her shoulders back, straightened her spine, and her face instantly lit up in a bright smile as she made a low bow. "Your Majesty."

Jude giggled.

Throwing a caution-filled glance at Russell, Sabrina straightened and turned to the bags on the island behind her.

"I hope it's not too forward." She dropped her voice to a whisper as Jude swung a Barbie around by her hair. "Growing up we got donuts for breakfast on our birthday. Quinn and I do it every year. I grabbed some in case you hadn't eaten yet and..."

She wouldn't meet his gaze. "I mean, if you'd rather not, I totally get it. Sugar coma before a party, probably not the kindest thing I could have suggested, but I wanted to bring them anyway, just in case."

He chuckled and rubbed the space between her shoulders before crossing the kitchen to grab plates. "It's a great idea."

"Yeah?" Her face lit up again. Her smile could melt the ice at the X, where his life-long favorite team – one he hoped to be part of some day – the Minnesota Wild, played. He wanted to keep her smiling forever.

He nodded. "What else you got in those bags?"

Her smile softened. "I brought a costume. I wasn't sure if anyone was dressing up, but I didn't want to miss out on a costume opportunity. And her gift is there, too."

"You brought a costume?" They heard Mom before they

saw her. But he didn't miss the flinching of tiny muscles on Sabrina's face.

She didn't miss a beat before replying, though. "Yes ma'am. I figured if nothing else Russell wouldn't be the only one dressed as a princess."

A faint smile played on Mom's lips. Was it possible she was warming to Sabrina's charm, wit, and all around awesomeness?

"That was very sweet of you. And coffee and donuts?" Mom leaned between him and Sabrina to help herself to a jelly donut. "Trying to impress?"

"With respect, ma'am. I think I've already impressed the only Stewarts I need to." Sabrina's face remained impassive, chin tipped high enough to radiate confidence, but not into cocky territory. Her eyes narrowed and determination shone in their depths as though challenging Mom to say something, but her smile only grew.

Pride surged through his veins, replacing the protectiveness that coursed through him when Mom started speaking.

Where had Sabrina's bravery come from? He had never been more attracted to her than he was watching her face off with his mother.

Mom glanced down at Jude who was still inflicting bodily harm on her Barbies on the floor, before nodding. "It seems like you have, yes."

The two women stared at each other in silence for a long moment, as though Mom was sizing up her opposition and Sabrina's moment of bravery had run its course. With a nod, Mom turned and left the room as quickly as she'd entered. "I'll get started on the party room."

Sabrina blew out a long, wobbly breath. "That woman is terrifying." Her voice shook and her face had turned almost green.

"For what it's worth? You're doing just fine. This is new territory for all of us."

Sabrina's hands still trembled and she sucked in slow breaths. "I don't know why I can't channel the same courage when it comes to my own family."

He didn't know why she couldn't either.

She shook her head like she was clearing thoughts out of her mind before clapping her hands. "Not the time. Alright, Your Majesty. It's time for dolls and donuts!" She grabbed a plate, two donuts, and some chocolate milk from the fridge, navigating the space like she'd lived there her entire life.

For a moment it appeared as though she was going to try to balance everything in her hands. The last thing he needed was for Sabrina to spill chocolate milk over Mom's precious white rug. "Here, let me help."

Taking the sippy cup and glass of chocolate milk, something warm sparked in his chest as Sabrina reached out to Jude, who didn't hesitate before slipping her tiny hand into Bre's.

"Let's go slay some dragons… and donuts."

Jude laughed up at Sabrina as though she was the funniest person alive. He glanced up in time to note Mom ducking her head back around the corner of the formal living room – which was less formal, more just a wide open space.

Russell understood caution, but in time, perhaps Mom could come around to the idea of him having someone else in his life.

He lived in hope.

"Haaaaappy birthday to youuuuu."

Cheers and claps rattled around the space as the song came to an end. Jude's cheeks puffed wide as she attempted to blow out the candles on her two tier, 3D superhero birthday cake.

Sabrina stood at the back of the room, dressed as Princess Anna, complete with an auburn wig, braided in pigtails over her shoulders. She held a jug of punch in her hand, refilling the empty cups of anyone who passed her.

Mom moved it so she could slice it onto paper plates and pass it out to the eight children sitting around the table.

Linc, Finn, and Sébastien hovered around the table of snacks, keeping to themselves, while parents of the kids from Jude's two weekly playgroups milled around the room chatting.

The kid next to Jude dropped his slice of cake on the floor as soon as it was handed to him. His bottom lip trembled and his eyes welled with instant tears.

Before anyone could act, Jude reached her palm to stroke the little boy's face. "S'ok. No cry." Without hesitation or seemingly a second thought, she picked up her slice of cake and handed it to him with a smile.

Russell's chest tightened and his throat clogged with emotion. His daughter's kindness and compassion knew no bounds. He had to look away or he was in severe danger of crying in front of his teammates at his kid's birthday party.

His eyes met Sabrina's. She dabbed at her eyes with a princess napkin, a warm smile on her face. She clutched the napkin over her chest. Linc said something to her and she giggled with a nod.

Her ease at chatting with his teammates was surprisingly comforting to him. Mom, on the other hand, jabbed at a piece of cake with a plastic fork. Her face flitted between disapproving Mom-frown and curiosity when he caught her staring at Sabrina.

He was sure the fact she'd worn a princess costume when no one else but Jude was in costume, had earned points for her, but maybe there was something more to it. Was Mom feeling replaced? Did she think Sabrina helping at the party was somehow bumping her down the list of importance?

Dad had left her for another woman, and perhaps she was simply scared of being made redundant from Russell and Jude's life too.

An hour later, Sabrina – still in full costume – hugged Linc and the guys goodbye before slipping into the kitchen as Russell and his mom handed out party favors and waved off their guests.

They found her, wig-off, sleeves up, Glad trash bag in hand, clearing down the garbage from the party room and kitchen.

"Oh! You don't have to do that." Mom darted toward her, reaching for the trash bag.

"I know. I want to, though. I've got this, if you want to go snuggle Jude. It's probably time for her nap, right? I saw her rubbing at her eyes."

Mom's face softened into a small smile before she nodded. "Sounds like a plan. Thanks."

"Where do you want me?" Russell held his hands wide and gestured around the room.

Her eyes flared with heat as she held his gaze. His lips twitched into a smile as he arched his brow. He cleared his throat. "Maybe later. What can I do to help?" His semi-hard dick objected to the change of direction.

"You can cut me a slice of the cake I didn't get around to trying, then wrap the rest of it up."

He saluted her. "Yes, ma'am."

A few minutes later, Mom appeared back in the kitchen.

"She's already asleep. I guess opening forty thousand birthday gifts will do that to a two year old." Her voice was laced with nostalgia. "Three year old."

Sabrina didn't miss a beat. "Yes ma'am, you officially have a threenager. Sooooooo much worse than the terrible twos."

"Wait, what?" Russell's stomach dipped. "W-worse?"

She had to be kidding. There was a state worse than the terrible twos? Why was there no instruction manual for kids to warn people of such things?

A warm hand cupped his face and she kissed his cheek. "I'm sorry to be the bearer of bad news, but yeah. It's a little known secret. My nephew seemed to have adopted a demon when he was three."

His mouth dried up. His vision tunneled inwards, and for a few seconds, he was blind with panic.

Was she stroking his arm and shushing him?

"Hey." She paused until he met her gaze. "It'll be okay. You've totally got this. You're a tough-as-nails hockey player. A tiny terrorist threenager princess doesn't stand a chance." She winked at him before dropping a light kiss on his lips.

Her confidence enveloped him like reinforced steel, and out of the corner of his eye, Mom nodded with a reassuring smile on her face. "Sabrina, would you like to stay for lunch?"

Bre dropped her hands like she'd touched an open flame. Her eyes widened, as though she'd forgotten his Mom stood watching the entire exchange.

"Thank you, but I have a shift at work to go to. I've got my uniform in the car."

He wasn't ready to let his ray of sunshine leave. He'd hardly seen her since she landed on his doorstep, a bundle of light and sugary snacks. He grabbed her hand and squeezed. "Come back for dinner?"

He didn't care that he sounded pathetically eager, nor did he miss the smirk and eye roll Mom didn't even try to hide.

Bre turned to cast a wary glance at Mom before giving a cursory nod. "I'd love to. I'd offer to bring dessert, but I feel like we'll all be eating cake for a week."

At her presumption she'd be around for cake-consumption, a ripple of anxiety and irritation passed through him. Were they at that stage? Was she part of his everyday life? Was this the logical next step for them to take together? Making plans and existing in each other's spaces?

Was he ready for that?

The idea of not seeing her or sharing cake with her left a sour taste in his mouth. Maybe he needed to be open to the fact he wanted this woman in his life and needed to just... go with it.

He swallowed hard. He'd never been one to just go with anything, ever.

"Russell?"

"Mm?"

"You look like you have indigestion. Are you okay?" Concern pinched Sabrina's face.

He nodded. "I was just thinking I might need to bring some of the cake to the team. I'm not sure we can manage it all. And if we can, I'm not sure we should."

She giggled. "True story. As tempting as it is to turn up to work dressed as Princess Anna, I should probably get changed and head in. If you're sure about dinner, I'd love to come back. But if things change in the meantime, just drop me a text to let me know."

Had she read his thoughts? Or was she simply so considerate of other people that she could tell the idea of such a commitment was causing a low-key freak out?

He'd never had a girl over for a family dinner before. While his stomach curdled like milk left out in the sun, he reminded himself that Sabrina wasn't anything like Jude's mom, Elise, and it was only a meal, not marriage.

CHAPTER 14
Russell

"Dinner was delicious. Thank you, Mrs. Stewart." Sabrina had seemingly found the secret to getting on Mom's good side. She'd asked for a second helping of Mom's veggie hot dish *and* helped clean up yet again.

He got the impression Sabrina wasn't intentionally trying to impress them. It was just how she was, and Mom – the feeder that *she* was – couldn't help but like someone who loved her food.

Mom kissed Jude on the forehead, ruffling the little girl's curls, before grabbing her purse. "I'm heading over to the nursing home to see grandma. She needs a few things now that she's out of the hospital. And cake, obviously. I'll be back in a few hours." She waved at Sabrina and left.

"That was... abrupt?" Sabrina's forehead creased.

"I think she's just upended by the fact I brought a girl home and she isn't sure how to deal. She's fluctuating between disapproval, consternation, and maybe even feeling conflicted 'cause she actually likes you." He chuckled. "It's just been the three of us for a while now."

"What happened to your dad?" She handed him a pot to dry and removed the stopper from the sink to let the water drain.

"He up and left one day. Made himself a new family with his assistant. Triplets, a dog, two cats, white picket fence; the whole shebang. I mean, he tried to be *present* for me... for a while. If we're counting throwing money at my mom to help her buy a car for me. But I guess it just got to be too much work, or I wasn't worth the effort. And if I hadn't needed his guilt money, I wouldn't have let Mom take it."

The poorly sutured wound in his chest from his father's abandonment threatened to come undone.

Sabrina dried her hands and squeezed his arm. "I'm sorry. Parents can be real dicks sometimes."

He nodded. "Mom's just protective. She'll come around though."

She arched an eyebrow, but didn't say anything.

"And if she doesn't, it doesn't matter. You were right. You have the only Stewarts on your side that you need."

He felt every bit of the surprise she was clearly fighting from showing on her face. Chuckling again, he put the pot away.

"What's next in your night time routine?"

Her genuine interest in his daily life chipped away at pieces of the wall he'd built around himself. "Bath and bed for the munchkin. You can help if you want, or you can hang here till we're done."

Her indignation was instant as she folded her arms and frowned. "And miss story time? Are you *kidding*?"

❇

Forty minutes later, Jude was bathed, dressed in a new pair of jammies someone had gifted for her birthday. She'd insisted on stories from both Russell *and* Sabrina, and now she was down for the night, he couldn't sit still.

He'd never been nervous around a woman before, but every nerve ending in his body was raw, charged with a bone-deep ache to be closer to Bre.

She bumped into his back when he stopped outside his bedroom door. "Oof! You need to come with brake lights."

His heart thudded wildly in his chest and his dick twitched as he chuckled. "Sorry." He turned to face her. Fighting the pull was futile, so he closed the distance between them, leaving less than a foot of space.

"You have serious face. What's wrong?"

"Nothing... I..." Scrubbing a hand across his jaw, he flicked his gaze to his bedroom door. "I don't wanna be the guy who assumes... y'know... or who drags you into his room to have his wicked way with you. Buuuuut I also don't wanna be busted by my mom again."

Heat radiated from his cheeks and neck. He sighed.

A smile tugged at her lips and she stepped toward him, palms flat against his chest. "Maybe I'll drag you into your room and have *my* wicked way with *you*." She led him into his room.

He slipped his hands around her waist, palms on her stomach, and rested his chin on her shoulder while she took in the space. His dick hardened against her ass and she groaned leaning into him.

She smelled like everything good in the world.

Brushing her hair off her neck, he dotted kisses along the curve of her shoulder, enjoying her muscles softening under his touch.

She led him to the bed and lay down on her side, patting the mattress next to her.

Lying next to her, the dark mass of hair falling over her face, her adorable button nose, the perfect curve of her lips, and her chocolate eyes swirling with intensity.

He gave in to the twitch in his fingers yearning to stroke the soft skin of her cheek. Cradling her face, he leaned to her. Brushing her nose with his, he enjoyed the soft sigh that escaped her before he covered her mouth with his.

What started out slow and sensual quickly built into a hungry frenzy. She clawed at his shirt, yanking it from his body between heated kisses before dragging her tongue up his chest, collar bone and neck, sending tiny shivers of desire straight to his already straining cock.

He slipped his hand under her shirt, caressed her skin as it trailed up her chest, and ran his thumb over the nipple straining against the thin fabric of her bra. "Fuck." He deepened the kiss, rolling her onto her back and covering her with his large form. Her legs parted and he settled between them, enjoying deep, unhurried kisses.

"Daddyyyyyyy!"

Their faces knocked together as they jolted.

"Fuck." He loved his daughter with everything he had, but if he didn't get inside Bre soon, he might die of frustration.

"Be right there, Princess!" He gave Bre a lingering kiss, toed off his jeans, threw on a pair of PJ bottoms, and attempted to rearrange the stubborn bulge in his pants before making his way into Jude's room.

When he returned twenty minutes later, Sabrina had fallen asleep on his bed. Her arm was draped over her face and her chest rose and fell with even breaths.

He pulled a blanket from the closet and covered her, before grabbing one of his t-shirts and a pair of shorts, leaving them next to her in case she woke up and needed to change.

The final credits of *Thor Ragnarok* were rolling when Mom came in announcing her presence. He chuckled. "I'm in here."

"I figured with the TV on, but I didn't want to, y'know. Oh. Is Sabrina not here?"

"She is. She fell asleep on top of my bed while I was putting Jude to sleep. I didn't want to wake her, so I came in to watch a movie."

"You really like her, don't you?"

He contemplated the question. "Like" didn't seem to do justice to the affection brewing for Sabrina in his chest, but fear was a 7ft tall, wide AF defender keeping him well away from thinking about the exact depth of his feelings for her. "Yeah. I like her."

Like was safe.

Like was neutral.

Like wasn't going to upend his entire life.

Like wasn't commitment.

Mom nodded thoughtfully, perching herself on the arm of the couch. "She seems nice."

Was she warming to the woman he'd chosen to spend his free time with?

"She is. Wicked smart, too. I'm glad she came to the party." He peered at Mom, waiting for her reaction, but her face remained unreadable save for a noncommittal 'hm.'

No complications or commitment had seemed a good idea, but if he truly didn't want either, why was his heart so keen for his mom to like his girl?

E ggs cooked in one pan while Sabrina flipped pancakes in another. Russell leaned against the doorframe, taking in her bare feet and his Snow Pirates t-shirt that fell to her knees. It left just enough visible skin to stir his dick against his pajama pants.

He'd slept in the guest room, opting to give her space, but her magnetic pull tugged at him all night interrupting his sleep with sexy dreams and a rock-hard cock.

The Beatles crooned softly from his old record player, and she danced as she cooked, pausing to sip orange juice as she slid another cooked pancake onto a growing stack on a plate next to the stove. The more intently he listened, the more he realized she not only could sing, but she knew every word of the song that was playing – which only served to make him want her more.

The Beatles were hardly a chart topping success these days. The fact she could sing every word as she shook her hips to the beat almost had him writing his vows then and there.

Across the kitchen, Mom stood in the doorway that led to the laundry room, arms folded. A small smile played on her lips.

He'd seen enough romantic comedies to know that one of two things were about to happen. Either Sabrina was going to turn around, her hands full of his breakfast, get startled at the sight of his Mom and drop everything on the floor in a cacophony of chaos. Or, he would sidle up to her, cup her hips and dance with her as she cooked.

His quietly grumbling stomach and semi-hard dick both demanded he do the latter.

Mom raised her brows and bugged out her eyes as if to ask what he was waiting for, before she flapped her hand at him, ushering him toward the seemingly still oblivious woman cooking in his kitchen.

Mom hitched a thumb over her shoulder and mouthed that she'd go get Jude. He threw her a thumbs-up before making his way to Sabrina.

"Good morning," he mumbled into her hair as his hands closed around her hips. Her muscles tensed for a moment as she startled, but she quickly relaxed against his chest. "Smells great."

"I hope it's okay. I guess I fell asleep early and once I woke up, I..." She leaned her head to the side so she could kiss his cheek over her shoulder. "I didn't know where you were sleeping to come for cuddles, so I figured I'd just make breakfast."

He nodded against her cheek, and a shiver spread through her body, presumably at his stubble meeting her soft skin. He chuckled. "It's more than okay. It's pretty perfect, actually. Can I help?"

She shook her head and flipped the pancake in the pan. "I've got it. Table is set, and the food is almost ready. I guess you could pour juice if you wanted." She covered his hand with hers. "I kinda like you right where you are, though."

A satisfied hum vibrated through his chest, and he tightened his grip on her, enjoying the little gasp that escaped her when his now fully hard dick nestled between her cheeks. "In that case, I'll stay right here."

She rocked back against him, the friction of her ass against his crotch sending shivers through his body. "Mmmm."

"Thank you for being the perfect gentleman last night. I appreciate the chivalry. I wouldn't have minded waking up to you lying beside me, though. Y'know... in case it ever happens again."

He dropped a kiss on her neck. "Noted."

She turned off the stove, placing the last of breakfast onto the heaped piles of food and covering them with foil.

"Daddyyyyy!" Jude and Mom made their way into the

dining space. Mom placed the still-sleepy bundle of cuteness in the booster seat strapped to a dining chair and set about getting juice from the fridge, giving him a moment to compose himself and coax his now throbbing cock to calm the fuck down.

"Morning punkin. Did you sleep okay?" He ruffled her hair and planted a kiss on her forehead as she chugged from her sippy cup.

"Good morning, Sabrina." Mom's tone was warm, but her face was wary.

"Good morning Mrs. Stewart. I didn't..." She waved a spatula between herself and Russell. "*We* didn't... I mean..."

Mom held up a hand, hopefully to put his now puce-colored girlfriend out of her misery.

Girlfriend?

Ooooooh, boy, was he in trouble.

"It's okay. I know you didn't..." Mom cleared her throat. She glanced at Jude, who was eating the pancake Russ had plucked from the stack, faster than he could chop it up for her. "But even if you did... you know... you're both consenting adults."

Mom rarely got flustered or embarrassed, but her face was darkening with a fierce blush. "I..." She swallowed and cleared her throat again. "I trust my son to be careful. And as long as he's happy..."

She met his gaze with welling eyes filled with love, concern, and the fear he felt in the pit of his stomach every single day for Jude. She sighed. "As long as Russell is happy, I'm happy."

Wow. That must have hurt her to say out loud.

Sabrina twisted a kitchen towel clutched in her fists, but a soft smile curved her mouth. "Thank you." It was almost a whisper, and her eyes were fixed to the floor, but if she felt even half of the relief that crashed into him like a flash-flood, she was dancing inside.

"Does that mean you're going to stick around?" Anxiety at the prospect of being rejected curled around his heart.

He didn't need her. He and Jude had been fine for so long without anyone other than Mom helping out. They'd be fine without her.

But damn, did he want her.

Bre glanced at his Mom, who was looking everywhere but at the two of them. "Honestly? I'm kind of afraid to say yes in case you run for the hills."

Mom snorted and both Sabrina and Russell snapped their attention to her. She held up her palms. "Sorry."

Russell laughed. He wasn't a commitment-phobe, he just didn't like things being out of his control. He didn't often have a desire to be with anyone.

But he wanted this, wanted Bre.

Stepping toward her, he picked up the free hand dangling at her side. "Be my girl, Bubbles."

She laughed and shook her head before squeezing his hand, giving him the mother of all eye rolls. "Already am, Stud."

Warmth fluttered in his chest. He opened his mouth to say something, but too many words rushed to come out, leaving him mute.

"More, please!" Jude had finished her pancake and tapped the table with her fork.

"Coming right up, Your Majesty." Sabrina waved the spatula with a flourish as she bowed to a giggling Jude.

They carried plates of food to the table, and near silence descended as they dug into their pancakes with eggs.

"Are you from Minnesota, Sabrina?" Mom sipped at her steaming mug of coffee.

"No, ma'am. My family is in Seattle. They uh..." She paused and swallowed. "They actually want me to make a trip out there in a couple weeks. It's my parents' anniversary party."

Mom didn't miss a beat. "And you don't want to go?" She sliced a segment of pancake and dipped it into the pool of syrup on her plate. She had that infamous Mom-look on her face that said there was more to the situation and she wasn't giving up till she found out what it was.

He gave Jude some scrambled eggs and stayed silent while Sabrina sighed. "I'm sure it'll be fine."

She was pissed at her family, that much was clear, but why hold back? Could she be afraid of the impression voicing her opinion would leave on him and Mom? She never had to censor herself in front of him, but perhaps making progress with her relationship with Mom meant she didn't want to rock that particular boat.

"I'm going to get more juice." Mom got up and walked into the kitchen. Had she picked up on Sabrina's reluctance to talk as well?

He raised an eyebrow at Sabrina. "We won't judge you for being honest about your family you know. You can talk to me about anything. Always." When she still didn't answer, he frowned. "You really don't want to go, do you?"

She huffed out a sigh and dropped her voice. "Honestly? No, I don't want to go. I know that sounds bad. Really bad. Like I'm confessing she was guilty of the world's worst crime." She swallowed like something tasted bitter in her mouth. "Talking about your family to people outside the home... especially people you don't really know... it's the worst form of betrayal. I don't want your mom to think less of me for complaining about my family. But since you asked and you're not letting it go... no. I don't think I can handle being made to feel like I'm the disappointment of the family right now. And I'm certainly not strong enough to withstand their henpecking to make me stay and help out with family while I'm there."

Her sad eyes twisted something deep in the pit of his stomach.

"Sorry, I know... I mean, I don't want to drag everyone down. I just... I feel so suffocated by family obligations. Being the youngest, having to fill my older sibling's shoes, live up to my parent's unreachable expectations... it's just..."

He reached across the table and squeezed her forearm. "You don't have to do anything you don't want to, Bre. I know people generally feel compelled because they're family, and we 'should' do things. But the only thing you *should* do is whatever is right for you to do. You're the only one looking out for your own interests and advocating for yourself."

He'd learned the hard way. When he'd made the decision that he wasn't going to be the only one making an effort in his relationship with his father, people kept saying "But he's your dad." That didn't mean anything if the person on the other side of the relationship checked out, or treated you like crap. "There's nothing I hate more than people saying, 'well that's still your mom,' or 'that's still your sister.' I don't know what the background is with your family, but I do know that toxic is toxic, whether it's family or not. You're allowed to create space, or walk away from people who constantly hurt you." He popped a piece of pancake into his mouth. "Don't let them pressure you into doing something you don't want to."

Mom returned to the table looking almost impressed as she nodded. She'd heard at least part of what had been said and Sabrina's eyes filled with unshed tears. Something stirred deep within his chest. He couldn't imagine not having any supportive family. Mom, overprotective as she was, had his back at all times, no matter what. But neither parent being in his corner? His heart pinched.

The quiver in her chin, and the sadness in her eyes told him that Sabrina didn't have that. His heart tore. She always did things for other people, helping and stepping up to take care of everyone else, but did she have anyone doing the same for her?

How many times had she been forced to be strong because she was alone and had no one to lean on? The tear in his chest widened.

"That said…" He pointed his fork at her as Jude smacked her sippy cup on the table. "If you feel as though you want to go visit your family. I'm happy to come along and have your back."

Sabrina dropped her fork with a clang and a gasp. "W-what? You can't mean that. We barely know each other. It's only been weeks… You can't…" She rubbed her palm on her thigh before picking up the fork again and biting the piece of pancake off the end.

He could almost hear the cogs in her mind trying to rationalize what he'd said. "I know you well enough to know you're a nice person, with a kind heart. And I care about you. If you want to go, and you're apprehensive, I can come with you. I'll be your date for the party."

She shook her head as her stare bored into her almost empty glass of orange juice.

"You have time to think on it, right? Not a lot, but some. I know last minute flights can be expensive. I'm sure I can pull from my savings."

Mom's silence was deafening. But he didn't care. The growing ache in his chest needed to offer to be there for her at any cost. If Sabrina was to face her family, he had to be there to protect her. They'd caused her enough hurt.

"I couldn't ask you to do that, Russell."

"But you're not asking him. He's offering." Mom sipped her coffee again. "Earlier you said something about Russell running for the hills if you mentioned commitment. Maybe that door swings both ways. Maybe you should let him be there for you when you need a buffer with your family."

What? She was advocating for him to go on the trip with her? Had he had a micro-nap and ended up in the Twilight Zone?

Mom squeezed his thigh under the table and gave a reassuring nod.

He was definitely not dreaming.

Mom sighed. "Relationships are tough. If that's what you two are embarking on... well... I know it's a cliché, but a problem shared really is a problem halved. And I'm only too happy to watch Jude while you go and I'll cover half of your flight if you want to go with her."

Shock tangled in the gob of emotions in his chest. Sabrina's jaw dropped.

He couldn't blame her. Mom not only trusted him to make his own decisions, but she was even willing to front the cash so he could be there for someone who was important to him.

Was it some kind of trap? Had Mom officially lost her mind?

Mom laughed at what must have been two stunned faces staring at her. "I'm not a monster. I'm protective of my family, sure..." She pursed her lips like she was thinking of the right words to say next. "I'm cautious of anything new that upends our carefully crafted routine. No one likes change. And I..."

She lowered her gaze. "There's nothing a mother fears more than her child not needing her. It's hard to accept you're not my little shadow anymore. You have your own life, your own dreams, and your own family."

She shrugged. "But I'm also not blind. You've never brought a girl home, Russell. You don't do *anything* without considering it every which way to Sunday. But the biggest clue? You're offering to take time away from Jude to be with her for a weekend. That speaks volumes. I can't promise it's going to be easy for me. But I'll do my best not to meddle."

Neither Sabrina nor Russell spoke. He simply stared, dumbstruck at his mother. It was as though he was seeing for the very first time. So many things to say raced through his mind, but none of them made their way out of his mouth.

"Thanks, Mom." His voice was raspy and thick with emotion.

She stood up from the table. "I'm going to get Jude ready and take her out for a walk."

He nodded. "Sure. We've got the cleanup."

"I might take her across town to visit Grandma. It's been a while since she's wooed the entire nursing home staff with her adorable smile."

That meant she'd be gone for a while. Understanding settled into his crotch and his dick stirred awake yet again. He was finally gonna get his girl naked. "Sounds good."

CHAPTER 15
Sabrina

Nerves fluttered in Sabrina's stomach like leaves dancing in a fall breeze.

Dishes rinsed and stacked in the dishwasher, extra pancakes put in the freezer, and countertops wiped down, she sat quietly on the couch, waiting for Russell to say goodbye to his mom and Jude.

His mom had finally told Sabrina to stop calling her Mrs. Stewart and call her Natalie, but it did little to unwind the tight knot of anxiety in her stomach. What must Natalie think of her for not being eager to go home to see her family? Sure, her attitude had softened toward Sabrina, but there was no way her familial issues wouldn't impact Natalie's opinion.

They'd only been seeing each other for a short time, and this was the first real opportunity that presented itself for them to get better acquainted. For some reason, it wasn't relief she was feeling.

She was finally going to be alone with Russell Stewart.

Alone, and his girl.

Her stomach flipped as the door closed behind Natalie and Jude.

What if they weren't compatible in the bedroom?

What if he was great with his tongue but awful with his dick?

What if—?

"Your thoughts are too loud, Bubbles." He slipped onto the couch next to her.

Her breath hitched as their thighs touched. Heat shot straight to her core. He unhooked her bottom lip from between her teeth and dragged the pad of his thumb along the curves of her mouth. "Are you nervous? Is that why you're gnawing on that beautiful lip and twisting your hands in your lap?"

An obnoxious laugh burst from her before she could stop it. Nervous energy charged through her, every cell primed with anticipation. She nodded. "I..." The words lodged between the uncertainty swelling in her lungs.

The brush of his thumb across the apple of her cheek sent a shiver down her spine.

"We don't have to do anything you're not comfortable with. I hope you know that."

She nodded. "It's not that I don't want it. I do." Closing her eyes, she tipped her head back, forcing out a hard breath. "I want it all. I just..."

When she opened her eyes again, concerned, tumultuous blue depths stared back at her. How was it even possible for someone to be so damn attractive?

She caressed his stubble with a featherlight touch, and he angled toward her, kissing her palm.

"Your anxiety is lying to you, Bubbles."

She sucked in a breath, ready to argue, ready to tell him everything she was anxious about, but his finger covered her mouth.

"Whatever it's saying, it doesn't matter. You're perfect."

Warmth spread through her like she'd stepped outside into

a hot summer's day. Every inch of her wanted to protest, but the firmness with which he said it, coupled with the flex in his jaw under her palm, and the determination in his eyes made her falter.

Brushing her lips across his mouth pulled a low groan from his chest.

The doorbell rang.

He growled.

She smirked.

Someone knocked on the door.

He swore.

She laughed.

Lincoln Scott's voice echoed through the house. "I saw your mom on the way out, Stewie. I know you're in there."

He held up his index finger. "Let me get rid of him."

Were they destined to be cockblocked forever? Would she never know what it was like to have her bare, sweat-slicked skin pressed against his washboard abs?

Russell swung the door open with aggressive abandon, it thudded against the wall. "What?"

If her panties weren't already damp, and her core wasn't pulsing with need, the one word snarl he spat at his best friend as he opened the door would have been all it took.

Was icing your lady garden a thing?

If it was a thing, she needed it.

Linc seemed wholly unfazed by his best friend's attitude. He leaned a forearm on the doorframe, casting a lazy smile at Russ. "'Sup?" He tossed a wave over Russell's shoulder. "Hi, Sabrina."

She matched his wave, biting the inside of her cheek to avoid the bubbling laughter vibrating through her body.

"Lincoln." Russell's entire body was rigid, tension coursed off him in waves, and Sabrina suddenly had zero doubts that he wanted her every bit as much as she wanted him. Her nipples tingled under her shirt, and heat rushed to her core.

Linc needed to leave before she either came undone in front of him, or Russell killed him. She didn't have time or patience to help dispose of a body before getting naked with Russell, and with any luck, she'd be too tired after. Searing desire burned the apex of her thighs leaving her almost blind with want.

"I don't mean to overstep any boundaries." Her voice sounded meek, reticent, but her resolve was strong. "But unless this is an emergency..." She cleared her throat. "I'm going to politely request you leave, Lincoln."

He grinned and folded his arms, turning so his back leaned against the frame. "Is that so?"

The muscle in Russell's jaw twitched again. She nodded. "I'm not sure if you noticed, but if Russell has to request it, it would seem he wouldn't be anywhere near as polite. From what I understand, Natalie has a thing about getting blood on the white rug."

Linc snorted and stepped towards Russell, who pressed a rigid hand against his chest. "Don't. Unless someone is dying, go. Everything else can wait."

He ground every word out between clenched teeth. It was as though she was watching a coiled spring in a mechanism right before it sprang into action.

If Linc was in any way intimidated by Russell's outright aggression, it didn't show. In fact, he laughed. He tapped Russ on the chest with an open palm. "Hit me up when you're feeling less..." He threw a knowing glance at Sabrina. "Pent up."

If her entire body wasn't already on fire and aching with need to be touched by her hockey player, she'd have had the decency to blush.

"You kids be safe." The words had barely made their way

out of Linc's mouth before Russell slammed the door in his face.

His hands flexed by his sides, curling into tight fists before unballing and coiling again. "I think I need a cold shower."

She stepped towards him, placing her palms on his shoulder blades and running them up to his head where she scratched his scalp. "I don't think you do."

He hissed out a long breath. "I don't want you to think I'm some raging sex maniac who can't slow down and enjoy the moment or who jackhammers his girl like a fucking pneumatic drill."

"I don't." The image of him driving into her like a jackhammer had her clenching. She slid her hands down his back, hooked them under his arms and carried on her journey down his chest and abs until she met the bulge straining his pants.

"Right now, I just want to fuck you senseless." His admission was quiet, his voice like gravel, tense, as though fighting to even form the words. His muscles were taut against her chest and his dick twitched under her hands.

She swallowed hard. "I'm okay with that."

He took a step forward and spun to face her. Fire flickered in his eyes and lust fizzed in the space between them.

He raised an eyebrow.

She nodded.

She'd barely sucked in a breath before his lips crashed against hers, tongue pressing against the seal of her lips, demanding access.

Every ounce of tension she'd been carrying, every question, insecurity, and all her anxiety melted into his touch. He picked her up by the waist, and with strong arms, locked her legs behind his back, his cock pressing against her damp pants.

She rocked her hips against his length, once, twice, then he was moving. Despite the precarious position, the threat of gravity, being forced to put her trust in the hunky, muscular hockey player cupping her ass and stumbling towards the bedroom, she'd never felt more safe, more secure, more wanted.

He lowered her onto the bed. Her chest heaved with panting breaths and her lips protested his absence while he yanked his shirt over his head, and toed off his pajama pants. Hot damn she wanted to lick something... anything off those chiseled abs, taking time to learn every well defined ridge and groove.

Hooking his thumbs into the band of his boxers, he paused like he'd just realized she was gawping at him. "Enjoying the view?"

"Well, duh. But I'm wondering why you're wearing boxers under your pj pants." She winced at her own lack of filter.

"A fruitless attempt at containing my raging hard-on in the presence of my mother? Bre?"

She raised herself onto her elbows. "Hm?"

"Naked. Now."

Waves of desire lapped low in her belly as she shimmied out of her pants. As she sat up to tear her shirt over her head, warm hands clasped at her back, unhooking her bra. She savored his impatience before he pressed her shoulders down to the bed.

"I'm on the pill."

His brows hitched, like his brain was processing the information. "You mean...?"

"If you want..."

His brows pulled low, forming a V between them. "I'd rather not."

Her stomach dropped and her heart squeezed. What guy *didn't* want to go bareback?

"It's nothing personal."

She nodded. "Of course." Foolishness swelled in her stomach. Why had she even offered?

She should have known better. A player like him was probably always concerned with STDs. Not to mention, Jude was very likely an unexpected bundle of joy and while he didn't regret her for a moment, he probably didn't want to take any chances of having another one quite so young. Or maybe at all.

Her heart quickened.

Maybe he didn't want more babies. Maybe he—

Her breath caught as he pinched her chin and turned her head to face his. "Come back to me, Bubbles."

She nodded. "Sorry."

His smooth hand sent little currents of warmth through her cheek. "It's not personal, Bre. And I appreciate the offer. Maybe someday..."

Someday. That suggested a future, but she didn't have time to mull over that thought.

The rock hard dick pressed against her belly was hard to ignore. "It's okay. I wasn't thinking." Her voice was light and breathy.

"I see the hurt in your eyes. This is 100% a me thing, not a you thing. Jude's mom... well, she told me she was on the pill, too."

Jude's mom had lied. It was no wonder he had trust issues. Mr. Control Freak losing control must have been quite the shit storm.

She didn't want him thinking of his ex while she was lying naked underneath him.

She didn't want him thinking of deception and being unable to trust the woman he was about to do the most intimate of things with.

She didn't want him thinking she was offended because he wanted to be responsible.

She wanted him inside her.

Skimming her nails along the defined muscles on his chest,

she was rewarded with a low vibrating hum as he closed his eyes and tipped his head back. She tilted her hips to grind against his length and his head lolled forward until his forehead and nose rested against hers.

Her heart quickened as she curled her arms around him and sank her nails into his shoulder blades, drawing a feral moan from his lips.

His mouth captured hers without hesitation. He somehow kept his balance enough to tear open the foil packet he'd plucked from the drawer next to his bed.

Sure, he seemed every bit as eager as she was, but was he at least going to check the oven was preheated before he—

A flutter crept up her spine, surprising her as his fingers slipped between her folds.

Like there had been any chance she *wasn't* preheated.

Sliding his fingers deeper inside her, he pressed her G-spot. She ground against his hand as his lips trailed a delicate path down her collarbone.

Fire shot through her skin as his tongue lapped at her beaded nipple. The friction between her legs wasn't touching her ache. She needed more and he did too.

He was clearly attempting to be a gentleman by taking it slow, when he'd already told her what he needed.

Palm flat against his chest, she rolled him onto his back.

It was time to give them both what they needed.

He opened his mouth, maybe to protest, but she covered his lips with her fingertips and gave a shake of her head.

Primal hunger spurring her on, she straddled him, wasting no time lining him up with her entrance. While he wasn't particularly long, he was girthy. Anticipation melted her bones as she sank onto his tip with a hungry pant. His face was full of wonder as he stared up at her.

Her walls clenched around him as she explored his chest.

The ridges of his toned abs, well-defined shoulders, and strong biceps, firm under her palms.

She sank a little lower, another inch, then two. His muscles twitched under her touch, and his jaw ticked with what seemed like restraint, but he didn't grab at her, or push into her.

He waited.

Rocking her hips, she exhaled the breath she'd been holding, as relief flickered through her at being able to take him.

"You okay?" His voice was almost pained.

She nodded. "I don't want to be that girl, but my, what a big dick you have."

They shared a laugh, and his body loosened beneath her.

She rocked again, pulling moans from them both. Large hands crept up her body, sending licks of pleasure through her nipples as he brushed them with his fingertips before pinching them and making her gasp.

She moved, slowly at first, but she didn't stay slow for long.

Neither of them needed slow.

Firm palms gripped at her hips as she rode him, chasing the sweet release growing in her core. Breasts bouncing, chest heaving, she ground down on him, enjoying wave after wave of undulating pleasure that rattled through every piece of her body.

"Holy shit." His hiss through gritted teeth was all the encouragement she needed to keep going.

He slipped a hand between them, thumb sweeping against her slick clit. His fingers coiled tighter around her hip as he came on a low grunt.

Disappointment and frustration tapped at her insides as he softened inside her, but he didn't let her go when she tried to climb off him.

Instead, he rolled her onto her back, pulled himself from

her and removed the condom, tying it and dropping it to the floor next to the bed.

Leaning over her, his mouth dipped to deliver a still-hungry kiss. His fingers found their way to her clit as she gasped and grabbed at the hair at the nape of his neck.

Jolts of pleasure streamed through her muscles as her orgasm grew. Her body trembled under his touch, her pants grew faster, and a bead of sweat trickled down her face.

His teeth nipped at the tender skin of her neck as he brought her closer to the edge, her hips bucking against his hand like a wild bronco.

Back arched, body tense and pulsating, she screamed his name as sparks exploded behind her eyelids. Her release crashed into her like a cloudburst. "Fuck."

He nuzzled against her ear, dotting tiny kisses on her cheek. His fingers still resting between her thighs. With every languid sweep, her entire body shook.

She shook her head, covering his hand with hers. "Too... sensitive."

He chuckled. "Don't care."

Somehow, his lips replaced his hand on her swollen bundle of still-tingling nerves, and his fingers curled against her inner wall, lighting her whole being up like a firework.

Her hands flailed at her sides, grabbing at whatever they could find. Sheets balled in one hand, clumps of Russell's dark hair in the other, her hips reared against his face as she ground against his eager tongue.

Breathless from the siege on her core, she sucked in short panting breaths as she careened towards another orgasm.

Russell grunted, before shouldering her legs over his back and pounding at her G-spot with two fingers. Dots danced at the edges of her vision.

"Don't... stop..." Her rasped pleas were met with a deep

chuckle as he feasted on her like he was at an all-you-could-eat buffet in stretchy pants.

With what could only be a reserve tank of energy she had no idea existed, her shuddering legs tightened around his head, forcing a muffled moan from him. His free hand grabbed at her hard nipple, squeezing and pinching.

The second wave hit her like a freight train. She bolted up from the bed, cradling his head with both hands so he couldn't move his tongue from her clit as ripples of bliss surged through her.

Collapsing back onto the bed, her muscles finally relented. She couldn't move. Every muscle had turned to jello, and none of her limbs were under her control. Spasms flickered through her muscles as she lay splayed out like a starfish in a patch of her own wetness.

Could she hear color? Were all hockey players so good with their tongues? Was it something about playing with their mouth guards that had them proficient in bringing a woman to a blinding climax?

When he reappeared, kissing her like he'd missed her, she hummed at the taste of herself on his lips.

"I'm sorry." Fighting her heavy, fluttering eyelids seemed to be a losing battle.

"What for?"

"I'm pretty sure you almost drowned."

A bark of laughter shook the bed.

"If you hadn't been wet, I'd be insulted." Trailing his fingers along the swell of her breast he circled her nipple. A shiver traveled through her lifeless limbs. "I like how... reactive... your body is to my touch."

As if he'd commanded it to, her nipple pebbled. "Don't get any ideas. I'm broken. None of my systems are reporting in. I have no control over my body yet. And I'm pretty sure I can hear colors."

He laughed again before dropping kisses along the curve where her shoulder met her neck. "We have a problem."

Her loose muscles tensed at his words.

"Shhhhh. It's not a real problem. Well, it might be. It depends."

"Will you spit it out so I can go back to enjoying this post-coital bliss, please?"

She'd never tire of the timbre of his laugh. It was like hot cocoa on the wildest winter night.

"While part of me is definitely sated." He trailed his tongue along her jaw. "I *most definitely* want a repeat of everything we just did."

"You do?" Her voice was a squeak.

"Don't you?"

The indignation in his voice made her laugh.

"Of course I do! When my muscles stop twitching, sure. But I wasn't sure if..."

"I know I have a rep for being a one and done kind of guy, Bubbles." He brushed his lips against hers. "But you're different. It's different with you. I want you."

He paused, dragging his finger along her stomach and circling her belly button. "I want every delicious inch of you. And when we're done, I want you all over again." He poked at her tummy. "It should be me apologizing to you for being a bit of a horn dog."

She smiled. "I like horn dog Russell." She clenched her core, a delicious ache throbbed from where he'd stretched her.

"I gotta pee."

"And they say romance is dead."

"I know, right?"

He pushed up from the bed, stepped on to the floor and cringed. "Ew."

"What's wrong?"

"Next time, remind me to dispose of the condom a little further away from the bed."

Naked, exposed, raw, and vulnerable in ways she'd never before let herself be, she erupted into delirious giggles as he stooped to pick up the condom. Her weight shifted on the wet patch under her butt, sending a chill up her spine.

She was officially in trouble. She was falling for a man who feared commitment.

CHAPTER 16
Sabrina

"Got your ID?"

Warm arms curled around Sabrina, forcing her to stop pacing. "Bubbles, I'm going to need you to take a breath. Please." Russell rubbed his palms along the length of her arms. "I have my ID. I've had it the last four times you've asked since we woke up, too. It's all going to be okay. They know I'm coming, right?"

Did they know he was coming? Her stomach had been in knots when she'd called to tell them she was bringing a boy home. They'd been elated, shot three million questions at her in a fraction of a second before the line went quiet and heavy with suspicion when she'd said his name was Russell.

Yeah. They knew he was coming. She nodded. Her jaw ached from clenching her teeth. "I don't want to go." Her voice was a trembling whisper as she buried her head in Russell's chest. Anxiety seeped from her muscles as he held her close.

"I'll be with you the whole time. You're going to be okay. I know you're anxious, but you really did want to go see your family."

Gnawing at the inside of her cheek, she nodded again. Her nerve endings were raw with apprehension and her head throbbed.

Spending time with Russell and Jude over the past couple of weeks had been difficult, to say the least. They'd stolen time where they could, an hour here, an hour there. They'd stayed over at each other's places, having frantic sex before their roommates came home, or lazy morning sex before they parted ways for the day.

Quinn had invested in noise cancelling headphones, making a point to leave the box in plain sight on the dining room table. Apparently Sabrina and Russ hadn't been as quiet as they thought they had.

Sinking into the warmth of the memory, she urged the angst lashing at her spine to settle down and leave her alone. But it was no use.

Even with Russell by her side, her insides twisted. What would her family have to say about him?

In their ideal world, she'd settle down with a "nice Indian boy," live next door, and give them thirteen grandkids that they'd help name and raise, and she'd never make another decision by herself for the rest of her life. Why would she when they were all on hand to help at every turn?

Concern pinched Russell's face.

Would he judge her family? How would he react to her mother's henpecking?

Or, worse yet, would he think she was overreacting?

Her heart contracted.

She needed someone on her side more than she cared to admit.

It would break her if he was blinded by their charm and missed the subtle jabs at her, or how they treated her differently to the rest of her siblings.

Nausea sloshed in her stomach.

"Hey." He cupped her face with both hands as they stood at her front door.

Her eyes snapped to his.

Overnight bags lay at their feet. If she wasn't so terrified at the prospect of emotional onslaught from her family, she'd be excited. Two nights by themselves – what wasn't there to like about it?

He had to leave early Saturday morning to get back in time for his game, but they still had two glorious child-free nights stretching out in front of them.

"Yeah?"

"If you really don't want to go – truly, in your heart, don't want to go. We can go somewhere else. Or stay right here. We'll have dinner someplace nice and you can wear the dress you got for your parents' anniversary party. We'll spend all day in bed watching movies, and I'll do that thing with my tongue you like."

He was giving her an out, protecting her, offering her an alternative option. Her heart swelled. "You'd do that for me?"

"Of course." His gruff dismissal that it wasn't even a question wrapped around her like a safety blanket.

"Even though you think I need to confront them head on?"

He pursed his lips and pulled her to him. "Not everyone is ready to face their demons at the same time, Bre."

"What if I'm never ready?"

His silence spoke volumes. What she'd give to have his bravery, his unwavering belief in everything he did, his confidence.

He squeezed her. "What's it gonna be, B?"

Steeling her spine, she mustered up the strength for a small smile. "Let's go." She picked up her bag, but he slipped his hand over hers and freed it from her grasp.

"I've got it."

She opened her mouth, but he kept talking.

"Yes, I've got my ID, too. Let's get to the airport before I need to figure out how to render you unconscious with my driver's license."

"Sabrina?"

Her ex-boyfriend's familiar voice froze her in place at the baggage carousel. The airline had gate-checked their carry-on bags and were taking their sweet time getting them out on the belt.

"A-Arnav?"

His wide smile under his sharp nose sent all the wrong signals through her body. She flinched as he opened his arms and stepped towards her, grabbing her in an awkward hug.

"Hey! It's been a long time. Aap kaise ho?"

Her brain short circuited. Arnav was studying to be a hot-shot doctor at Johns Hopkins in Maryland. He had no family there… they'd moved after he finished high school… no business being in Seattle, unless…

Bands of anxiety ratcheted across her chest.

They wouldn't.

They couldn't.

Except it seemed like they not only could, but had.

"I-I'm good, thanks. W-what are you doing here?"

"I'm here for your parents' party. They didn't mention they invited me?"

She shook her head. Surely she'd misheard. "When did they invite you?"

"Two… maybe three weeks ago?"

Right around the time she'd told them she and Russell were making the trip. Warmth radiated through her shirt as Russell's hand braced against her lower back.

Claiming her.

Please God let him be claiming me.

He reached out to Arnav. "Russell."

Arnav didn't break eye contact with Sabrina for a stretched-out moment before tossing a wary glance in Russell's direction. "Arnav." He accepted the handshake, but the tightness in his jaw and suspicion in his eyes suggested reluctance.

Russell dropped a kiss on her cheek. "I spy our bags, I'll be right back."

She nodded, already missing the warmth of his palm against her spine.

"Who's that?"

"Russell."

His nostrils flared, presumably at her sarcasm. "Boyfriend?"

She nodded.

"Serious?"

Russell's voice came from behind her as he dragged a bag across the floor. "Well, I flew across the country to meet her parents, so I'm going with yeah, pretty serious."

A giggle rattled between her ribs as a cornucopia of emotions flickered across Arnav's face before settling on a scowl.

"Ready to pick up the rental car?"

Was Russell really not bothered by Arnav's presence?

Did he not realize who he was?

Did he know and not care?

Did he know and care but was hiding it?

So many questions.

Russell didn't wait for her to reply before continuing. "Arnav, do you have a ride sorted? Do you want to ride with us?"

How was Russell being so blasé about everything?

Anxiety stabbed at her gut. It was a short, fifteen minute drive from Sea-Tac International to her parents' house in Salt Air Hills. Standing in the presence of her ex-boyfriend, with the knowledge her parents had gone behind her back to invite him, had her struggling for a full breath.

Arnav's frown deepened before giving a sharp nod. "Sure. It'll save me getting a cab or an Uber."

Russell picked up both bags and led the trio to the rental car desk. Twenty minutes later, they climbed into their Chevy Cruze. Russ pulled up GPS on his phone, and they were on the way in a heavy, awkward silence. She needed to do something. She needed to channel the nervous energy flooding her system.

"I probably should have warned you." She cleared her throat, taking in Russell's profile. "Car karaoke is my jam."

Russell grinned and shook his head. "I'm not sure you want to subject the world to my noise pollution, Bubbles. But I could listen to you sing every day and twice on Sundays. Go for it." He gestured at the car radio.

They both ignored Arnav's repetition of "Bubbles?" from the back seat.

"I'll make a deal with you. Whatever song comes on the radio when I turn it on, we'll sing it together, loud and proud."

His face crinkled as he scrunched his nose. "I feel like this is a very, very poor decision on your part. But fuck it. Let's do it."

Ecstatic that he was playing along, she sent up a prayer to the car karaoke gods it would be something they both knew the lyrics to. When Celine Dion belted through the car speakers, she couldn't help but laugh.

Russell loved the classics, his music taste was well and truly rooted in the 80s and 90s. He opened his mouth and a tone deaf version of *All Coming Back to me Now* burst from his lips.

She cringed. But he kept going. The noise was so bad, she could only laugh. He knew every word and sang like his life depended on it.

She let him sing for what felt like three hours, her entire body vibrating with laughter at his silliness. Chest sore and tears rolling down her cheeks, she cupped her hand over his mouth. "We're going to get kicked out of Washington if you don't stop singing."

He plucked her hand from his face and linked their hands together, resting it on her thigh.

Arnav cleared his throat. "So... how long have you guys been together?"

"A while." Russell's piercing stare pinned him in the rearview as something stirred in Sabrina's stomach. She loved how he wasn't afraid to be warm and squishy with her in the presence of a stranger, yet he somehow stayed guarded and protective of her at the same time.

"Where'd you meet?"

"In the men's restroom."

Sabrina snorted, unable to contain the obnoxious noise behind her hand. "I thought you forgot about that."

"Forgot about meeting the most beautiful woman in the world while I was peeing? Nice try."

Arnav had paled in the backseat. "You didn't."

She shrugged. "I needed to pee. Girls take too long."

"Did you...?" He met her eyes in the mirror. "Y'know... use the urinal?"

It was Russell's turn to snort.

"I used a stall, Arnav."

"I don't like how you say my name anymore. What happened to Arnie?"

"He wasn't what I needed him to be." She crossed her

arms. Maybe the pressure against her chest would somehow loosen the bands refusing to budge.

Russell's jaw ticked, and his eyes darkened.

An uncomfortable silence descended on the car as they turned into her parents' street. Their porch light lit up the path as they parked. She sent up another silent prayer that her mom had made something for dinner that wouldn't set Russell's tongue on fire or give him a wicked dose of the shits.

Pulling her shoulders back, she straightened her spine, took his hand, and led him up the path to her childhood home. It was time for him to meet the parents.

CHAPTER 17
Russell

Russell didn't like him.

In fact, he hated him.

Could you hate a complete stranger on sight?

Regardless. He did.

Arnav. The guy standing way too close to Sabrina for his liking, clearly her ex-boyfriend – he'd be talking to her about that gross mistake at a later date – gave him the creeps.

The way he held himself, from his chin tilted with an air of indifference that said he was better than everyone, to the arrogance that dripped from every word he'd spoken since they'd met, was sickening.

He hated him.

How could Sabrina have ever lowered herself to date such a douche canoe?

He didn't have time to ponder the question as the front door burst open, and a myriad of smells and sounds assaulted his senses. They were ushered inside in a wave of greetings. An older man and woman – presumably Sabrina's parents – stood ready to welcome their daughter back into their home. Their polite smiles looked almost pinned to their faces.

Behind them, two tables had been joined together and set with beautiful red and orange linens, ornate place settings, and shining silverware, ready to host a banquet fit for a king.

Was this a regular Thursday night dinner in the Sharma household? Had they done this to celebrate Sabrina's return?

Smiles wide, they hugged her, then quickly moved on to Arnav, who they fussed over as though *he* was the prodigal child returning from afar.

Sabrina met his eyes and gave a sad shrug.

Manners be damned, he wasn't going to stand by and watch her be discarded so easily. He stepped forward, arm outstretched. "Hi, I'm Russell. Sabrina's boyfriend."

There.

He'd said it.

It hung in the charged air between them like a grenade with the pin pulled.

It was their move now.

Her father accepted his hand, closing it in a firm grasp, shaking it twice. "Vishal. Nice to meet you. This is my wife, Aneka."

"It's nice to meet you both at last." He smiled as he shook Aneka's hand.

"Come, come, let's get you inside. I hope you brought your appetite." Aneka ushered Arnav into the room behind her.

"She made enough to feed the neighborhood. As usual." Vishal draped an arm over Sabrina's rigid shoulders and guided her into the dining room where a heavily pregnant woman sat with a small child bouncing on her knee.

A man stood next to her, scrolling on his phone, and two other small children sat at the table coloring.

Aneka sat Arnav next to Sabrina, leaving Russell across the table from her. The sadness and anxiety held in her every cell made his chest ache. Something inside him clawed like an untamed animal to protect her.

While he hadn't witnessed much of their family dynamic, whatever had happened in the past was enough to have her bent wholly out of shape.

Part of him wanted to pick that smug bastard Arnav up in his chair and switch places with him so he could curl a protective arm around her shoulder and offer whatever support she needed.

But he'd play nice, for the moment.

Or until Sabrina gave him a sign that she needed him to step in.

He cursed himself silently. He should have come up with a code word for her to drop into conversation if she reached her capacity for her family. Something obscure so he'd know she needed to be rescued.

Or a traffic light series of code words, so he'd know she was approaching her limit of discomfort before needing escape.

Reaching across the table, he squeezed her rigid hand as it clutched the fork in front of her. Her smile was brittle, forced, and her eyes swam with emotions he couldn't quite decipher.

If Russell's mom had invited his ex to a family weekend behind his back, Russell would feel a typhoon of emotions as well. Mostly betrayal.

What the hell had he waded into?

Sabrina pointed to the dishes spread out on the table, giving him a run-down. Slow-cooked dal, potatoes and peas (aloo gobi), paneer in creamy tomato yoghurt gravy, chapattis, peas pulao and biriyani with raita. They tucked into the steaming plates of fragrant food in silence, but the quiet didn't last for long.

"Arnav, how is medical school going? Have you chosen your specialty?" Aneka scooped bread around a small pile of rice on her plate and bundled it into her mouth.

As far as Russell understood, Sabrina hadn't seen her parents since the summer. Surely they should be catching up with her and not the asshole who gatecrashed their gathering.

Was Russell the asshole who gatecrashed?

Sabrina pushed vegetables and rice around her plate, head lowered, hair falling in front of her face. Where was his upbeat, lively girlfriend with her beautiful smile?

Irritation lashed up his spine. Arnav was chatting to Aneka about having chosen the same specialty as she had, cardiology.

Perfect. It wasn't enough for the smug fuck kiss-ass to be in medical school. No, he had chosen the same path as Sabrina's mother.

Russell shoveled another forkful of biriyani into his mouth, hoping the spices would burn his tongue off so he didn't speak out of turn. His eyes bore into Sabrina as her parents engaged everyone at the table but her.

His knuckles turned white as he clutched the silverware, and his jaw ached from holding his mouth shut. Every now and then, she met his eyes and gave an infinitesimal head shake.

"Sabrina?" Vishal sat only three places away from her, but his voice echoed around the large room.

Her head snapped up. Her lips pulled into a soft smile, and her eyes lit up. Was he finally going to acknowledge his daughter?

"Pass the chapatti."

His heart dropped.

Her eyes pleaded with him to stay silent, and just let it happen.

Let it happen.

Like hell.

It wasn't in his nature to *let* anything happen. It took everything he had not to speak up on her behalf.

When dinner finally ended, they rose to leave.

"I made up your old bedroom, Sabrina." Aneka was already busy cleaning the dishes Russell and Sabrina had cleared from the table.

"Thank you, Mrs. Sharma, but we don't want to impose. We booked a hotel for the weekend."

Sabrina looked every bit as surprised as her parents at the announcement.

"Dinner was delicious, thank you so much for having us."

"Aren't you staying to help your mother clean up?"

Sabrina froze.

"Actually, sir, we've had quite a long day, and we have an early start in the morning. I'm sure Arnav wouldn't mind helping."

At the mention of his name, Arnav spluttered the chai he was drinking. "What? Oh, yes, uh, sure. Of course I don't mind."

Sabrina's lips tugged at the corners and light kindled in her eyes.

"We'll see you all at the party tomorrow evening. It's been a pleasure to meet you all, and I can't thank you enough for welcoming me into your home." His words were polite, but his tone was glacial.

Sabrina's sister, Avni, gave him a warm smile and mouthed "thank you" as he placed his hand on Sabrina's back and guided her out the door and into the car.

Once out of sight of their house, Russell pulled into a parking lot. Sabrina was yet to speak a word, but they needed a place to stay for the night, and from the heaving breaths coming from her side of the car, she wasn't yet ready to unpack the evening.

A few minutes and a discount travel site later, they were booked into the Hampton Inn and Suites for two nights.

Tiny shudders shook her body. He took her hand, gave a

squeeze, rested their interlocked hands on her thigh, and didn't let go until they pulled into the hotel parking lot.

He circled the car, opened her door, and held a hand out to help her out of the car, but she still didn't move. "Come back to me, Bubbles." He crouched next to her, brushing her hair back from her tear-soaked face.

"They're going to be so offended I walked out on them and left with you."

This wasn't about them. This was about her. "I don't care if they're offended. I care about you!"

"I'm sorry." Her small, gravelly croak split his heart in two.

He had to take a moment to school his raging emotions before he answered. "You have nothing to be sorry about, Bre." He shook his head. "Do you hear me? And the mere thought that you do... That you're somehow to blame? That... that's part of the problem."

"I know you think I should have stood up for myself. I saw you. You wanted to say something."

"Of course I wanted to say something!" He erupted to his feet, pacing three steps forward and back and waving his arms as he ranted. "I hated every second of watching them treat you like shit, Bre."

She nodded and stepped out of the car, closing the door with a soft click. "I tried once." Her voice was quiet as she walked to the trunk and pulled out their bags.

Nervous energy buzzed through him, the animal in his chest still rattling against the bars of its cage. "What happened?" His words were almost a grunt as they forced themselves out of his clenched mouth.

"They didn't engage in the conversation." She shrugged. "I guess it was selfish of me to ask, right? Selfish to need time, selfish to want answers, selfish to leave without washing dishes... That's me, Selfish Sabrina."

Bitterness dripped off her every word as she played with the handle on her bag.

He surged toward her, cupping her face with both hands, forcing her to look at him. "You're not selfish, Sabrina. You hear me? You have a heart as big as Texas. You constantly put people before yourself. And if we're putting labels on people, it's clear to me as an outsider that your parents are the selfish ones in this equation. Not you."

Her smile didn't reach her eyes. One conversation wasn't going to change something she'd clearly believed about herself for her whole life. And while he was overwhelmed with the depth of dysfunction in her family, he couldn't let her believe something that was so blatantly untrue about herself for a moment longer.

Part of him wanted to run, to flee from the wall of the commitment he had somehow run into face first. But the other part, a much bigger, fiercer part, wanted to wrap her into his arms and never let her family say another bad thing to her for as long as he lived.

War raging in his chest, he picked up the cases, locked the car, and led her inside.

They checked in and made their way to the bedroom. The door was barely closed behind Sabrina before she pressed him against the wood, kissing him with the same urgency that was charging through his veins.

He dropped the bags and dotted hungry, wet kisses down her neck as he tugged the hem of her shirt up to reveal her perfect lace-clad tits. Freeing them out of the fabric he lapped his tongue over her hard nipple, while he palmed at the other.

His cock throbbed against her thigh, aching to be inside her.

"Russell..." Her needy gasp of his name as he slid his hand up her long skirt shot white-hot sparks of desire into his very soul.

"Please..." Her nails scratched at his scalp.

Head tipped back against the door, eyes closed, lips parted and tits hanging out, the single word yelled a demand for him to help her forget. To help her feel something other than the shitty feelings her parents had left her stewing in after dinner.

Unzipping his jeans one-handed, he freed his dick, pulled a condom from his back pocket and tore it open with his teeth. He might not be able to fix her family issues, he might not be able to convince her that everything they said was a lie, but he sure as shit could fuck her till it didn't matter anymore. Even just for a few minutes.

Sheathed and hard, he pulled her panties to the side, finding her slick and ready for him. "Do you want me to slow down?" He at least owed it to her to offer even as beads of precum leaked from his pulsing cock.

Her fingers curled into his hair as she shook her head. "I need you."

Their lips crashed in a messy kiss as he slid his hands under her thighs and raised her against the door. In one long moment, he slipped into her on a low moan.

Balls-deep, he paused. Her eyes were alive with lust, and her chest rose and fell with heavy breaths. Her body loosened in his grip, muscles softening. He shuffled his feet apart a few inches, and swallowed her sigh in a ferocious kiss.

Wrapping his arms around her, he paused again, she pulled her head back enough to scowl and nod. "Fuck me, Russell."

With a grin, he did precisely that. With every thrust her back slapped against the wooden panel door, and she panted like his dick was pumping air straight into her lungs.

She kissed him frantically, clawing at his shoulders and hair as he rammed her against the door. The familiar tingling built in his balls as he pounded into her. The only sounds in the room were the slapping of skin on skin as he drove deeper and deeper into her and their heavy breathing and grunting.

He'd be damned if he would let himself come first this time. Shifting his weight so he could support her with one arm, he slipped his other hand between them. He strummed at her slick clit like she was a perfectly tuned instrument. He was the virtuoso and she would only play under his fingertips.

A deep shudder ran through her as her muscles tightened. "So... close..." Her words were breathless pants as she closed herself around him, burying her face into his neck as her muscles stiffened.

Would he ever get tired of making the woman in his arms come undone around him?

Her hot, wet pussy clamped his dick with such force, he saw stars and felt it everywhere. The scream that ripped from her chest as she fell apart on his cock would have been enough to get them kicked out of the hotel, but he didn't care. He drove into her, hard, fast, vision blurring at the edges as his own release flooded his system.

Her body shuddered in his arms as he struggled to catch his breath. Was she giggling? A whimper escaped from her against his throat.

Shit.

Not giggling.

Still inside her, he carried her into the bedroom, and sat on the edge of the bed. She tucked her legs around him and held on tight with both arms wrapped around his neck. He shushed and stroked her back, holding her as the wave of emotions hit her.

"I'm s-s-sorry. T-t-this is so embarrassing."

"That's enough. I'm not naïve enough to think I can fuck the sad out of you, Bre. Or make anything better with my cock. But I sure as shit can hold you while you process things."

"I'm n-not crying 'cause of the sex."

"Shhhh. I know." The collar of his shirt grew wetter, but eventually her sobs stilled to muffled hiccups.

This wasn't what he'd signed up for. Her family drama and emotional baggage were stifling. But every cell in his body screamed at him to hold her, to comfort her until it passed. He wasn't used to feeling others' pain. Since Jude was born, she was the only person in the world that mattered to him other than his mom and his teammates.

Until now.

Now he cared about someone else.

Now he wanted to take her pain and suffer it for her.

Now he wanted to hurt those who hurt her with such passion and ferocity, it took his breath away.

He didn't know for sure what was developing in his chest for Sabrina, but he knew it was scary as fuck. And dangerous.

When she quietened in his arms, he pulled back to see her face. His heart squeezed. Hair stuck to her tears, mascara smudged under her puffy eyes.

"I'm going to need you to move before he gets any ideas." He jerked his head toward his crotch.

She swung her leg and removed herself from his lap. He hissed through his clenched teeth. His semi-hard dick was already getting ideas. Tying off the condom, he took it into the bathroom, tossing it in the trash before peeing.

When he returned to the room, Sabrina was out cold. Fully clothed, tits still hanging out of her pretty bra, breathing heavy and even.

As he tugged off her shoes and positioned her under the blankets, he wondered how he was going to get through the anniversary party without losing his shit at her parents.

CHAPTER 18
Sabrina

Plates and glasses clinked, and servers waited on their 100-person strong, formally dressed group of family and friends with military precision. The chandelier overhead sparkled, and a string quartet played Mozart in the corner.

"So, Russell, what are you studying?" Arnav's question was almost a sneer, as though he knew no matter what Russell's answer was, it wouldn't come close to his training to be a cardiologist like Sabrina's mother.

Arrogant asshat.

Sabrina's eyes darted between Russell and Arnav. Her parents, in what had to be another laughable mis-aimed attempt at match-making, had sat the three of them together at a ten-person table. Avni and Viren, her oldest sister Jayshree, and their oldest sibling Raj sat next to them. Raj's girlfriend, Sajjani, was seated next to Raj, and next to her sat her other brother Vijay.

Her four older siblings regarded Russell with varying expressions from curiosity to caution.

Russell took a sip of water before answering. His spine was

straight, his shoulders square, but loose, and despite the occasional twitch in his jaw, he leaned back in his chair with an openness suggesting he was comfortable with his surroundings. "French and Computer Science."

"Major, minor?" Raj, the computer science grad of the family's intrigue had obviously been piqued.

"Double major."

Raj, though scowling, whistled. "Huh." It was hard not to be impressed by a double major, especially when one wasn't even in English.

"And you play hockey?" Avni was the only sibling who had asked about Russell before their visit. Sabrina had told her a little about him, but the fact he had a child was something that hadn't yet come up.

Guilt stirred in her stomach. If she was honest with herself, it was more that she knew her family – namely her parents – would be judgmental. Sabrina had cowered away from that, like she had all other confrontations with her family for as long as she could remember.

It would come up, though.

Probably in the next few minutes.

She'd expected to feel embarrassment at the idea of her family finding out about Jude, but all she could find when she searched her soul was a fierce protection of the little girl and the gladiator that was her father.

Russell nodded. "I do."

The awkward tension hanging over the table was suffocating. If nothing else, Russell looked damn fine in a suit.

"Are you any good?" Arnav's smug arrogance was grinding her gears.

The fact he even had to ask the question said enough about his knowledge of college sports. It didn't matter what their reply was, he probably wouldn't get it anyway.

She opened her mouth to say something about his stats,

but Vijay beat her to it. "Very." He tore apart the still steaming naan bread in his hand and popped a piece in his mouth. "Rumour has it the Minnesota Wild has been scouting him." He arched an eyebrow and directed his full attention to Arnav. "That's a big deal. National league team." His stage whisper made Sabrina giggle. Russell snorted.

A blush stained Arnav's cheeks. "I knew that."

Vijay had always been softer with Sabrina than the rest of her siblings. He threw her a wink across the table and didn't seem to even try to hide his smirk.

"You sound incredibly busy." Raj was still scowling. Overprotective and every bit their father, her eldest sibling appeared to be firmly on Team Arnav.

Russell mopped up the last of his dhansak with some roti. "Yeah." His eyes darkened and his questioning gaze spurred her to nod at him. Understanding passed between them. With a warm smile he continued. "Between school, hockey, and my daughter, I'm definitely kept on my toes."

The gasp came from Sajjani. Sabrina's two sisters joined Raj in his scowling, but Vijay was nodding as though crazy impressed.

"You have a daughter?" Dad's voice sent prickles of irritation and discomfort across the back of her neck.

Russ turned to face him. "Yes, sir. I do."

Disapproval etched across his features, Dad walked away, presumably to tell Mom all about their daughter's boyfriend's dirty little secret.

Avni softened first, clearing her throat. "Do you have a picture?"

The smile that burst onto Russell's face was sunshine and more genuine than any she'd seen since they arrived at her parent's house. He pulled out his phone and unlocked it.

"She's called Jude, and she just turned three." Pride laced

every word Sabrina spoke. "She loves princesses and superheroes."

Russell squeezed her thigh before handing his phone across to Avni.

She clutched at her chest. "Oh! You both look so cute together."

Warmth spread through her chest. "Aren't they adorable?"

"I mean you and Jude." Avni turned the phone so Sabrina could see the picture. She was holding Jude at her birthday party, Jude's head was thrown back in a spurt of open-mouthed glee. Sabrina was gazing at her with adoration painted clear across her face.

She hadn't seen the picture before, but the more she stared, the more she realized that warm feeling holding strong in her chest, was most definitely love.

A jolt of recognition struck her as she studied Russell's profile.

Love... for both of them.

Her heart tripped over itself in her chest.

She didn't have time to explore that particular feeling at the dinner table, but she'd need to circle back when she had some space to process.

"Click the photo album and scroll. There's a bunch in there."

Jayshree scooted closer to Avni and the two ooh-ed and aah-ed as they flicked through the pictures.

Vijay asked Russell about his hockey plans since he was a lover of all things sports. While they chatted, Sabrina's face burned with the judgement radiating from Raj and Arnav's matching scowls.

Despite the two year age gap between Raj and Arnav, they'd been friends in high school before Arnav had left to study medicine. Raj had always been convinced she would find her way back to his friend. He was going to be hard to win over, but she'd hoped the party would go a ways to getting him onside.

That was before she'd bumped into Arnav at the airport.

"He has a child?" Her mother's hiss from behind Bre's was loud enough for the whole table to hear. Russell's face betrayed no reaction, but she was reacting for both of them.

"Yes, Mamma, Russell is a single father."

"And what about the mother? Where is she? How does that work with your relationship? Is this truly what you want for yourself? A broken family and someone else's baggage?"

Embarrassment spread across Sabrina's body like she'd stepped in a fire ant hill, rendering her mute.

Arnav cleared his throat. "Your mother is right to be concerned for you, Sabrina." He flared his nostrils as he glared at Russell and back to Sabrina. "It doesn't feel like a good fit."

Russell's jaw twitched. None of her siblings said anything to refute either her mother or Arnav. Not even Vijay. Her father stood stoic and silent at her mother's side, his mouth taut in a grim line.

It was how it always went. They ganged up on her for being young, naïve, foolish, convinced her she was wrong, and no one stepped up for her or cared to listen to what she had to say.

But nothing about the feelings in her chest *felt* wrong. In fact, when she was with Russell and Jude everything seemed to align just right.

Except for now. Poorly contained rage and indignation oozed from his pores, and his whole body was rigid. It must have been painful for someone who faced life head-on to witness the exchange or rather lack thereof.

Russell cleared his throat. "With all due respect." He pushed back from the table and stood. "Though god only knows why I'm extending respect to any of you, given how despicably you've not only spoken to me but to your own daughter. Sabrina is a grown and capable woman, and to my knowledge, she's not asking any of you to sleep with me, so it's none of your concern." He held out a hand to her, ignoring the gasps and mutterings around the table.

Warmth radiated up her arm as she slipped her palm into his.

"C'mon. Dance with me, Bubbles. I can't have you sitting at the table looking stunning all evening. Let me show you off in that dress."

She bit the inside of her cheek, but a smile tugged at her lips. While her mom, sisters, and Sajjani had all opted for the traditional Indian sari for the soiree, Sabrina had gone in a different direction.

She'd chosen a British racing green, floor-length gown with a small band of diamante stones under her bust. It wasn't revealing, but her meager handful of cleavage certainly looked impressive, cradled by the fabric. The back of the dress buttoned at the top, but had a slit revealing a modest patch of her back.

She shivered when Russell's hand met her skin as he guided her to the dance floor. She didn't miss the gawking stares of her family as she left them to dance with her boyfriend.

Russell

Fury consumed every fiber of his being. Who the fuck did they think they were?

He didn't give a shit about their judgments of him. He was used to people hearing he was a single father and making their own assumptions.

What he cared about, however, was the fact they were railroading Sabrina, ganging up on her, making her feel bad about her choices and the path she'd decided to walk.

"You keep looking around." She stroked at the space where his hair met the skin on the back of his neck. He was dangerously close to purring like a contented cat.

"Honestly? I'm trying to find a dark corner to drag you to and fuck you senseless. I've had a raging hard-on cutting off the blood flow to my brain since you stepped out of the bathroom. You're lucky I let you leave."

The musical laugh that erupted from her was almost worth the pain from chafing against his boxers. She softened in his hands and a flicker of relief sent a shiver along his spine.

"You know they're still staring, right?"

"Fuck them." He barely contained the growl rumbling in

the back of his throat and the urge to slip his hand toward the curve of her ass as they swayed. If she wasn't so overtly afraid of them, he'd have done it, but he didn't want to upset her further.

"I'm sorry."

"Nope. Not accepting an apology you don't need to make."

The song changed but their pace stayed the same. If he focused on anyone else in the room, his body trembled with anger, so he kept his gaze firmly fixed on the beauty in his arms. "Why do you let them talk to you like that?"

A bitter chuckle escaped her as they navigated couples on the dance floor. "Distance helps. It's much easier to ignore their bullshit when I'm not surrounded by it."

He nodded, but she still hadn't answered his question. He was about to ask her again, when her mother interrupted their dance by grabbing Sabrina's arm and pulling her to the side of the dancefloor.

"Your father and I think you need to come back home." She threw a narrow-eyed glare at Russell who had followed. "For good." She held up a hand to silence any protests that might make their way out of Sabrina's wide-open mouth.

"It's best for the family. If you're going to give up everything to mother a child that isn't even yours, with a damaged man, then you might as well give everything up and look after your family. Your family who have given you every opportunity to make something of yourself. You can go to a local school, but also be here for your grandmother."

"Are you kidding me?" Russell couldn't keep the words from forcing their way out into the space between them. "What about what Sabrina wants? Or what's best for her?"

The crow's feet at the corners of Aneka's eyes were more pronounced as she glowered. The severe look on her face was probably one she'd used on Sabrina her entire life, but it didn't work on him. "This is between my daughter and her parents."

True story, it was.

And if he thought for one moment Sabrina was ready or strong enough to stand up for herself in the moment, he'd have stayed quiet. But the surge of hostility that hit him at her mother's patronizing tone shook him to his core.

"No." Sabrina's quiet voice was almost inaudible over the noise of the party.

Aneka's frown was replaced by a smirk in Russell's direction. "See? Tell him. It isn't his place to create drama." She gestured at him. Vishal appeared behind her shoulder, face stern, arms crossed.

If steam wasn't spurting from Russell's ears at his barely contained rage, it would be a miracle.

"I meant no to you, Mama, not Russell. I won't be moving back to Seattle." Strength seemed to reinforce her spine right in front of his eyes. She pulled her curled-forward shoulders back and set her jaw.

"I'm happy in Minnesota. I have a life there. I love my classes, I get good grades, I have wonderful friends and a supportive boyfriend." Her fingers slipped between his, and he gave a reassuring squeeze, silently urging her to keep going.

A bluster passed her father's lips, and her mother's face creased with a deep scowl.

"I know I'm not a doctor like you, or top of my class like Raj, or happily married to a nice Indian boy with kids like Avni. You know why?"

Her words picked up speed as she went. There was no stopping her, even if he wanted to. Whatever dam had been keeping all her feelings and reactions to her family contained was leaking.

Her free hand clutched in a ball by her side. "Because I'm not them. I'm me. Sabrina. The only one of your children born in the US. The only one with an American name. The only one who gets constantly shit on from everyone in the family, and I take it because that's how I was raised to be."

She held his hand in a death grip. If she was drawing strength from the contact, he wasn't going to let a little numbness or a potential broken bone disrupt her flow.

Pride welled inside him at his girl finding her voice. She might regret it when they got back to the hotel and had time to process. She'd probably feel guilty for blurting out things she'd held onto for years, but watching her come into her own was a sight to behold.

"I know I'm not the perfect daughter. I don't live nearby to help take care of grandma." She checked off her sin on one finger. "I don't visit for holidays, and I don't call three times a day to check in." She kept counting on her fingers.

Her breath was shaky as the words erupted from her mouth and her chin trembled. "I picked the program I wanted to – not medicine or law, or whatever – at a college far away from my family, but I needed to breathe. So maybe it feels like abandonment. But I needed to grow. I needed space to spread my wings and find myself, and before either of you say anything, I know you're going to say I'm selfish. It's what you always say, and if you don't say it out loud, it's how you make me feel. How you all make me feel. The weight of responsibility for this family is too heavy, and I can't take it anymore."

Sabrina's open-mouthed parents at least had the decency to cast their eyes to the ground at the announcement of how they made their daughter feel.

He willed her to stay strong. Not that crying made someone weaker, but that was how it was perceived. Crying, even angry crying, was always somehow a losing move in an argument.

No doubt her family would feel the same and use it against

her. He squeezed her hand again, running his thumb along hers. He could only imagine the overwhelming stress of confronting her parents, never mind in the middle of a formal dinner party, surrounded by her entire family and her parents' lifelong friends.

Sabrina huffed out a breath at his side. "This might not be the place for this discussion, but you invited it. Storming across the room to demand I move back home like I'm incapable of making my own life choices. And why?" She put her free hand on her hip but didn't let go of his.

"Because Russell is a single father, and it might somehow reflect poorly on the family image?"

Her mom shifted, and her dad glanced up at the ceiling.

"Is that it? Because I didn't swoon at the sight of Arnav in the airport and run back into his arrogant arms? I don't even care what your why is. Shame on you. Shame on you both. Russell is smart. And funny... and strong. He loves his daughter with everything he has, and he's raising her right. And Jude..." She sucked in a breath as though the words spilling from her lips were exhausting to say.

"Jude is everything good about the world. She's as kind and fierce as her father and so full of sunshine and love, it's hard not to love her." Her eyes brimmed with tears as she spoke about his daughter. "And I do... love her. I love them *both* and that might not work for you, but it works for me and that's all that matters."

She loved him? Wow. Fear coiled like a readying serpent low in his gut. Something else lay there, too, but he had no time to pause, Sabrina's emotional dam had burst, and while she didn't outwardly seem to need him, her arm trembled against his and her leg twitched as she spoke.

"I knew coming here was a mistake. I knew something would happen where I'd be made to feel like shit for my choices. I ignored the feeling in my gut and came anyway."

Her face turned to stone. "I won't be making that mistake again."

Her mother stepped forward, hand clutched at her chest, mouth open, poised to speak, but Sabrina charged ahead.

"No. I've bitten my tongue for too long. Shoving down my thoughts and feelings because that's what was expected of me, but no more. If my life choices aren't good enough for you, if you believe I'm selfish for wanting my own life, then I'm sorry, but that's a you problem, not a me problem. Now, if you'll excuse us, I'm done here."

Hurt flashed in her eyes. Somewhere along the way Raj and Avni had joined the group and presumably heard every word their sister had thrown at their parents. Avni plucked at a cuticle and Raj's scowl appeared as though it was a permanent fixture.

Was no one going to speak?

Didn't they feel ashamed of themselves and their behavior?

Russell let go of Sabrina's hand and slipped his palm low on her back. "Let's go, Bubbles."

They walked to the car in silence.

Sabrina stared vacantly out the window as he drove, never letting go of his hand. Her voice was laced with heavy sadness and exhaustion when she finally spoke. "Where are we?"

He jerked a thumb out the window. "You barely touched your food, Bre. We're here to carb-feed our emotions with a side of ooey-gooey cheese."

She reached for the door handle.

"Wait." He grabbed her arm. "I forgot to ask... Are you a pineapple-on-pizza kind of girl? Please say no. It'll be torturous trying to find a replacement."

Her brow and lips quirked. "I'm tempted to say yes, simply because you look like the idea of fruit on pizza is a personal insult to you. But no, I don't like pineapple on pizza."

Russell blew out a breath. "Thank fuck for that. Let's eat."

Ten minutes later, he folded a fully loaded slice of pizza into his mouth. Despite the layers of meat on top of the triangle of bliss, the base remained crispy, and he could still taste the flavor profile of everything in one single bite.

Perfection.

Sabrina's moan reflected his own feelings of the pie they were sharing.

"Maybe we should have ordered two." He chuckled as her eyes rolled and fluttered closed before her head tipped back.

"So fucking good!" She didn't open her eyes as she took another bite.

Affection spread through him at the woman sitting in front of him. She'd told her parents she loved him, but he couldn't help but wonder if she had simply been caught in the heat of the moment.

Did he love her?

If not, could he?

He'd never been in love before, so the tangled wad of emotions weighing on his chest was intimidating. As far as his parents were concerned, love ended in heartbreak, abandonment, and even hate. He forced down a mouthful of pizza as unease rattled through his bones.

He couldn't love her, because love wasn't a Disney movie or a Broadway musical. Love wasn't some beautiful, perfect thing wrapped up in a pretty bow. It was tough. It was messy and complicated. And it was hard work.

Love was dangerous.

As she took another bite of pizza, she smiled across the table at him, warmth flickering in her eyes. "What?" Her hand flapped up to her face. "Shit, do I have stringy cheese on my chin?"

He chuckled and nodded. "You do, but that's not what I was staring at."

She brushed her fingers across her chin, and he laughed again. Smacking his bicep, she joined him in his giggling. "Jerk. There's no cheese on my chin."

Shrugging, he wiped his hand on a napkin before gliding it over the apple of her cheek. "Made you look."

"So what are you staring at?"

"You, Bubbles. I'm just staring at you. You look incredible tonight, sure. But your inner strength, standing up for yourself, finding your voice with your parents... I'm kinda impressed at just how much of a fucking badass you are."

"You are?" Her voice was small as she picked at a piece of bell pepper from her pizza.

"I'm so proud of you."

Her eyes remained glued to the table but her small gasp arrowed straight to his soul. Had anyone ever told her they were proud of her before? Gratitude welled inside him, wrapping around the shards of heartache for her. Despite his parents' divorce, he'd never once questioned whether Mom loved him or was proud of him.

What must life for Sabrina have been like? Always coming in last to her siblings must have been exhausting. His chest compressed.

"I mean it, Sabrina." He hardly ever used her full name, so, as expected, her head snapped up.

"You don't think it was too much?"

He shook his head. "I think you still managed to hold back despite the runaway train of emotions that crashed into you on the dance floor." He paused, dipping his crust into the marinara dip. "I think you gave them a lot to think and talk about. And I think you're going to have the emotional hangover from hell tomorrow. But I got you."

Her bright smile didn't quite reach her eyes, but it was a start.

"I wasn't sure you had it in you yet, Bre."

Her eyebrows shot up her forehead.

"Ah – wait, don't get me wrong. I knew you had it in you, I just didn't think you were ready. I was all wound up and ready to be your knight in a fly-as-fuck suit. Which you haven't even commented on tonight, Bubbles. Don't think I haven't noticed. I'm pained by your lack of mention of how hot I look." He gestured at his chest and pouted.

He wiped his greasy fingers on a napkin. "But you didn't need a knight of any kind. You didn't need me, you didn't need anyone. I knew you were fierce, I knew you were strong. But I didn't think you were ready."

"What if…" She ran her finger around the rim of her water glass. "What if they don't talk to me ever again?"

He grabbed her hand and squeezed. "Look, I know this doesn't help but sometimes that's how it goes. When you put down boundaries for those who have been allowed to take up space in your brain and heart, they don't like it. There's going to be a period of adjustment and settling into a new normal – for all of you."

She sat agape.

"If they decide they don't like your boundaries and don't want to talk to you, that doesn't mean you're wrong. That's the lesson. That's the most important part. Don't compromise yourself because they make you feel like you're somehow at fault for having healthy boundaries."

"You sound like you're speaking from experience."

"Mom and I haven't always been as close as we are. When dad first left…" He sighed and raked his hand through his hair. "It was awful. For a while I split my time between his house and hers. She'd ask me about him, peppering me with questions about any girlfriends. Or worse, she'd ask me to ask him things."

He shook his head. "It was toxic. And her overprotectiveness kicked into high gear. We argued a lot – I was a teenage boy with a lot of testosterone and feelings about my parents' divorce. I went to therapy for a while, we both did. I think she still does to be honest. But my therapist told me that setting boundaries to protect yourself is never a bad thing. In fact, it's something I not only needed to do for myself, but for Jude."

"For Jude?" Her button nose wrinkled as she scrunched it in confusion.

"If I didn't have healthy boundaries, and reinforce them, it would allow Jude to grow up believing it was okay for Mom, or anyone else, to treat me like that. Including Jude. I needed her to know that it wasn't okay, that it's not okay for anyone to treat you in a way you don't like to be treated. And just because they're family, they don't get special dispensation for being dickish."

"You're such a good dad, Russell." Her words tumbled out on a sigh.

He shrugged. "I figure if I can't bring myself to do things for myself, I at least owe it to Jude to make sure the toxic shit stops with me and doesn't get handed down to her."

She sniffed. "I hope you do some things for yourself and not everything is just for Jude."

A non-committal noise escaped him. Hoping she didn't notice him bristle, he sipped his water, and eyed the last slice of pie between them.

He'd never been enough, not for his dad, not for Elise, and some days not even for his mom. He spent every day pushing himself that little further, just to make sure he was enough for his daughter.

"It's all a work in progress. We all are. And you made huge progress today, Bre. You need to acknowledge that. Laying down those first few beams of the barriers between toxic people and your heart? That's no small feat."

"So this is celebratory pizza?"

He chuckled and nodded. "I guess it is."

"Then I guess that means you won't mind if I claim the last slice of pie."

"Damn. I didn't even see that one coming."

Not only did he let her have the last slice of pizza but he'd bought tickets for them to see a musical for her birthday. This woman.

A warning rang somewhere in the darkest recesses of his mind, chirping on repeat like a smoke alarm needing its batteries replaced.

Sure, he was in Seattle with his girlfriend, but he was getting in way too deep, and he wasn't sure how to stop it. She'd been in his life for a few months, but already the tug in his chest, his desire to see her every single day, was driving him to distraction.

He had no time for distraction. He had shit to do and goals to achieve. He needed to bring his A-game every damn day to ensure he gave Jude everything she could possibly need and more.

Maybe he was overthinking it. Maybe they weren't in as deep as his thudding heart seemed to think. Or maybe, as was more likely, he was just full of shit.

CHAPTER 19
Russell

"You're doing what?" Lincoln raised his voice and cupped a hand around his ear.

"I'm pretty sure you heard me." Russell met his volume, tugging off his pads.

A post-win locker room resembled a zoo. Nervous energy buzzed around the space; the team, energized by victory, were loud, animated, and everyone talked at once.

"I heard you say you're going to a theater to see a musical."

Russell grunted in response.

"Are you sick? Did an alien possess your body in Seattle? Is this some kind of distress signal?"

Finn snorted, presumably at the exchange. Linc wasn't wrong, Russell wasn't exactly a theater kind of guy.

"Probably why he didn't suck as bad as usual." Johnny tossed the insult over his shoulder as he passed.

Russell growled. Johnny cast a smug grin in his direction before disappearing into the showers.

"Don't let him get at you, Stewie." Finn patted his shoulder. "You know he feeds off it."

Most of the other guys on the team could tune out Johnny's incessant assholeness, but Russ never could. Johnny didn't know when to quit and always seemed intent on ending up with someone's fist ramming his face.

Russ couldn't figure out his deal, nor did he want to. Did Johnny just wake up every morning and choose violence?

He didn't like the guy, and seeing him talking to scouts for two games in a row chafed at his competitive bone. He puffed out a laugh. "I'm fine."

Finn shook his head. "Surrrrre you are. That's why we can hear your teeth grinding to dust in your mouth, right?"

Linc chuckled. "I think it'll be fun. The musical thing. They're actually not bad."

Finn's eyes widened at Linc's announcement.

Linc shrugged. "I have sisters. Their lives are basically musicals. It wasn't a day ending in Y unless one of them burst into song at the drop of a hat for no apparent reason at all."

"It's cute that you're doing something nice for your old lady, Stewie. Expand your horizons and all that." Finn hadn't moved to take off his gear, he crossed his legs at the ankles and put his hands behind his head before leaning back. "Fuck I was good tonight."

"I guess we spoke about topics other than Finn being a god on the ice for too long. His ego needs stroking." Russell shook his head, and Linc crammed his pads into his kit bag.

"It's not my fucking ego that needs stroking."

Russ snorted.

"Good game tonight." Will slapped Linc's bare shoulder. "Let's keep it up over the weekend, yeah?"

The three men groaned. After a losing spell, getting traction for the big W was hard enough, but keeping the momentum for more than one win was proving to be even harder.

"Yes, sir, Captain Will, sir." Finn gave a salute to his best friend. "We'll get right on that."

Will rolled his eyes. He was hovering. Fully dressed, ball cap pulled on backwards, wet strands of hair poking out from under it, he was clearly ready to leave. What was he waiting for? Finn wasn't going anywhere fast, so unless he was going to pull up a pew and take a load off, there was something else their fearless leader wanted to talk about.

"How's Sabrina?"

Russ's head jerked up so fast his vision blurred. "My Sabrina?"

Will nodded, holding up a hand. "I'm not after her."

"Good." The rumble in his chest surprised him. He hadn't seen her for three days since they'd returned from Seattle. He'd convinced himself she needed time to settle back into her life and process everything that had happened over their weekend away, but the truth was, he just needed space.

Or at least that's what he thought he needed.

He rubbed absentmindedly at the knot in his chest. He missed her. He missed her scent, her smile, her sass... and he hated himself for it.

"Okay, well. Bye."

Linc's frown lingered until Will was gone. "That was weird."

Finn sat up and leaned forward. "Did he take a hit to the head out there?"

Russ didn't answer, his gaze remaining on the door Will had left through. Jealousy exploded under his skin, and acid burned the back of his throat as anger simmered deep in his chest. Why had Will wanted to talk about Sabrina? And why was it drawing such a visceral reaction from him?

He finished getting dressed in silence. On the way to his car, he pulled out his cell phone to message Will. If he didn't figure out why the hell he was asking about Sabrina, it would eat him up all night.

There was already a message waiting for him.

> Will: Honestly man, I'm not after your girl. I was talking to Molly and she said Sabrina seemed upset or something. I was only half listening, but it occurred to me it could impact your game if your girl was having issues.

> Will: I couldn't figure out how to broach it in the locker room though. My bad. I definitely fumbled that pass, sorry.

Sabrina was upset?

Guilt curdled in his stomach. Was she upset because he hadn't talked to her since they got back from their trip? Was it her family?

He'd know what was wrong with her if he hadn't been taking space for the past few days. He'd been so blinded by trying to maneuver his own feelings that he'd dismissed hers out of hand. He scraped a hand through his hair. This was the exact complicated emotional bullshit he didn't have time for.

Johnny wasn't standing around feeling guilty about a woman or getting so tangled in a web of emotions that it was compromising his life. That's probably why scouts were talking to him and not Russell.

Okay, so maybe he was exaggerating the situation just a tad, but it was just another reminder that he didn't have enough hours in the day to accomplish everything he needed to.

His heart squeezed. Torn between his future, doing everything he needed to do, and his growing affection for Sabrina, he thumped the steering wheel.

Linc's words still rattled around in his head, warning him against keeping people out. He sighed and unlocked his phone. Nerves fluttering, he pulled up her number. His thumb hovered over the end call button as he waited. Maybe he shouldn't have called. Maybe she was busy.

"Hey, Russ."

His dick woke at the mere sound of her voice, but her sad tone made his guilt grow.

"Great game tonight."

He hadn't seen her in the stands. "You were at the game?"

"No. Watched at home. Wasn't feeling being peopley."

"Everything okay?" He plucked at a loose thread on his shirt, heart racing.

After a heavy moment of silence and a sigh, she answered. "I'm not sure."

It wasn't her nature to stride toward confrontation. If she was upset at him, she likely wouldn't say it, not unless he pulled it out of her somehow.

"I'm sorry I didn't call after we got back."

"I'm sure you were busy..." It wasn't a question, but her tone suggested she wasn't even convinced by what she was saying. "It's only been a few days..."

Her sadness stoked the inexplicable righteous indignation building in his gut. Sure, things had leveled up on the trip, but if he was busy, he was busy and she'd just need to accept that he couldn't afford her every free moment of his time.

He sucked in a breath. Was he actually pissy with her for wanting to spend time with him? Was he more upset about Johnny fucking White being headhunted by scouts than he was allowing himself to acknowledge? Or was he simply running at the first sign of real commitment to an amazing woman he enjoyed spending time with?

Maybe it was all of the above.

"Russell?" Her voice was a whisper. Something ruffled against the speaker. Was she already in bed?

"I'm here."

"I know. I can hear your thoughts from here. Usually it's me who thinks too loudly."

He chuckled. "I don't know how to do this." He'd never

been one to beat about the bush. Telling her what was concerning him was the only way to navigate the indecision and stress pressing against his temples.

"This being... ending things?"

"What? Why is that your first thought? Is that what you want? Shit, Bubbles, I meant relationships. I don't know how to be a boyfriend. The only real relationship I ever had... well..."

She gave a non-committal hum.

"We both know my reputation before I met you. I'm a one-night-stand kinda guy, Bre." The words tasted sour in his mouth, but he needed her to know where he was coming from. "Purely physical. Scratching an itch. No strings."

"Love 'em and leave 'em." Bitterness hung on every word.

He swallowed. "Yes. It's what had to be to ensure Jude never got hurt. It was best for everyone if I stayed single and..."

"Played on and off the ice?" A mirthless chuckle erupted from her. "Are you saying you want no strings? Because..." She sighed. "It's too late for that, Russell."

"No... I..." He scratched a palm over the back of his neck. "I'm saying I want strings. With you. I want the strings, I just don't know how to do the strings. Sometimes I'm not going to get it right. Sometimes I'm going to be a selfish ass and take space without thinking about how it affects you. I don't know how not to be that person. But I'm trying."

She snorted.

"Okay, fine. I wasn't trying very hard, but I'll try harder from now on."

Her soft laugh seemed to expel some of the tension between them. "Where are you? It sounds weird."

Outside the car, his teammates were climbing into their vehicles and driving away. Linc threw him an "Okay" sign with his hand and Russ nodded, sending a thumbs up in return. "Outside the rink. In my car. I was going to go home and call you from there, but I guess I just didn't make it that far."

"I miss you." Her voice was small. "I thought maybe…"

He urged her to finish her sentence. To confront him about what he'd done that had upset her. Tell him how she felt.

She blew out a wave of air that hissed through the speaker. "I thought my family drama had scared you off."

"It kind of did." He didn't miss the small squeak that escaped her. "It's a lot."

Someone smacked the hood of his car, causing him to jump. "Fuck."

Johnny White was flipping him off through the window with a twisted smile on his face. "Fuck you, JW."

Johnny couldn't hear him, but Russell felt better for grousing at him.

Asshole.

"You okay over there, hot shot?"

"Yeah… sorry. Johnny was being his dickish self. What was I saying?"

More shuffling against the phone. The idea of her turning over in bed sent sparks of desire to his crotch.

"My family drama shook you."

"It did." He nodded, even though she couldn't see him. "I have a lot going on in my life. I just… got overwhelmed I guess? I know you probably needed support these last few days and I'm sorry I got wigged out. But, like I said…"

"You don't know how to do this."

She didn't sound convinced, and he wasn't sure if that feeling low in his belly was guilt or shame. But there was no judgement in her tone, only sadness. Like she wished he could be what she needed.

While he wasn't sure he could, another wave of indignation crashed into him. Damn it, he wanted to be.

Maybe in time he'd figure out how to balance the pieces of his life and take better care of the people he loved.

Loved.

He meant cared about, right? There was no way they were already in love territory.

Except wasn't that what love was? Wanting to put your partner's needs and wants before your own?

He was screwed. Jumping without a parachute. Driving without GPS. Flying blind. He had no fucking clue how to traverse relationship terrain and that frustrated the fuck out of him. Of the many things he hated, not being in control was definitely in the top three.

"It must be scary." She continued when a lengthy silence fell between them.

Was she a mind reader too?

"I don't like admitting I'm afraid."

"No one does. It leaves us exposed for people to exploit and use against us, right?"

He nodded again. "Man. My parents' relationship really fucked me up." A nervous laugh rippled through him. "I truly am sorry, Bre. I realize this is, like, high school boyfriend bullshit. My whole world has been Jude, from the minute she was born. And I only had one serious girlfriend, her mom, so I feel like I missed a bunch of the how-to date, y'know, the learning years."

"Do you want me to ask Quinn to come to the show tomorrow night?"

"Of course not! I told you I'd go and I want to go." The voracity in his voice surprised even himself. He really did have it bad for this woman, even if he didn't quite know how to handle it.

That only made him madder.

Madder at himself for not taking the time to learn how to have relationships with people.

Madder at his parents for conditioning him to believe love was a weakness, a danger, something to be feared.

Madder at Elise for disappearing into thin air and leaving him holding the baby.

Literally.

He'd always been a hands-on learner. Reading about things never truly worked for him. It's why he was learning both French and computer science – hands-on things that involved practical application of the lessons. Things he could put in motion and practice in action.

He had to accept that dating was no different. He had to hope he'd improve the more he did it. He only hoped Sabrina's patience would last long enough for him to figure shit out.

"You ready to go?" Sabrina slipped into the front seat of his car and pulled the door closed behind her.

Dressed in jewel tones, she was stunning. Her shimmery eye shadow caught the light making her eyes pop and sparkle. She wore little gold chandelier-type earrings that jingled with every small movement. Her glossy lips parted in a big smile as she leaned across the center console to air kiss his cheek.

"You clean up well, Mr. Stewart."

"Gotta keep up with my girl." He wanted to be as excited as she was, but Jude was running a low-grade fever before he left and he couldn't shake the parental guilt and anxiety that came from leaving your child when they were sick. Especially for something as flippant as celebrating a birthday.

Her face fell. The all too familiar tendrils of guilt coiled around each vertebrae in his spine and squeezed, forcefully expelling air out of his body. His muscles wilted.

"What's wrong?"

He sighed. "Jude has a low-grade temp. I know she's fine, Mom has her, it's just... I feel guilty going out and having fun."

Her hand fluttered to her chest. "You should absolutely go be with her, Russell. I don't mind, I'll go alone or get Quinn to come with me."

The seeds of irritation permanently sown in his gut sprouted like weeds. "It's fine." The jolt of her eyebrows at his snapping made the guilt surge even more. "She's fine. It's fine. Let's just get moving, okay?"

Her eyes slipped to clutched hands in her lap. "If you're sure…"

"I'm sure."

Perhaps she didn't mean to sound like she was questioning his parenting, but that's how it felt. Like she was somehow judging him more than he was even judging himself for being out while his baby was suffering.

He'd made the right decision. Mom knew how to handle a sick baby, and if she needed him home, she'd tell him as much. He was going to swallow down his guilt and show his girl a good time for her birthday.

"You wanna come back to my place?"

They'd made it through the show – which Russell didn't hate – but he was only paying about 65% attention to it. He'd spent the evening covertly checking his phone to make sure he wasn't needed at home.

He thought he'd gotten away with it or at least not been too disruptive to the enjoyment of the musical. Mom had texted during the second act to say Jude was sleeping peacefully, temp normal, and to enjoy himself. He'd tried. But from the downturned lips and the deflated way with which Sabrina held herself in the front seat of his car, he could tell she was upset.

"It's okay." She stared out the window as he drove. "I should probably get back. I have an early start in the morning."

Her flat voice irritated him. So he'd been distracted, so what? Her being withdrawn instead of calling him out on his bullshit ground at his raw nerves. Passive aggression was a pet peeve of his. He wouldn't be guilted by anyone for worrying about his daughter, and if Sabrina had something to say to him, she should just find some balls and spit it out.

He flexed his hands. Frustrated energy coursed through him. A good fuck would probably sort him right out, or at least take the edge off, but from the way she was angled away from him, head hung low and hair over her face, that wasn't going to be an option.

Her sad smile before she turned to open the door, as they idled curbside outside her apartment building, melted his heart. He was being an irrational asshole, and he couldn't even pinpoint the why.

Not that it mattered.

It wasn't her fault. She was trying to be her nice, people-pleasing self at every step of the evening, but the more she tried to accommodate him, the more it rubbed him the wrong way.

Reaching toward her forearm, he hesitated for a moment before curling his fingers around her wrist. "I'm sorry."

She nodded but didn't look at him. His heart ached. Why was this so hard? She was a fantastic woman and he enjoyed being around her but everything was complicated and irritating.

He tugged her to his chest and snaked his hands around

her, holding her against his body. "I really am sorry. When it comes to Jude..."

"You don't need to explain yourself to me. I just... I guess I wish you'd taken the out when I offered it, stayed home with Jude so I could have enjoyed the show. Or even both of us stay with Jude. Whatever. This... it just didn't work."

He nodded, grudgingly admitting she was right.

"It wasn't all bad. I had fun, and the show was amazing." Her eyes welled with unshed tears. Either at the memory of the show or the situation they found themselves in, he couldn't quite tell.

"I'm glad." His voice croaked. "I didn't mean to ruin your birthday celebration."

"I know." She ran her nose along the curve of his jaw. "You didn't. I just think it could have been handled... differently, y'know?"

Story of his life.

So many things he'd done or not done could have been handled differently.

No matter what he did, or didn't do, it seemed someone always ended up upset with him. He sighed. Maybe one day, he'd finally figure out the key to being enough for everyone.

CHAPTER 20
Sabrina

"You gonna eat that?" Russell's fork hovered over Sabrina's plate.

She arched her eyebrow, fighting a grin. "Maybe I am." She folded her arms and leaned back in her seat.

Schedules permitting, they'd met for dinner every night over the past week. Which meant every night he wasn't at the rink. While he wasn't a terrible cook, he didn't come close to her skills in the kitchen. He'd already wowed – or rather disgusted – her with his blue-box mac and cheese talents. While Jude loved her daddy's ready-mac, taking Sabrina out meant neither of them needed to do dishes either. Win-win.

Things were almost back to normal between them, and the more time they spent together, the more she adored him.

"Y'know... a person might think your body language and lack of defensive position over your plate might indicate you're fine with me stealing your food."

She grinned and jerked her chin. "How do you still have room to eat?"

He speared the pasta on her plate, sliding it across onto his own and tucked in. "Mmm. Why didn't I get the Alfredo?"

"Because you knew you'd end up getting some of mine anyway?"

He waved his fork at her. "I'm not one to make assumptions."

Her snort drew a smile to his face that sent spurs of lust to her core. "Sure you're not, Hot Shot. How was practice last night?"

Reaching across, he gave Jude's sippy cup a shake. "You good, Princess?" Jude nodded, waving her sauce covered fist clutching a fork in his direction. "Practice was... exhausting."

Frowning, Sabrina leaned forward and picked up his free hand.

"Are y'all alright? Can I get you anything else?" Their server's arms were laden with dirty dishes and a bead of sweat trickled down her temple.

"We're good for now, thanks." Russell crammed another piece of chicken into his mouth, and Jude smacked the fork off the table. The server looked at Sabrina who nodded before leaving them to it.

"Have you thought anymore about what you're going to do next?" Her voice was quiet, and her eyes fixed on her glass of soda on the table.

Part of her wanted him to tell her what his plans were, but the other... her heart tugged, reminding her that he might end up leaving her. Worse still, reminding her that she might not be a consideration in his future plans at all. Her stomach fluttered. She had no idea what she wanted to do after college.

Maybe she could become a teacher? Or a social worker? Maybe she could become a translator? Nothing she'd considered had imprinted on her like it was what she was born to do.

She knew he was being ripped apart by indecision at the thought of the draft. While June was a ways off, he needed to have a strategy in place when it happened. Either he'd be drafted or he wouldn't – and both options needed to be planned for accordingly.

"I don't know." He rubbed his thumb along the back of her hand. "If I don't get picked up by Minnesota... the idea of either leaving Jude with Mom and moving or upending Jude's life and finding a nanny wherever I go..." He swallowed hard as though the food turned to ash as he spoke.

What about her? She hadn't made the list of people he was concerned about. Did he think this was a flash-in-the-pan romance and they wouldn't last? Pressing down her own emotions, she turned his hand over and traced circles on his palm.

"Don't tell me the King of Cold is having feels – what'll the team say?" She winked, ignoring his eye roll. "Hey..." She waited until he met her gaze, so he'd know she wasn't being flippant. "I'm sure your mom would move with you, Russell. Her job can be mobile, right? She's freelance and can edit books from anywhere in the world. Digital nomads are in right now."

She was trying to lighten his spirits, but indecision wasn't usually something he was plagued with, and it wasn't something he particularly enjoyed either. It must have been fraying at his nerves.

He cleared his throat. "I need to figure out what I want, then I can pursue it relentlessly."

Smiling, she nodded. If ever someone needed to define Russell in two words, "pursues relentlessly" would work for his personality both on and off the ice. "I thought you wanted to play for the Wild?"

He nodded, tearing apart the last breadstick in the basket and mopping up the Alfredo sauce pooled on her plate. "I did. I do. I just... I don't know. Maybe I'm not good enough. Maybe I just want to play pro because I know I'll make enough money that I can squirrel it away and take care of Jude. Maybe they won't want me. Maybe—"

She curled her fingers over his kissable mouth, drawing a laugh from Jude. The butterflies in Sabrina's stomach grew more restless as anxiety ratcheted up her spine. "Look... I know it's not my place. I know I don't have my own child." She glanced at a still-watching Jude. "But I can see your brain unravelling as you talk, and while we don't always know all the answers, I think it's important to take a breath right now."

He stayed quiet, eyes narrowed. Was he pissed at her for speaking out of turn? Was he keen to hear what she had to say? Ugh. Why was his resting bitch face the same as his tell-me-more face?

Deciding to be undeterred, she rolled her shoulders. "What if it was Jude? What if she was nineteen and wanted to pursue something, anything, and started questioning herself? Wouldn't you tell her to follow what was in her heart? If you want to play pro hockey, play pro hockey, but don't chase a dream that isn't yours."

He wiggled his jaw as though to speak, but she held firm, still covering his lips. "If you're intent on playing because the money's good and there's a kind of safety net to provide for Jude, that's different to chasing your own dreams. That's responsible dad Russell talking and while it's admirable, it could lead to resentment later in life that you didn't follow your heart. But if parental responsibility and chasing your dream collide and both point to playing at a national level? Well... Fear of failure isn't a valid reason not to do something." She finally freed his mouth and booped his nose. Jude giggled again, and Sabrina booped her nose, too.

"That needs to go on a T-shirt." He kissed her palm, spreading warmth through her chest. "Thanks for that, though. I think I get so caught up in what I should do, that when I think about what I want to do, even if it's the same as what I should do, I freak out."

"Everyone freaks out, Russell. It's how you move through the freak out that really matters. Don't sweat it. It's not June yet. You have time." She pulled wipes from the diaper bag and started working on Jude's sauce-covered everything.

How kids managed to paint their entire being with a few tablespoons of sauce was beyond her. Russell had even asked for the sauce on the side and drip-fed it to the toddler to avoid chaos. As it turned out, chaos and toddler were synonymous.

"Worry about today's problems today. June will figure itself out." Squeezing his hand before letting it go, she shuffled back and took a sip of her drink.

"What about you?"

Heart racing, she wiggled her tongue around, her mouth drying up at the swift change of subject. They hadn't talked about her family since he'd told her the drama was overwhelming. She'd been reluctant to bring them up, not wanting to add to his stress or give him any reason to run or push her away. She dropped the dirty wipe onto her plate and used another to busy herself cleaning the table in front of Jude. "What about me?"

"Any word from your family?"

Shifting in her chair, she willed the unease sitting heavy in her gut to shift. "My sister messaged. She didn't say anything about my... outburst. She just asked whether I was going to visit after the baby's born. And by visit she means help."

His face was almost entirely impassive, save for the slight twitch in his jaw. He probably expected her to run from every confrontation again, that her growing a spine and standing up for herself was a one off. "Did you answer her?"

She nodded, bone-deep sadness making her limbs heavy. "I almost said yes."

Falling silent again, he canted his head. Standing up for

herself wasn't something that came naturally, and it took a lot for her to push back. Pre-anniversary party Sabrina would have groused about not wanting to go, or how they made her feel, but still would have done what they wanted regardless of how she felt. The fact she hadn't up and left at their first message and had dismissed it so quickly, was a testament to how she was reinforcing her new boundaries – even if it hurt.

"I didn't though. Say yes, I mean." She searched his face. Was she seeking his approval? Validation? Some form of emotional head pat that she was doing the right thing? "I told her I'd see how the semester goes, but I hadn't planned on going home again any time soon. My family doesn't really celebrate Thanksgiving or Christmas, and I have stuff to do here. But mostly I just don't want to be there. Especially since they haven't reached out."

"Hopefully they're just processing everything and they'll realize they're being asshats."

From the tension on his face and the dullness of his eyes, he was only saying it for her benefit rather than believing it. Something warm pooled low in her belly at his attempts to make her feel better. She squeezed his hand. "Either way, I found my voice with them now. I feel better about dealing with them, and while it's tempting to fall back into old habits in moments of weakness, I know this is for the best." She swallowed. "For me."

Jude had upgraded from smacking her fork on the table to pushing silverware off the edge of the table and banging her sippy cup. They were on borrowed time.

With a nod and a smile tugging at his lips, he picked up the diaper bag. "Let's go before we're barred from your favorite Italian restaurant. Wanna come help put Jude to bed?"

❄

An hour later, Jude was fast asleep, Natalie had gone to visit Russell's grandmother, and with no dishes to clean up, they'd bought themselves a small window of alone time which she planned to thoroughly enjoy.

Need pulsed between her thighs as she snuck a glance across the couch to where Russ sat, staring right back at her. The edge of his mouth tugged into a knowing smile. "Tired?"

She pulled her lip between her teeth. "Hungry."

"But you just ate." His voice was light, playful, and charged with faux innocence, but desire flickered in the blue depths of his eyes.

"And yet I'm still not sated." She reached out and palmed the bulge in his pants. "Feels like you're not either." She pinched the bands of both his sweats and boxers and tugged, freeing his erection.

One hand curled around his length, she pumped twice, enjoying the shining bead of precum already glistening at the tip. She pumped again, increasing the pressure and reveling in the groan she pulled from deep in his chest.

Rotating her hand at the top of his shaft, she slid it back down, scooting closer to him so she could comfortably lean forward and tease the end with her tongue. She grinned up at him as a shiver rattled through his muscles.

Fingers weaving into her hair, pressure mounted on the back of her head, forcing her to cough. "Don't rush me, Hot Shot."

She licked her lips and rocked her hand back and forth a few times before trailing the tip of her tongue along the head of his cock. Sliding her mouth over the tip, she hummed in approval, not missing the hiss of breath released through his teeth.

He didn't push her head, and a thrill shot through her that he might actually be relinquishing control of... well, anything.

Still clasping his length, she bobbed her head and hand up and down, licking and sucking, slowly at first but soon picking up speed as his body reacted under her touch.

Muscles corded and tight, breathing in shallow, rapid pants, and eyes rolled back in his head, he tugged at her hair. "Gonna... come... Bubbles."

She hummed in acknowledgement but didn't slow down, determined, slurping on his cock like she might suck his soul out if she tried hard enough. In her periphery, he crammed his fist in his mouth and she grinned around him. Neither of them wanted to wake Jude, but the strain on his face as he fought to be quiet made her giddy.

With her free hand, she cupped his balls and gave a gentle squeeze before jets of thick, creamy liquid hit the back of her throat as he came on a strangled groan. She dragged her tongue along his slit, picking up every drop of his release. Fingers rubbed her scalp as he pulled from her mouth. "Oof. Gimme a second, Bre. I... I..."

She smirked, planted a kiss on his tip, and sat up, licking the salty taste from her lips. Walking her fingers up his stomach, she dragged his shirt up over the ridges of his abs, gliding over every crease and ridge. A few faded scars dotted across his abdomen.

"Appendix." His voice was a raspy whisper as he answered her unasked question.

"This one?" She swept a fingertip across a less surgical looking scar.

"Skate to the gut." At her gasp, he kept talking. "It was a freak fall. I got lucky." He traced his thumb over her crinkled brow. "It's okay, Bubbles. I survived. And all I got for my trouble was this lousy scar." He winked at her.

"How old were you?" She couldn't pull her skin away from his, feeding off the contact, energy sparking under her fingertips.

A chime she'd never heard before echoed from his phone and he bristled, his entire demeanor shifting in a fraction of a second. Surely he wasn't going to pick up the phone when they were in the middle of... well, they weren't exactly in the middle of anything considering she'd just swallowed his load. But she'd assumed it was going to develop into a toe-curling, fist-chewing O for her as well.

He picked up the phone and paused. Something on the screen creased his brow in a severe V, and if she concentrated hard enough, she could hear his teeth squeak against each other as he ground them.

"I haven't heard that ringtone before..." She was nothing if not subtle.

She waited, but all he did was stare in silence, nostrils flaring, eyes vacant, his chest rising and falling in labored breaths. What the hell was on his screen?

"Russell?"

Still nothing.

He pressed at the screen once, probably to unlock it, but the staring resumed. She sought out any clues about what was going through his mind, but came up empty. Always so guarded, walls so high and impenetrable. All she knew was someone unexpected had sent him a message that shifted him from down and dirty to dark and broody – and not the hot, Angel from *Buffy the Vampire Slayer* kinda brooding. Squeezing his thigh made him jump.

"What?" Irritation, impatience, confusion, a myriad of emotions flickered across his face and dripped from the single word he'd spoken.

"I..." She pulled her hand from his leg. "You checked out there for a second. Are you okay?"

"I don't know."

"Who was the message from?" It was none of her business, and what's more, she knew it. But they were in a relationship, and it was kind of her place to know, right? And if it wasn't, he'd undoubtedly tell her as much.

"Jude's mom, Elise."

"Wait, what?" His words crashed into her like a freight train. She had to have misheard, Jude's mom was dead, right? "Jude's mom? B-but I thought she was dead?"

His already impossibly deep frown somehow deepened. "No, where'd you hear that?"

She raked through any previous mention of his ex, panic creeping through her veins and hurt spreading in her chest. "You said she was gone." Her voice was a shaky hushed whisper. He hadn't told her outright that Elise was dead, but the tone and the way he'd said it... she'd assumed.

Gone. Not dead.

Embarrassment clawed at her throat, and the pain in her chest spread further. Would they get back together? Be a family together? Would Elise travel to whatever state Russell was drafted to and take care of Jude? A choked gasp suffocated her as possible scenarios rammed her mind. Would she have to say goodbye to Jude?

"Gone, Sabrina, yes. But I never said or even alluded to her being dead." Irritation oozed from his every word, but his eyes remained on the screen. He offered no other explanation, no further information, he simply glowered at his screen.

"W-what does she want?" She chewed at a loose cuticle around her thumb. Of course she'd want him back. Who would be crazy enough to leave such a beautiful family?

He sighed, as though her question took effort to contemplate. "To meet."

"Are you going to see her?"

Something flared in his eyes as he dragged them off the screen and pinned her with a glare. "She's the mother of my child, Sabrina."

His child, right. She had no claim to Jude and from the

coolness with which he was regarding her, she had no right to question where his affections lay either.

She's the mother of my child, Sabrina.

Like that should have been all the answer she needed for any questions she might've had. Sweeping her clammy palms on her thighs, she rose to her feet. "Okay, well, I should go. It's getting late."

His fingertips brushed against hers. "You don't have to go."

He didn't mean it, his dim eyes, his flat tone, and the fact he was still burning a hole in the screen of his phone with his laser focus had her leaving before he could get up from the couch.

When she got outside to the street, she sucked in a deep breath but her tight chest refused to loosen. This was the man she defended to her family, stood up to them for: what if it had all been for nothing? Maybe she was overreacting. Maybe he'd race out into the darkness behind her and tell her she was, that he loved her as much as she loved him, and that he didn't want anyone else but her. Did he even love her at all? He hadn't said it back.

With each step toward her car, the weight in her stomach grew heavier. He didn't follow. And as she drove away, she couldn't help but wonder what the hell that meant.

CHAPTER 21
Russell

"Must admit, I expected to find Sabrina here this morning when I woke up." Mom stood leaning against the kitchen counter, hands cradling a steaming cup of Joe.

Shaking his head, he hit the coffee pot hard, and poured the elixir of life into the biggest mug they had and taking a sip.

"Black coffee kind of morning, eh?" Her piercing gaze and carefree tone suggested she knew something was up. "You tossed and turned a lot last night, Russell. Anything you want to talk about?" She toed at the cushioned, anti-fatigue mat in front of the sink.

He tossed some cream and sugar into his mug, stirred, and threw the spoon into the sink. "I think I fucked things up with Sabrina." Scanning her face for any trace of relief, or satisfaction, he found none.

"Wanna talk about it?"

"Elise texted. She wants to meet me tonight after the game."

She frowned and crossed her arms, jolting her mug almost spilling it. "Does she want to get back together as a family?"

Was that fear coating her voice? It sure as hell wasn't excitement, or hope.

"I don't know, Mom. She said it was important and she needed to meet, that's all I know."

"And is this what messed things up with Sabrina?"

Jude stirred in the other room. Her chattering to her toys could be heard throughout the house thanks to the monitor he still insisted on using every night.

He tilted his head. Mom sounded almost disappointed that Elise was back and disappointed that things with Sabrina were going to hell. Shouldn't she be happy things were falling apart? It wasn't as though she loved Sabrina. She was only putting up with her because he liked her, right? "We were on the couch when the message came through." Heat shot up his neck, settling in his cheeks. "Getting... uh..."

She held up her hand. "I get it."

"Right. Well. Yes. Anyway. The message came through, and she asked who the chime was for and I said Elise. I guess I must have been short and shitty with her because next thing she was leaving."

"You guess?"

The timer on the oven beeped. Mom put her mug on the counter, grabbed an oven glove, and opened the door releasing a sweet apple-and-cinnamon gust of warm air toward him. "Is that French toast hot dish?"

She nodded. "I figured you could use some cheering up. Or bribery to talk to me if you weren't forthcoming with your feelings this morning."

"That's kind of savage, Mom. I like it. So yeah, I was a jerk to Sabrina and she left."

She grabbed plates and a serving spoon, heaping a steaming pile of deliciousness onto each. "Then what happened?" She handed him a plate and put Jude's in the fridge to cool for a few minutes.

"I let her?"

"Have you spoken to her since?" She scooped some onto her fork and blew before popping it into her mouth. Jude was still chatting with her toys, probably telling them how awful her mimi and daddy were for leaving her in a cage while they enjoyed a hot meal and uninterrupted grown up conversation. He shook his head, guilt souring his stomach.

"Oh, Russell." The disappointment drenching those two simple words crushed his heart. "If you don't want to be with that girl, you need to let her go."

Did he want to be with her? He thought so, but things were getting more and more complicated. If Elise was back in town, at best he'd need to be civil and accommodate her into Jude's life. He had no interest in rekindling whatever they had together. He couldn't even if he wanted to – the trust was lost.

If she wanted, she could press for shared custody, or worse still, try to take Jude from him.

Dread soaked him like a downpour. There was no way he would give up his baby without a fight. Things with Sabrina would have to wait until he figured out what Elise wanted and how to handle her. He only had the bandwidth to deal with one woman at a time.

Legs burning, heart pounding, and adrenaline coursing through his veins, Russell crushed his opponent into the boards and sailed the puck to the nearest white shirt on the ice. The victim of his epic check, Jeremy Lewis, hit the ice with a dull thud. The home crowd cheered.

"Dafuq is your damage, Stewie?" Rolling onto his stomach, Jeremy sucked in a few breaths before pushing himself to standing.

Ignoring Jeremy's question, Russell focused on the puck,

not sparing him a backward glance. The Snow Pirates were 2-1 down with only minutes left to go in the third. Both conceded goals were because of him. Distracted, angry, and sloppy – that's what Will had groused at him during the period break, and from the glares Coach Swift was giving him, he was going to get his ass handed to him post-game as well. All he could do was concentrate on the last few minutes of play. He wasn't letting anything else get near their damn net.

"Someone piss in your Cheerios this morning, Russ?" Lewis's chirping was like sandpaper on a raw wound, but Russell wouldn't let his anger get the better of him. Try as Jeremy might, Russ wasn't getting drawn into conceding a penalty and giving the Mustangs a man advantage with only minutes to go.

"Fuck you, asshole."

Jeremy nudged his elbow and slid his stick in front of Russ's, the clack of stick-on-stick stoking the rage pooled in his belly. The other time they'd faced each other, Jeremy hadn't been so aggressive or such a dick on the ice. But something about his narrowed eyes underlined with dark circles and firm-set jaw suggested Russ wasn't the only one having a shit time of things.

"You wish, Stewie. You fucking wish." Jeremy flashed the grin that caused bunnies to lose their mind – and their underwear – and surged forward to meet the puck.

Over my dead body.

Russ met Jeremy's pace and their sticks cracked and clinked as they fought for possession. Just as Jeremy pulled the puck back, the buzzer sounded.

Sweat trickled into Russ's eyes, and his pulse thumped in his temples. Jeremy threw a coy grin over his shoulder and pushed against Russell's crotch with his ass. "Back up, boo. I'm not that kinda guy." Pushing off Jeremy's still-extended butt, Russ skated away.

"Aw c'mon, Russ. Talk to Uncle Jeremy. Tell me all your women-woes."

If it wasn't for the arena full of people he'd have told Uncle Jeremy all about his women-woes with his fucking fist. But since his ex was on her way to meet him after the game, he didn't have time for the fun shit.

"Feel better?" Finn coasted up to his side and draped an arm over his shoulder. Russ grunted in response. "I know I'm not your bestie or anything, but... I mean... even I can tell something's eating at you, man. You sucked out there tonight."

Russ growled and spun to face him. Finn held his hands up. "Just stating facts. You know it. I know it. We all have those games, it's no biggie." He narrowed his eyes. "But if it is a big deal, if something's going on and you need help... We got your back, Stew."

A wad of emotion swelled in Russell's throat, like a cotton ball soaking up water. He gave a sharp nod before continuing across the ice to the tunnel. "Thanks, man."

Finn skated away, only to be replaced by Linc. Russ held up a hand. "Don't say it."

"Sayin' nothin'. I don't have a fucking death wish, man. You going to see her now?"

"Yeah." Nausea swished in his gut.

"Where are you meeting her?"

He swallowed and shook his head, knowing before he said it that it was a bad plan on every level.

Linc's hand slammed against his chest, pushing him against the wall of the hall leading to the changing rooms. "Oh no, Russ. Are you suicidal?"

Russ groaned. "It was her idea."

"And you couldn't have said, oh I dunno, let's go somewhere else. Is Sabrina working?"

Russ dropped his gaze to his skates and shrugged.

"Didn't you say she just... left... when you got the message from Elise last night?"

Russ nodded.

"And you haven't talked to her since, right? So showing up to her place of work with your ex... fuck, Russ, that's low."

"I tried to talk Elise out of it at first, but then I kind of figured it would be reassuring for Sabrina to see us together and know it isn't a date. It had seemed like a good idea last night, but now... He winced and looked to Linc for reassurance. Right? She'll see us, just two people co-parenting our child together over dinner, and... and..."

"Fuck." Linc pulled his helmet off and ran his hand through his sweaty hair. "You thought, what? She'd be cool with it? Dude." He bopped Russ on the head with an empty glove. "How can you give out such sound, solid advice and be so fucking dense in your own love life?"

Russ snorted. "Takes a special somethin' somethin' I guess. This is going to be a disaster, right?"

Linc cringed, bugging out his eyes. "You think? Fuck. You're toast. She's gonna filet your balls and stick them on the grill. I'll pick up some beer on the way home."

Bre hadn't replied to his message asking if she was working, which meant she was either ignoring him or she was working. Nerves speared his stomach and knots rolled down his neck, settling in his shoulders.

He and Jude sat on one side of a table tucked in the corner. Elise had texted to say she was running late, and while he hadn't yet seen Sabrina anywhere, a heavy sense of foreboding clung to his every cell, making it hard to breathe.

"This was a bad plan, Princess. Daddy is in big doo doo."

"Doo doo!" Jude giggled and offered him her doll.

Sabrina and Elise both arrived at the same time. Yeah. This was definitely a bad idea. Recognition dawned on Sabrina's face for a split second before she schooled her face. His heart twisted.

"What's she doing here?" Elise slipped into a chair facing him.

Russell wasn't sure whether Elise was talking about Jude or Sabrina, who was standing tableside, and whose chocolate eyes seared into the side of his head as Elise took her seat. Bre cleared her throat but wouldn't meet his gaze.

Fuck was he ever in trouble.

"Can I take your order?" Her voice was flat and quiet.

"Just two waters for now, thanks."

"Three, please." Russell scowled at Elise for not thinking to order a drink for Jude.

Sabrina turned and left before Russell could fully react to her presence. Thus far, Jude hadn't seen her yet.

"I asked what she's doing here, Russ." Elise gestured at Jude who was attempting to chew on the crayons he'd given her from his bag.

Redirecting her hand to the page, he searched Elise's face for... something. "You mean Jude?"

Elise nodded.

"She's your daughter, Elise. I figured you'd want to see her." He gritted every word through clenched teeth. If she wasn't there to see her child, why had she come?

"I'm aware she's my daughter, Russell."

"Here are your waters. Can I get you anything else, or do you need a little more time?"

"I'll just take a cheeseburger and fries, please." She handed her menu to Sabrina without a second glance.

"B! B! Beeeeee!" Jude gesticulated wildly with her crayon.

Sabrina's smile was warm and genuine as she curtseyed.

"Your Majesty. What a surprise to see you this evening. Are you hungry?"

Jude nodded through her laughter.

"Mashed potatoes?"

The toddler nodded again.

"What can I get you, Russell?" Her eyes flicked from playful to frostbite-inducing as her attention shifted to him, and a chill shot up his spine.

"I'll take a crispy chicken tender salad."

"Sure. Veggies and tenders with Jude's mashed potatoes?"

"Yeah." His eyes darted from the creases on her forehead, to her cold eyes, to the rigidity with which she held herself, and his chest ached. He reached out to touch her hand, but she pulled away.

"I'll get that started for you." She flashed a brittle, fake smile at the table and left. She was a few feet away when Jude slipped off her chair and gave chase. Damnit, this was why she usually sat in highchairs. He needed to screw his head on right.

"B! Beeeeeeeee!" Jude launched herself at Sabrina's leg and clutched it as though it was a buoy in a raging storm.

Bre placed the menus she was holding on a nearby empty table and swooped picking Jude up. Elise watched the exchange, curiosity etched across her face. Warmth crept through his body at the affection between his daughter and Sabrina.

Bre spun Jude around before returning her to the table and leaning close to Jude's ear to stage whisper. "Maybe if you eat all your veggies, your daddy will let me bring you a treat."

Wide, hopeful eyes turned to him, and he flashed her a grin before ruffling her curls. "If you eat all your veggies."

Sabrina held his gaze for a beat, then two, before picking up the menus and disappearing into the kitchen.

"She's cute." Elise tipped her head in Sabrina's direction.

"If you're not here to see Jude, why are you here, Elise?"

"All business. Got it. Guess I deserve that." She pulled a manila envelope from her bag. "I want to sign over all my parental rights to Jude."

Flickers of anger took flight in his stomach. Why didn't she want to be a mother to the most beautiful, perfect little girl ever to walk the earth?

His mouth dried up. "I thought…"

"I know. But this is better for all three of us."

He reached a tentative hand out to the envelope, stopping and pulling it away as though it might scorch his skin. She wasn't there to fight for custody. In fact, she didn't ever want to see Jude again. She was handing over all her maternal rights to their child.

His heart cracked in his chest that the woman in front of him could just sign their daughter away. But he wasn't going to beg her to reconsider; she'd clearly made up her mind. He forced indifference into his tone. "You're sure?"

She gnawed on the inside of her cheek. "I'm sure. I'm not cut out to be a mom, Russie." She gave him a sad smile. "That much is never going to change."

After a few minutes of heavy silence, Sabrina's colleague Gregg appeared with Jude's food. "Here you go, lil lady." He placed the plate in front of her with a flourish that made the toddler laugh.

Before walking away, he pinned Russell with an intense stare that made his skin itch. Had Sabrina given their table to Gregg to wait on for the duration of the meal? He was fucked. He scraped a hand over his jaw.

"Know what? I'll take my food to go, please." Elise filled the awkward silence hanging over the table.

Gregg's brows shot up as his eyes widened. "Uh… okay. Sure." His gaze landed on the envelope sitting on the table between them.

With any luck, he'd go back into the kitchen and tell Bre

that Elise was leaving and had left an official-looking envelope in her wake. Maybe she'd even come back out to see them again, and he could find a way to tell her he was falling in love with her.

His stomach flipped and his heart flared.

Okay, fine. He'd tell her he'd already fallen in love with her and he was sorry for being such an epic douche nozzle.

CHAPTER 22
Sabrina

Cowering behind the swinging door to the kitchen, anxiety expanded in Sabrina like someone had mixed vinegar and baking soda in her stomach. Her hands trembled. From where she hid, she couldn't see Russell's table, or see the pretty blonde sitting across the table from him.

Her heart pinched and she idly rubbed at the ache throbbing in her chest. Why would he bring his ex to her place of work to reunite? Why would he rub salt in her wound like that?

The more she wrung her hands together and chewed at her lip, the more she realized he wouldn't. Russ, for all his flaws, wasn't spiteful. Straight talking, confrontational... sure, but never cruel.

Why would he have brought his ex where she worked then? Did it matter? If he was getting back together with Elise, this was Sabrina's only shot at telling him how she truly felt. If she was going to lose him, she wasn't going to just stand by and let it happen.

With behemoth effort, she pushed herself away from the

wall and heaved a breath. Rolling her neck, she forced her shoulders away from her ears and swung the door open into the bar. The woman was gone. Perhaps she'd gone to the restroom.

"She didn't. She left." Gregg appeared beside her, hands laden with dirty dishes.

"I was thinking out loud again, wasn't I?"

His eyes turned sad. "I know you're hurting, but I don't think that..." He jerked his head at Russell's table. "Well, I don't think it's what you think it is. I'm not getting kissy kissy make up vibes from them. Maybe you should go talk to him? I'll cover your other table."

Her legs were like lead as they carried her on auto-pilot to his table. She'd barely slipped into the seat opposite when he started talking.

"I'm not getting back with her."

Some of the apprehension resting on her sternum uncurled, and she blew out a puff of air.

"In hindsight, agreeing to meet her here without talking to you first..." He rubbed a hand around the column of his neck. His eyes were heavy and tired, his skin pale, and she longed for his down-turned lips to curve into his bright smile. "I thought it might help you seeing us together. To know it wasn't romantic, that I wasn't sneaking around with her behind your back. I guess, it wasn't my smartest idea."

"No sh—ugar." She widened her eyes. That was close. Jude was copying everything she heard, and all Sabrina needed was Russ's mom to hate her for teaching her granddaughter the word shit.

Sitting quietly and waiting for him to explain was painful, but pushing him would only make things worse. His shoulders were tense, and his overall demeanor radiated solid don't-fuck-with-me vibes. She didn't want to poke the bear.

He gulped down his water and smacked his lips, pulling a

giggle from Jude. He reached over, cupped the little girl's face and caressed her nose with his thumb. "Elise is giving up her maternal rights."

His voice was flat, and his tone suggested this wasn't the good news it seemed to be. "I need to get a lawyer to look everything over. I... I don't trust her. She's manipulative, and for all I know, she's left a loophole in here, allowing her to swan back in at any time and take her from me."

It sounded unlikely, but the idea alone shot bolts of panic into *her* chest. She couldn't judge him for wanting to be thorough.

"I know I have no right to ask for your patience right now, but I need it. I..." His splayed hands covered his face before travelling through his hair. Pleading eyes met hers, and her heart cracked in two. "I'm struggling right now, Bre. I... I'm spiraling. I sucked on the ice, I barely scraped a pass in my last French paper, now Elise... I just..."

When his voice cracked, she reached across the table and squeezed his hand. "It's okay. We'll get through all of those things."

His eyes widened like he might not believe her. She wanted to wrap him up in her arms and hold him until the storm passed, to lend him her strength until he felt strong again.

Eyes welling, she sniffed and shook her head. "I gotta get back to work, but I'll grab treats and bring them right over, okay?"

The sadness in his eyes made her tummy ache as he nodded. She kissed Jude on the forehead. While Sabrina was still low-key cranky that Russell had just shown up at her place of work with his ex, part of her couldn't help but wonder if it was because he knew she'd be there to support him. She turned to leave but a warm hand slid into hers, tugging her backward.

"Hey."

Casting a glance over her shoulder, gratitude swam in his eyes. "Thanks for everything, Bubbles."

Delight radiated through her body at the weight of his simple words. She squeezed his hand. "Any time, Hot Shot."

The next day, despite being busy, Sabrina and Quinn had managed to nab their favorite table next to the window in the Sugar Bean. Their oversized mugs brimmed with hot chocolate. Quinn had chosen pumpkin, refusing to admit fall was over and winter was already in town, and Sabrina gleefully sipped on her chocolatey peppermint deliciousness, embracing the warmth seeping through her being.

"So you just left him there?"

"Technically, he and Jude finished their food and left. I'll probably call him later, I just… he seemed so overwhelmed, Q. I don't think he's used to having so much go wrong all at the same time."

Quinn dragged a finger through the whipped cream on top of her drink and licked it off. "Any word from your parents?"

"Actually yeah."

"What? You're kidding? Were they giving you shit? Do I need to smack a bitch?" Quinn's fiery red hair and almost unrealistically green eyes coupled with her hot temper made for a walking stereotype. She was quick to anger but would have Sabrina's back no matter what.

"Stand down red alert." Sabrina sipped at her drink. The door to the café opened letting in a blast of cold air, and a collective groan rippled around the space. "Mom called to check in. We actually had a conversation about how I'm doing."

"Did she ask you to go home again? Lay on a sprinkling of guilt about how hard it is to take care of everyone? Top it off with a side of passive aggression?"

Despite Sabrina's smile, sadness crept into her bones. She sighed. "Not this time. She asked leading questions, listened to what I had to say, told me she loved me, and that was that."

Quinn's squint and pursed lips echoed the cynicism Sabrina had felt earlier in the day when mom had woken her up for a 'chat.' "Maybe they're..." She paused. "Changing?" She screwed up her face as though the word tasted gross in her mouth. "Sorry. I know they're your family and all, but I just... they've been so super self-absorbed, I just don't see how they can wake up one morning and suddenly not be damaging to your mental health."

Quinn held her hands up. "I hope I'm wrong and being overly suspicious. Of course I do. But at the same time, I don't want you to get hurt, and I don't want you to undo all the good boundary work you've been doing either."

Sabrina chewed the inside of her cheek. "I know, you're right. I admit my suspicious bone tingled when I saw her name on my screen. Other than calling at 7AM – I mean, who the hell does that unless someone's dying or in labor? It's not like I'm an early riser."

Quinn snorted. "That's for damn sure."

Hope flickered in Sabrina's chest. Maybe this time would be different with her family. Perhaps speaking up for herself was all it would take to break the cycle. But she'd need to prepare herself for the fact that their behaviors were so ingrained that they couldn't be changed, no matter how much she wanted them to.

"What if they aren't different? Are you prepared to walk away?" Quinn's striking green eyes watched her from over the brim of her mug as she drank.

"I dunno, Quinn. I feel so much better, freer, lighter now

that I'm not constantly dreading my phone chiming with messages admonishing me for whatever I did on a given day to piss them off. I'm sleeping better, too. I feel like that's telling, right? The hen-pecking, the judgement, the accusatory messages that I'm somehow always to blame for things, or I'm too selfish and need to do what's best for the family... I'm doing okay without all that."

Quinn reached across the table and squeezed her hand. "Girl, families are hard, sure. But there's definitely a line. I think we're raised to put our parents on a pedestal, like they are somehow above, more than, not mere mortals like the rest of us. We're taught to obey and respect them simply because they're our parents. And when we get older, I dunno. I think we realize they're human like everyone else. They make mistakes, they aren't always right, and while they believe they have our best interests at heart, they don't always know what our best interests are. You're right to draw lines and make space. Family don't get to treat you like shit, just 'cause they're family."

Sabrina nodded. "I know. It's hard though. I miss them." After a sip of her quickly cooling drink she cast her eyes around the busy coffee shop. "Or maybe I miss the idea of them. The idyllic family picture I had in my head as a kid. Y'know, before I grew up and realized all those things you just said."

Quinn nodded. "It's more common than you might think. I mean, I love my family. But I'm one of the lucky ones. I think the fact my parents have a..." She cringed, and trailed her finger around the rim of her mug. "... Complicated relationship with my grandparents on at least one side has meant they broke the cycle and wanted things to be different for me. And for that... well, I'm forever grateful."

Sabrina drained the last of her drink and leaned back in the oversized chair. "I feel like such a drama llama right now."

"Well, we can't both be drama llamas at the same time, right? We'd lose our shit. Taking turns works much better for us and the rest of the world." She winked. "Hey, isn't that Russ and Linc?"

Russell and Lincoln stood in line to order, their backs toward them. "Mhmm."

"That grin is wicked. I don't even want to know what you're thinking about right now, Bre."

Sabrina picked her phone up off the table and typed out a text.

> Sabrina: You think if I asked the really hot guy in line at the coffee shop to take his winter coat off so I could ogle his ass in those sweats, he'd say yes?

Her eyes flitted between the man and the screen.

"What did you say?"

"You don't wanna know."

Quinn tossed her an eye roll as the three dots started moving on Sabrina's screen, then stopped. Russ slipped his coat off, clenched his ass cheeks and wiggled in her direction.

"You're such a freakin' pervert." Quinn shook her head.

"I'll buy you new pearls to clutch for Christmas. You can wear them with your devil horns."

Quinn's snort drew looks from the girls at the table next to them. "I'm just jelly 'cause I'm not getting any."

"You said it, not me." Sabrina's phone vibrated in her palm.

> Russell: Enjoying the view?

> Sabrina: It's a bit distant. Kinda hard to get a good view from all the way over here.

> Russell: All 15 feet, eh? LOL. I'll endeavor to bring the goods closer. Refill?

"He wants to know if we want refills." At the quirk of Quinn's eyebrows, Sabrina frowned and pointed at her. "Friends don't let other friends overdose on hot chocolate alone."

Quinn waved a hand as though she had no real power over the decision anyway.

> Sabrina: We could be convinced to have a second round.

> Russell: Pumpkin and peppermint, right?

> Sabrina: Got it in one.

> Russell: Got room for this fine ass at the table? Or do you just want me to stand close by and jiggle my junk periodically?

Sabrina laughed and beckoned him over. He'd turned to face her while he typed. The din of the busy coffee shop was easing off as people left. With any luck, her hearing would return before Russell and Linc joined them.

"Your face is going to break from all that smiling." Quinn's sing-songy whisper taunted her from across the table. "Have you told him yet?"

"Told him what?"

"That you're head over heels in l—"

"Ladies. Thanks for letting us join you guys. It's dog-eat-dog in here. We weren't sure we'd find seats when we first walked in." Lincoln dropped into the seat next to Quinn, careful not to spill his... blended frozen drink? Was the man insane? It was fucking winter outside and he was drinking frozen drinks? Sabrina shivered. He deposited Russell's drink on the table.

"Not to mention, this table is probably the warmest in the room." Russ handed Sabrina and Quinn their hot chocolates. Sabrina reached for her purse but stopped at the frown and shake of his head. "I got this, Bubbles."

Their eyes locked in a battle of wills, broken only when Quinn sipped from her mug, hissed and swore. "Thanks for the drink, Russ."

Sabrina threw an incredulous look at her friend. "I'd have thought Miss Gender Studies would have put up more of a feminist... argument... something..."

Quinn shrugged. "Meh. Sometimes you gotta let the caveman provide the food." She raised her mug, a smirk ghosting her lips, and took another sip. "But if you're going to insist on buying his next drink to make up for it, I'm tapping out. Two hot chocolates in one morning is my absolute limit."

"Death by chocolate, though. What a blissful way to go." Linc leaned back and tilted his head toward the ceiling as though contemplating drowning in chocolate.

Russell's warm fingers slipped between Sabrina's own as he captured her palm in his and rubbed his thumb along the back of her hand.

"How's Cleo, Linc?" In an attempt to ignore the whispers of pleasure radiating from their touching palms, she grasped for conversation. It had only been a few days since they were last intimate, but it might as well have been a lifetime. Lust fizzed and bubbled low in her belly, and the desire to blurt out that she was madly in love with the brooding, blue-eyed man at her side was almost overwhelming.

The smile that lit up Linc's face was telling. "She's good, thanks. I'm meeting her after class and taking her to lunch."

Russell's phone lit up on the coffee table. "I gotta take that. It's my lawyer."

Quinn and Linc made small talk while Sabrina tracked Russell as he slipped his jacket on and walked outside.

"Linc?"

Linc snapped his attention from Quinn.

"Does it get easier to read his resting bitch face? I feel like I never know if it's good or bad with him. His face never gives anything away. It's just... so frustratingly impassive!"

He chuckled and shook his head. "I can safely say that Russell Stewart's poker face doesn't get easier to read over time. But I will say, he'll always be upfront about which it is, good or bad."

She busied herself sipping on her cocoa when Russell returned to his seat, trying to listen to pieces of the discussion Quinn and Linc were having, but she couldn't focus. She didn't want to pressure Russell for information or overstep her bounds, but she was bursting to know whether the lawyer had found anything suspect.

When he returned, he rubbed his palm up and down her back and brushed a kiss against her cheek. "Nothing untoward in the papers she brought. No drama. It's all good. I just need to stop by the lawyer's office and sign them, then I can be done with Elise for good." He sank into the chair with a sigh.

She took his hand and squeezed it. "I'm so glad she's not here to cause trouble."

He nodded before taking a sip of his coffee. "I really am sorry we had crossed wires about her. I don't like to bring her up. I didn't mean to give you the impression she was dead."

She nodded. "I know. I appreciate the apology though."

"He doesn't give them out often." Linc's chirp from across the table reminded her she wasn't alone with Russell.

Russell's scowl made her laugh. "Do you have plans later? It's not a practice day, right?"

Linc wagged a finger. "Every day's a practice day. We had

an off-ice gym session this morning where Will tried to kill us all."

"I have to go see Coach after class later, too. He hasn't kicked my ass over last night's loss yet, so that needs to happen."

A weight settled heavy on her chest. She wanted to curl up on the couch together and watch the next Marvel movie on his list. She needed to be folded in his relaxed arms, his breath tickling her neck, comfortable and happy. Aching to be in his arms... his strong... firm...

"Bubbles?"

Her head snapped up. Their eyes locked, humor reflecting in his blue depths. Busted.

"Were you just ogling his arms?" Quinn sounded every bit as amused as Russell looked.

Sabrina flipped her off, then Linc smooshed a napkin into her hand.

His deep chuckle sent shots of heat straight to her cheeks. "You might wanna mop up your drool there, Sabrina."

"I will not be shamed for... staring... at my boyfriend's... assets." Her face burned. "You were saying?"

A smile tugged at the corners of Russell's mouth. "I asked if you're free tomorrow night. We could watch another Marvel movie if you're not sick of your Marvelducation."

"That's not a thing." Sabrina sipped at her drink. If possible, the second mug of hot chocolate tasted even better than the first, and there were most definitely more marshmallows floating on the cloud of whipped cream. "Oh hey. Why did we start with Captain America?"

His nose crinkled as he pursed his lips. Lincoln groaned, covering his face with his palm.

"Why wouldn't you?" Quinn looked up from her phone. "That's where it all began."

"The internet says Iron Man is first."

Linc groaned again. Russell smirked and waved a hand at Quinn as if to say, "Do you wanna take this, or should I?"

Sabrina turned from her best friend to her boyfriend. "Well? Who's going to explain it?"

"Iron Man was released first, but Captain America's movie is literally called 'The First Avenger'... chronologically speaking, Cap comes first. If you watch them out of order, you mess with the timeline and that just fucks it up for everyone."

"Couldn't have said it better myself." Russ grinned before taking a sip of his coffee. "It's the only way to watch Marvel movies."

"Who knew?" Sabrina shrugged.

"Everyone. I'm amazed he hasn't gone over this with you before now." Linc dug his straw into the corner of his cup and slurped at a stubborn mound of frozen drink.

Bre laughed. "I keep forgetting to ask. I'm sure he'd have been only too eager to nerd out with the explanation, but I was checking the list the other day to see what came next to try to wow him with my know-how, but I just ended up more confused!"

Russ patted her palm. "Don't worry, you'll be a Marvel pro in no time."

Quinn licked her lips. "I still called dibs on Cap, though." They shared a laugh.

Mugs empty, coats on, they had no other reasons for avoiding the chill outside the coffee shop. "I'll see you tomorrow?" Russ rubbed his nose against hers, sending warmth through her body.

She nodded, somehow breathless at the touch. "I can't wait."

He thumbed at her lip, releasing it from between her teeth. "I can't either. I miss you." Pulling her against him for a hug, he shifted his jacket so his hard-on pressed against her stomach.

She hissed out a breath. "Suddenly I can't feel the cold anymore. Wanna blow off responsibilities and have sex in my car?"

With a groan, he dropped his forehead against hers. "Do I ever. But I can't. I gotta keep Coach sweet so I don't get kicked off the team."

"Tomorrow."

He nodded. "Tomorrow."

Longing rippled through her, telling her to launch herself into his arms and take him right where he stood, but Quinn tugged at her arm.

"Yes, yes, you'll get laid tomorrow. We get it. Now let's go before he gets frostbite and his dick falls off."

CHAPTER 23
Sabrina

"Sabrina? It's Natalie. Uh, Russell's Mom?"

Something in her tone sent a chill of dread straight to her soul.

"Sabrina? Are you there?"

"Y-yes ma'am." Her voice was a quivering whisper. "What's wrong?"

"Don't panic."

Sabrina hated when people told you not to panic. As if that wasn't the one thing destined to make you do just that. Prickles of fear sent gooseflesh over her skin before she realized Natalie was still talking.

"Wh-what?"

"They were in a car accident, honey. They're okay. They're in an ambulance heading to the hospital to get checked out. I was wondering if you wanted me to pick you up on my way there."

"Please. I'll just put some shoes on. I'll text you my address." She hung up before Natalie had time to reply and sent her the address to her apartment.

Quinn's narrowed eyes studied her from across the room as she shuffled toward the door. "What's wrong?"

Shoving her feet into her shoes, she reached for the door handle.

"Bre? Stop. What happened?"

"Russell and Jude were in an accident. I have to go to them." She turned back to the door, reaching again for the handle.

Quinn bolted across the room, grabbing her by her biceps. "Okay. And you will. But I think you might want to take your pjs off and put some real clothes on. If for no other reason than it's a cold night out there and you don't want your nipples falling off."

"What is it about you and body parts falling off in the cold?"

She shrugged. "Got you to smile, didn't it? Fine, it got you to grimace, whatever, close enough. Do you want me to come with you?"

Sabrina shook her head as she pulled off her pj bottoms and replaced them with leggings. "Could you call Gregg and ask him to cover my shift tomorrow please? His number's..."

"On the fridge, I know. I look at it every day, B. I got Gregg." She paused and pointed at Sabrina's boots. "You might wanna upgrade to jeans and Ugg's instead of leggings and sneakers."

Sabrina nodded. "Right."

Quinn ducked into Sabrina's closet, the screeching of hangers indicating she was rifling for something.

Sabrina shivered. Natalie had said they were fine, but her voice was every bit as shaky as Sabrina's. She wrapped her arms across her body and rubbed her biceps. It was a good thing Natalie wanted to pick her up and take her to the hospital, right? Definitely progress that she was being included in something so major.

Quinn emerged with Russell's Snow Pirates hoodie Sabrina had *borrowed* one night after they'd watched a movie together. It still smelled of him, and comfort settled over her as she slipped it on. "Thanks, Q."

Her friend nodded. "I gotchu, B."

When Sabrina slipped into the passenger seat of Russell's mom's SUV, Natalie gave her a fragile smile and told her what happened. Russell had taken Jude to see his grandma at the care home after dinner, while Natalie had stayed behind to finish up some work since she'd been to visit with her mom first thing. Someone in a pickup truck had run a stop sign, and while it wasn't a major collision, it was enough to set off the airbags, so the EMTs insisted on checking them both over at the hospital before they could go home.

The rest of the drive to the hospital was silent. The anxious, hyper-aware kind of silence that filled every pore with apprehension. Every red light felt like an eternity, and no words Sabrina could think of felt like the right words, so she stayed silent and wrung her hands in her lap.

The emergency room was bustling, but not crammed with people. Natalie's face was a veil of collected calmness as she approached the nurses huddled at the desk and asked where her son and grandbaby were. She'd clearly shoved her own fear and worry into a deep pit somewhere in her chest and was projecting a confidence Sabrina wished she herself could find. They followed a nurse to Russell's room.

"Mom!"

Natalie's eyes welled with tears as she darted across the small room Russell and Jude had been put in and hugged her son. Sabrina waited next to the door, not wanting to crowd the family. Jude curled into Russell's side, sleeping peacefully. There didn't seem to be any injuries, but Sabrina could only see half of the little girl.

Russ on the other hand had sutures holding together a cut

on his forehead, his arm was swollen and already bruising. He held out his good hand to her and relief quenched the ache in her belly at the small gesture. She squeezed before intertwining their fingers together.

"What have the doctors said?"

"Jude's all clear. The car seat did its job and protected her. She came away without a scratch." He shook his head as though he couldn't quite believe it. "I guess all that stuff about extended rear facing is true. Legit, not even a bruise."

"A-and you?" Sabrina kept her voice quiet so as not to wake Jude.

"They want to keep me in for observation. I hit my head and have some blurred vision so they did some scans, and I'm waiting for X-ray results for this." He winced as he raised his still-swelling, still-darkening hand. "The airbag deployed and sent my hand shooting into the visor."

"Ouch." Sabrina's chest ached at the sight of him in the hospital bed. He shifted his weight on the mattress and reached out to pick up the jug of water in front of him. "I can do that for you." She shot forward to pour him a drink, but he frowned and shook his head. "I got it."

"But you don't have to have it. I can do it."

"I said I've got it." Water sloshed over the edge of his cup as the stubborn ass poured himself a glass of water.

"Do you want me to wait around a while to talk to the doctor? Or do you want me to take Jude home and put her to sleep in her own bed?" Natalie swept his hair from his forehead, working around his wound.

Sirens screeched as an ambulance pulled up to the bay doors of the ER right outside Russell's room, reminding Sabrina that they were actually standing in a hospital. She shivered. Footsteps slapped on the linoleum floor as medical staff raced down the corridor outside the room. Loud voices called for medical equipment, and the pained sobs of a loved one pleaded with whoever was in earshot for them to save her daughter.

Russell's accident could have been much worse.

"I—"

"I can take Jude back to your place if you want to stay to talk to the doctors, Natalie." Sabrina needed out. She needed a blast of cold air to the face. She needed a deep and cleansing breath that didn't smell like hospital. Panic still held her chest in a vise, and her head throbbed behind her eyes.

Russell frowned, then winced and pressed the heel of his hand to his forehead with a hiss. "It's fine."

What was fine? Nothing was fine. Why was he being so weird? Did concussion turn people into jackasses? It was misdirected anger. It had to be. There was no way he could be so grouchy with her for something that wasn't either of their fault... right?

"That might be helpful, Russell." Natalie's soothing voice seemed to do little to quell his irritation. "Shit." His mom pressed her fingers on the bridge of her eyes. "I have things to do in the morning... appointments... It's usually the morning you're with Jude. I..."

Sabrina reached out and patted Natalie on the shoulder. "I can help. Please let me help. I can blow off class and sit with Jude, or I can sit with your mom at the care home if that's what you need, or I can run errands... I..."

"Stop. Just... stop!" Russell's outburst caused Jude to shift and everyone held their breath for a long moment before they even moved again, much less spoke. "I don't need your help, Sabrina. I get that you want to, but you're just being so... much. Take a breath. This isn't about you."

Ouch.

"Russell." Natalie's hushed whisper was stern. "That's not fair. I get that you're feeling crappy, but that's no excuse to take it out on Sabrina."

Wasn't that what her parents always said to her? *Stop being so selfish. This isn't about you.* Except this was about her. Wasn't it? He and Jude were part of her life, part of her heart. All she wanted was to help. She wanted to climb into the bed next to him, trace circles on his chest until he fell asleep, to help him handle his life for a day or two until he was feeling better and fighting fit. Yet it seemed all he wanted was to push her away and handle everything by himself. Alone. Without her.

He really hadn't let her in at all, had he?

Hurt crept up her throat, squeezing every molecule of oxygen from her body. Even when he was hurt and feeling like shit, he couldn't acknowledge that he might need help from anyone, not even her.

Didn't they say people lashed out at those closest to them in moments of stress? Was that all this was? Or was it a pattern of behavior just like that of her own family? Had she traded one kind of toxic influence in her life for another?

She cleared her throat. "It's okay, Natalie. I'll give you guys some space." She backed toward the door.

"But you didn't drive here, Sabrina. Wait for a little bit, I can give you a ride home."

Sabrina picked at a cuticle on her finger. "It's okay, I'll grab an Uber. I don't want to be any trouble." She had the door already open and was halfway into the corridor before she called back. "Let me know if you need anything, Natalie."

"Don't scream. I'm on your bed." Quinn's voice met her from the darkness.

"Hey."

"Your text suggested you might need a hug."

Sabrina crossed the room, shucked off her Ugg's and jeans, and flopped onto her mattress. "All I said was 'On my way.'"

"Yeah, and it was enough to suggest you might need a hug." Quinn repeated her words as though she was addressing an idiot. "I speak Sabrina, remember." She brushed loose hair from Sabrina's face and stroked her cheek. "What happened, B?"

"I really don't know." Sabrina flapped her hands on the bed. "All I did was offer to help and he got mad about it. I feel like he's mad at me a lot lately."

"Not *at* you." Quinn slid down the bed so she was lying face to face with Sabrina, giving her hand a squeeze. "I know it feels like he is, but he isn't. He's blowing off steam. Doesn't make it much better though."

"I'm tired of being a punching bag, Q. I just got done building up some boundaries so my family stopped doing it. Why is it okay that he's doing it too?" Tears she'd fought all evening trickled down her face without her permission and racked her body in shuddery sobs.

"It's not, B. It's really not. He's not being fair to you at all."

"Are you just saying that because you're my best friend? Am I really exaggerating? Am I being unfair?"

"I'm saying that because from the outside looking in, he hasn't done much to fill your bucket lately, and I don't like seeing my best friend hurt and sad."

Sabrina nodded as tears shook through her. Heavy tiredness pulled her toward sleep, but not before the realization hit that she needed to take a step back from the man she'd unwittingly given her heart to and his beautiful baby girl, even if it killed her.

❄

"Bre?" Quinn's quiet knock on the doorframe startled her from her trance-like state. "Are you in there?"

Sabrina groaned and turned away, pulling the quilt high over her head. "Sabrina isn't here right now, please leave a message or try again later."

When Quinn didn't react, she turned back. "What's wrong?"

"Russ is here."

"Here? Like... now?"

Quinn pursed her lips and nodded. Fuck. Of course he was there. Bolting from her bed Sabrina wrangled her unruly hair into a high ponytail before slipping on a pair of leggings. She was still wearing his hoodie and her shirt and underwear from the night before, but if he so much as threw her a judgy look for her swamp-witch-chic appearance, she'd punch him in his freakin' junk.

"I'm heading out. Are you going to be okay?"

Sabrina nodded. In the last fifteen hours, she'd tossed, turned, and flip-flopped about whether or not she truly needed, or wanted, to do what she had to do. Anxiety and dread strained every muscle, and a ball of pure, burning agony rested heavily on her chest.

She followed Quinn into the living room, and tossed her a thin smile as she left. Russell had showered and changed. His face was already turning a myriad of colors and his arm was bandaged, but not in a cast. Natalie had texted when she got home from the hospital with Jude to let Sabrina know that they didn't see any fractures or breaks on the X-ray, and his concussion didn't appear to be too serious.

"I'm sorry." He took a step toward her, arms outstretched, but she pulled her arms tighter across herself and stepped back.

Confusion and pain passed across his face as he stepped back again.

"I know." She sighed. "But I can't keep being your punching bag, Russell. You told me that I can't keep allowing people to hurt me just because I love them." The silence that followed her statement was all-consuming, suffocating. "I think we should take some space."

"You're breaking up with me?" The anguish in his eyes had her questioning every life choice she'd ever made, but she needed him to understand the level of hurt he'd caused her, too. And know that he needed to be all in, or she was all out.

A rueful smile passed her lips. "I tell you I love you, and you ignore it and jump straight to the negative. I said take some space. If you're not in a position to meet me halfway, then I guess, yeah. I'm breaking up with you."

His brows pulled into a deep frown, and he flexed the muscles in his cheek before opening his mouth to speak. "I—"

She held up a hand. "I've tried to meet you halfway and I feel like I've gone beyond. I gave you space when you needed it. I bit my tongue when you were overbearing because I know you like to be in control of... well, everything. I tried not to ask for too much or make any demands on your time or energy. I tried."

Hot tears coursed down her cheeks. "I understand that Jude comes first. I do. But I feel like I don't even place at all, Russell."

He stepped toward her again, and she scooted back. If he touched her, her resolve would crumble and she'd fall into a sobbing heap in his arms.

"I don't need someone who always puts me first. I've never been that person because my family never really permitted it." She winced at how bitter her own voice sounded. "But I do need to be with someone who acknowledges that it's okay to have my own needs, who loves me just for being me, who doesn't get frustrated when I want to be helpful."

She sniffed and wiped her nose with the back of her hand, tears dropping from her chin onto her shirt. "You have a lot going on right now. And I feel like taking a step back is the only thing that might have any chance of saving us."

As usual, his face remained expressionless. What was he thinking? What was he feeling? Was he feeling the same heart shredding pain rattling through his body that she was? Had his stomach bottomed out and his brain turned to mush?

She had no fucking clue. Because he, and his stoic AF face, just stared back at her as though she'd asked what he wanted for dinner.

"So... like Ross and Rachel on a break? Like... seeing other people?"

She groaned. "If you have to ask, I think you have your answer. Go see whoever you want to see, Russell. Just..." She waved a hand toward the door. "Close the door on your way out." She left him standing staring at her and kept her head high as she retreated back into her bedroom. The door closed behind her with a click before she slid to the floor and wept.

CHAPTER 24
Russell

"Wanna talk about it yet?"

Jude had gone to bed for the night, and Russell sat in silence on the worn couch in the living room, still mulling over Sabrina's tirade from the day before. His body ached, his head throbbed, but the worst pain of all was the broken organ in his chest. She'd broken up with him after a car crash. What the fuck kind of person did that?

Anger poorly hid the crushing feeling of inadequacy that soaked his every cell. She'd left him. When things got hard, when life got overwhelming, just like Jude's mom before her, just like his father, she'd left him.

"Russell?" Mom handed him a steaming mug of tea before plopping down onto the armchair perpendicular to the couch. "You wanna talk about it yet?"

Tendrils of rage snaked through his body, tightening every muscle, and irritating every nerve. "She broke up with me."

Expecting a gasp, or some form of extreme reaction, his head snapped toward her, making the room spin and his vision swim. "You're not surprised?"

She shifted in her seat, staring into her mug, and sighed heavily. His chest tightened. Was this really on him? Had he broken the best thing, other than his daughter, to ever happen to him? Was he really not enough?

Shit.

"Mom?"

She sighed again, picked up the remote and turned off the TV he forgot he'd even turned on. "No sweetheart, I'm not. I mean aside from you thumping around the house like a T-Rex with a sore head for the last 48 hours, you were a real jerk to her at the hospital the other night." She paused and searched his face. "But I don't get the impression it's all because of how you spoke to her just that one time."

He opened his mouth to defend himself, to tell her everything that had happened, all the accusations she'd laid at his feet.

"I don't need to hear the details, to know the details, Russell. You're my son and I'm always going to love you. But this is your first serious relationship since you broke up with Jude's mom. It was never destined to be easy."

"Isn't love supposed to be easy?"

"All the very best things in life take dedication and hard work. Especially relationships." She leaned forward in the chair, resting her arms on her knees, cradling the mug in her palms. "We never really talked about what happened with Elise. I know you guys argued a lot, and more than once, I heard her mention having an abortion."

Russell ground at his eye with the heel of his uninjured hand, hoping to press away the aching throb in his head. "She up and left without a trace and never looked back, Mom. At least not until she showed up to wash her hands of us for good."

"I know." She nodded thoughtfully. "And your dad left too... And now it feels like Sabrina has left as well. But—"

His derisive snort cut her off. "That's exactly what she did though, Mom. She left. Shit got hard, and she ran."

Something about the look on her face suggested she wasn't buying what he was selling. "What?"

She shook her head. "I don't think you're ready to hear what I have to say. But I also don't think she's fled in the way you think she has fled, son. I know your whole life is spent protecting yourself. I know Elise hurt you by disappearing and leaving you to be a young, single father."

Her voice softened and dropped. "I know she tried to control your entire relationship with her pregnancy, using it to make you bend to her will, give her everything while she strung you along the whole time, making you believe you'd be a family together. I know your dad and I hurt you with our divorce, with him leaving…"

His insides turned to soup, sloshing around under his skin. They hadn't talked much about their divorce or about Elise. She and Russell had gone to bed one night as a family, newborn Jude sleeping in the co-sleeper next to the bed. He'd woken up a single parent. And that was after she'd made his life hell throughout the entire pregnancy. Looking back, it was probably some form of punishment for her decision not to have an abortion.

He hadn't forced her to keep the baby, and he hadn't pressured her. He'd simply told her he wanted to have their child and that he'd be there for her, no matter what. She'd tested that to the extreme.

Tears shone in Mom's eyes as she thumbed the handle of the mug. "I understand. I do. I know you must feel it's not okay to be vulnerable or to trust anyone. I know it seems like every time you do, you get betrayed and people leave."

She placed her mug on the coffee table and picked up his hand, cradling it between both of hers. "I'm sorry I didn't do a better job of protecting you from everything you needed protecting from. And I'm sorry I contributed to your need to protect yourself from the world."

She met his eyes with a sad smile. "I know it's none of my business. I know I'm overstepping. You're a grown man who can do what he wants, and I should just leave you to stew over everything and work through this painful dark moment all by your big boy self. But from the looks of it, that's exactly what my mistake has been this whole time."

He opened his mouth to speak, to tell her it wasn't all her fault, to tell her he'd forgiven her for whatever she thought her crimes were, but she shook her head.

"I know I had my doubts about Sabrina to begin with. I was guarded and wary about letting someone new into all our lives. But I saw the way you looked at her and how she looked at you. I saw how selfless and adoring she was with Jude and how she'd walk through fire for either of you."

Guilt rattled up his spine as he tried to set aside his hurt that Sabrina had left him to process what Mom was saying.

"Take some time. Sleep on it, heal, do that detached and brooding thing you do to process all your feelings, then reevaluate." She paused and inspected her nails as though she was contemplating something. "Look, here's the thing. You might not be ready to accept this, but I feel like you need to hear it anyway. Then make your own decisions. But I truly don't think Sabrina ran away from you and Jude. I think she needs you to fight for her, show her she matters to you, and that you love her just how she is."

What if she was right?

❋

Finn sent a shot sailing across the ice toward where Russ stood. It smacked against the boards in front of him, making him start, despite the fact he saw it coming. "The hell, man?"

Finn shrugged, breaking off from the puck handling drill they were working on and skated to him. "Just checking you were paying attention. You were staring at the ice like it done you wrong, Stewie. Still off the bench?"

Irritation warmed his stomach as he picked up his still wrapped hand. "They might as well have cut off my dick."

Cringing, Finn cupped his crotch. "Don't even joke about that shit. Did they say how long it would take to heal? I imagine more than the, what...? Four days it's been since you had your accident?"

Embarrassment heated his cheeks. "Something like that."

"He's hiding. Let the man hide." Linc joined Finn at the edge of the rink.

"Hiding from...?" Finn's confusion would have been comical if Russell wasn't so vexed by just about everything and everyone. "Who could you be hiding from at this time of day?"

Linc patted Finn's shoulder pads. "Everyone. Everything. The whole world. The rink is his thinking place. Know how some guys think on the shitter? Russ here, he thinks best when he's crunching people into the boards or sending pucks down the ice at 80MPH."

Finn nodded twice. "I think best on the shitter."

Russell chuckled as Finn returned to practice.

"Hanging in there?" Linc's face turned serious. "Heard from her yet?"

Russ shook his head and kneaded at his chest with the heel of his hand. Other than second hand information from his mother – who texted Sabrina daily since the accident – he hadn't spoken to her. He'd watched her from afar in their shared classes, but he hadn't yet found his balls or his voice to say the things he needed to tell her.

Had it really only been four days?

She'd asked for and taken space. But he didn't want to give her so much space that he'd lose her forever.

He needed to shove his pride, his arrogance, and most problematically, his fear, aside and tell her what she meant to him, before it was too late. If only he could figure out how.

CHAPTER 25
Sabrina

"It's been three weeks, B."

"You think I don't know that?" Grousing from the couch in sweats and her stained Snow Pirates hoodie she refused to return to its rightful owner, Sabrina speared at an open tub of ice cream.

"That's also your third pint this week."

A growl vibrated in her chest as she jabbed the spoon toward her friend. "And?"

"And it's only Tuesday, Sabrina. When you get up to pee, there's an impression of your ass on the couch. Showering twice a week does not constitute good personal health, and we need to get you some vitamin D... or at least socialize a little. You've gone full-tilt-feral, girl."

"So sue me for being fucking heartbroken, Quinn." Sabrina rammed another spoonful of ice cream into her mouth and turned her attention back to Scarlett Johansson on the TV in *Black Widow*.

"I'm not suing you for being heartbroken, B. But you're nearly at the end of your epic Marvel binge, and I'm not sure either of us can handle the inevitable breakdown you're going to have during *Infinity War* and *Endgame*. I hate to bring the tough love, but you really do need to step outside for something other than class."

"Ha! I go to work, too." She hadn't become a complete hermit, no matter how badly she might want to.

Quinn nodded, lips pursed. "Sure you do. Lunchtime shifts so you don't see..." She paused.

Sabrina's eyes filled with tears. She couldn't say his name. She couldn't hear or even think his name.

Quinn cleared her throat. "Pirates."

Sabrina huffed out a shaky breath as Quinn dropped onto the couch beside her.

"Gregg misses you. Hell, I miss you, B. I get that things went to shit between you and... the Pirate, but I'd be a terrible friend if I let you wallow in your heartache."

The pain that laced her best friend's voice arrowed straight to Sabrina's heart. "And say I was ready to take off the sweatpants... what would you have in mind?"

Quinn's face lit up. "I love it when you speak *Friends* to me, girl." She clapped. "Pucks is having... eh... speed dating this weekend."

"Nope." Sabrina popped the P as she booped Quinn's nose with the spoon and took another bite.

"It's not a game weekend. I checked. There won't be a slew of Pirates there post-game. Pleeeeeease, Bre? For me? Pretty please? My vagina's so dusty, there's probably tumbleweeds blowing in a deserted town breeze in my pants."

Sabrina choked. "That... is quite the visual. You could go without me..."

And you could call Russell and talk to him, but you won't.

"*Or* you could stop being a sad Sally and take a shower. You're stinky, B. And you're taking the natural hair oil being good for you to the extreme. It'll be fun. Chat to a bunch of random, non-Pirate guys, drink some cosmos..."

And move on from the hockey player who broke you into tiny pieces – the unspoken part hung between them as Quinn pleaded silently for her to reconsider.

"I don't think I'm ready to people yet, Q."

"That's why this is perfect. You get a finite period of time with everyone. I think they can ask to buy you a drink, or for more time, I dunno, I didn't read the rules 'cause I thought you'd dismiss it without thinking about it. But I can check. It's quick, like three minutes per person... you don't need to hang out with people... It's just... small talk."

Small talk. Could she do small talk? Could she force a smile on her face for three minutes to tell strangers her favorite color was green or that she was an overnight Marvel fan for the sake of her best friend?

Quinn had put up with a lot from Sabrina over the past month, without as much as a single complaint, it would be nice to do something in return to thank her. Sabrina sighed, pinched the bridge of her nose and rolled her eyes. "Fine. When is it?"

"This was a mistake." Friday night in Pucks sports bar and grill was still a hive of activity, despite the lack of home game. Sabrina's palms were clammy and her heart, heavy. She'd washed her hair at least, well, all of her really, since Quinn threatened to drag her ass outside and turn the hose on her if she didn't.

While she showered, Quinn had invaded Sabrina's room, collected all her dirty PJs, her Snow Pirates hoody, and bedding, and started her laundry.

Sabrina tugged at the side of her bra, encouraging the underwire to quit poking at her. Wearing a dress with a bra that wasn't a sports bra and shoes that weren't slippers was definitely progress, but she yearned for the comfort of her couch.

People milled around the space, chatting animatedly in small groups. Tables lined the room, and a smiling red-headed woman stood at one end with a bedazzled clipboard and a tiara.

"It's not a mistake. I'll be right back. I'm going to put our names down before you flee." Quinn weaved her way through the bodies toward tiara woman while Sabrina did a slow turn, scanning to see if she knew anyone.

Panic seized her chest when Finn O'Brien clinked his bottle of beer against Will Morrison's as they leaned against the end of the bar. Maybe they were the only Pirates in the room. Maybe they weren't signed up for speed dating. Maybe luck was on her side and—

"Fuck." Blinking back the tears making her vision swim, she shook her head, but his face didn't disappear. Russell stood with Linc a few feet away from Finn, but as far as she could tell, he hadn't seen her yet.

Was he there for the speed dating? Did he choose to come or had he been forced to attend by his teammates? She had questions, and the more questions that peppered her brain, the more the air was choked from her body.

When Quinn returned, Sabrina grabbed her arm. "I need to leave. He's here. He's fucking here." Quinn paled as she peeked over Sabrina's shoulder. "I can't take watching him flirt with other women, Q, I can't do it."

"Alright everyone, listen up. If you could take your seats, we'll get started in just a few minutes. Ladies on this side, and gents, if y'all wanna sit over there."

"Okay." Quinn patted her hand. "Well, from the looks of it, it's just Finn and Will sitting down. Linc and Russell are standing chatting. I think you're good."

Good? Nothing about the situation she'd found herself in was good. She should have listened to her gut. Her gut told her there was a pint of Ben and Jerry's with her name on it back home.

Quinn guided her to a seat, and on autopilot, she sat, unable to tear her eyes off her sexy as sin, smoldering, son-of-a-bitch ex. He still made her insides turn to lava without even so much as looking at her.

Hoping he'd leave before the first timer started, Sabrina kept her eyes focused on the man taking a seat across the table from her. He was cute in a nothing-at-all-like-Russell kind of way. Where Russell was dark haired and blue eyed, the guy at her table was blond with green eyes. Where Russell had a few days' growth over his jaw, blondie – whose name was Brad, from the sticker tag on his pec – was clean shaven with a chin dimple.

She zoned out during the explanation of the rules, her foot jumping under the table, shaking her whole body with nervous energy. When the first bell went, she gave Brad a polite smile and held out her hand. That's what people did when they met, right? Shook hands?

"Hi, I'm Sabrina."

"Brad."

After a few minutes of awkward conversation, a new guy took Brad's place. Patrick. Serious, skinny, sleazy. His black hair was slicked to one side and his leer was anything but attractive. She fought the urge to wipe her palm on her leg after shaking his hand.

She knew the minute Russell spotted her without having to look in his direction. The skin on the side of her face tingled and heat crept up her neck. She gritted her teeth and forced herself to finish out the three minutes with Patrick.

Fuck. Had it only been three minutes? She ran a finger around the collar of her dress, tugging it away from her throat.

Was the temperature still rising? Was he still looking at her? If the shivers at her core were to be believed, he was.

When Patrick was replaced by Mark, she snuck a glance past Quinn to Russell, gasping when their eyes met. Shit. His unreadable face was as kissable as ever. But his eyes... his eyes swam with anger and the fire of a raging inferno. Guilt churned in her stomach. She shouldn't have come. She shouldn't be making small talk with other men when the only man she wanted to talk to still made her feel like crawling into a hole and crying until her tears ran dry.

Not breaking eye contact with him, she leaned closer to Quinn's ear. "I need to leave."

Without a word, Quinn glanced at Russell, before nodding. "I'm sorry. I didn't think he'd be here. I wouldn't have made you come if I'd known. Do you want me to come with you?"

"No, it's okay. It's still early and we aren't far from home. I'll be fine."

Turning back to Mark she made her apologies, told him she had food poisoning, and fled.

She was barely fifteen feet from the bar before she doubled over and sucked in frantic breaths. Would it hurt like that forever? Would the pain in her chest ever ease? Three weeks of not seeing him, kissing him, or laughing with him and his beautiful daughter.

Her chest pulsed at how much she missed the adorable little threenager. She needed to leave, to put space between her and the man she loved with every fiber of her being, the man who didn't love her back.

She stumbled as she started to walk, catching herself on the edge of a wall with a small squeak.

A sweaty hand curled around her wrist and tugged. "Hey now. A pretty girl like you shouldn't be out by yourself on a night like this." It wasn't a voice she knew, so she pulled and took a step forward. Anger, impatience, and the overwhelming desire to be at one with her ice cream rose in her chest.

"I'm fine." She jerked her arm, but he didn't let go. In fact, his skinny fingers coiled tighter.

"Why are you crying, sweetness? Boy break your heart? I could take you home, show you a good time. Show you what it's like to be with a real man." He licked his lips as fear and disgust prickled over her skin.

"I'm fine, thanks," she mumbled, attempting to unwrap his fingers to escape.

"The lady said she's fine." Russell's cold voice cut through her panic like a hot knife through butter. Ever her protector, even when they weren't together anymore. Her heart squeezed at the thought. "But you won't be if you don't let go of her arm real quick."

Her attacker glared at Russell for what had to be a full minute, perhaps he was weighing up the potential damage to his face if he didn't let her go. Dropping her hand, he shrugged. "Don't like foreigners anyway."

Russell surged at him, ready to strike, but the man simply laughed and sauntered back toward the bar, slamming the door behind him. The pair stood in silence for a long moment, neither speaking, their ragged, heavy breaths turning to clouds as it hit the frigid night air.

"We gotta stop meeting like this, Bubbles."

The Band-Aid over her heart burst open at the nickname, and a fresh wave of pain surged through her. She held up a hand and stepped back. Her tooth pierced her lip and a coppery taste touched her tongue. She gripped her lip harder, fighting the wailing sob building up within.

He smelled so good, and if she held her eyes closed for just a fragment longer than a blink, she could recall just how safe and warm his arms felt when they were curled around her. She could feel the planes of his chest against hers, the warmth of his corded muscles, and the firmness with which he held her against him.

But when she opened her eyes, she remembered he wasn't hers anymore. How did he look so good, so composed, so...*fine* when her entire body forgot how to function at the mere sight of him?

It was as though her broken heart made her forget how to breathe, forget how to move, forget how to speak... All she felt was a soul-deep, incurable ache in her chest, and she had no idea how she'd ever be able to move on from the hockey player who held her heart.

He reached out to touch her face, but she couldn't. She couldn't let him touch her, she couldn't talk to him, and she couldn't pretend she was fine when she was anything but.

So she did the only respectable thing any woman in her position would do. She wiped her tear-stained cheek with the back of her hand, turned, and ran home as fast as her jello-like legs could carry her.

Quinn burst through the door with the force of an elephant stepping on a watermelon. "Are..." She gasped. "You..." She waved a hand and covered her chest, bending like she'd just run a marathon and was about to pass out from exertion. "Okay?"

Cross-legged on her bed, cuddling Russell's hoodie, tears soaked Sabrina's shirt and her heart still ached. "As okay as I can be, I guess? How'd you know? Bestie sense a-tinglin'?"

She shook her head. "Russ." She sucked in another breath. "Fuck. I am all-the-way unfit."

Her traitorous heart flickered in her chest. "Russ?"

"He found me in the bar and told me I needed to come to

you. He said he'd found you outside, upset, but you ran off and he didn't want to upset you more by chasing after you."

The irony of Quinn's words seemed lost on her. He didn't want to upset her more by chasing after her? What a fucking moron. Chasing her was everything she needed from him. A sign that she was important to him, not disposable, not needing to change who she was, a sign that he fucking loved her, not that he was fine with her leaving.

"Why are you growling?"

"He's an idiot." She wailed through a fresh wave of tears. "I *want* him to chase me." She clutched her chest like it might keep her heart from falling out. "He gave up. He let me walk away. He didn't follow. Why didn't he follow?"

"He was afraid of upsetting you, so he got me," Quinn repeated, as though Sabrina had simply not heard her.

She shook her head. "Weeks ago. Why didn't he follow me weeks ago, Q? Why did he let me go?" Sobs shook her body as her friend climbed onto the bed next to her and pulled Sabrina's head to her shoulder. "And why the fuck did I let him let me go?"

"Shhhhhh. It's okay. I don't know what was going on in his head. But I know that you'll get through this, and if you don't, it'll kill us both because I'm not letting you sink alone."

CHAPTER 26
Russell

"Welcome back, Stewie." Finn raised his stick in a wave. "Fuckin' took you long enough."

"I'm touched you missed me, Obi." Russ chuckled and shook his head. "He knows I've been skating this whole time, right?"

Linc was still laughing. "He does, but skating with the team and doing leg day at the gym so you didn't lose your fitness isn't the same as playing with us. We missed you out on the ice, brother." Linc grabbed him in a headlock and rubbed his glove over Russell's helmet. Releasing him with a shove, Russell fought to catch his balance.

"Did you check in with Quinn? Is Sabrina okay?"

"Honestly, I think okay is a stretch." Russell rubbed his glove over his face. "You should have seen her, man. She was so fucking sad... so..."

"Broken?"

Russell nodded. His heart had been fractured since she'd walked away three weeks ago, but when he'd happened upon Sabrina outside the bar, something inside him just plain broke.

He turned the stick in his hand, rotating his wrist and testing how it felt.

"You gonna get her back?"

"I have to, Linc. I can't take much more of this distance. I hate being on a fucking break." He made quotation marks with his gloves, which just looked like he was waving his hands around. "It feels like the damn break has broken us and neither of us knows how to fix it."

"You know it's gotta be you, right? You need to fix this."

Fans trickled into the seats as the teams warmed up on the ice. Nerves flapped in his stomach as he skated with Linc. "I know. I do. I just don't know how."

An hour and two periods into the game later, the Snow Pirates led 3-1 against Michigan. Despite training daily, Russell's body reacted like it had been hit by a bus. Legs heavy, muscles burning, and sweat streaming into his eyes, he was suddenly filled with a renewed respect for athletes who returned to their sports after a serious injury. A busted up hand and some cuts and bruises had left him winded after two periods. He shook his head as he hit the locker room.

"You need a grand gesture, Stew." Finn's voice sent a chill up Russell's spine and his yelp of surprise echoed in the tunnel.

"A grand what?"

Finn stepped beside him and nudged his elbow. "A grand gesture. Don't tell me you've never seen a chick flick before, man."

At the blank stare on Russell's face Finn shook his head. He pulled off his helmet and slicked his hair back, shaking droplets of sweat onto the floor as they walked. "Jesus. Right. Well. In the movies, when the guy fucks things up for him and his girl, he does some grand gesture to win her back."

"Like Cleo wearing my shirt in the stands."

"Yes!" Finn hi-fived Linc. "Fuckin' kudos to her. That was

the grandest of gestures. I bet mini-Mo had something to do with that one."

Linc raised an eyebrow. Russell ignored the comment, not wanting to open that can of worms.

"I feel like he needs to figure his shit out before he embarks on a grand gesture, Finn." Linc shook his head and shrugged. "I'm not sure he's all-in yet."

Something surged in Russ's chest, shaking him to the core. "I am."

Finn patted him on the arm. "Any woman that can make you go caveman like that is gotta be worth it. You were a chest beating away from declaring yourself Tarzan."

Linc covered a snort behind his hand. "Guy's got a point, Russ. But if you're sure that Sabrina is who you want to be with, then we're bound by brotherhood to help you win her back."

"Damn fucking straight." Finn fist-bumped Linc. His mischievous smile should have been a warning, or triggered alarm bells, but Russ just wanted her back in his arms, and he didn't give a flying fuck what he had to do to get her there.

It was the night before school broke for Christmas vacation, and he had two classes and a hockey game to face before he was free to overindulge on food and play Santa to his baby girl. But he still couldn't get 'in the festive spirit.'

Truth be told, his spirit felt pretty fucking broken. He still hadn't managed to figure out how to win back his girl, and the distance between them seemed to stretch farther than ever.

Days apart had turned to weeks, and with only two weeks to Christmas, he'd expected to be snuggled up watching

Endgame with marshmallows bobbing in oversized mugs of peppermint hot chocolate.

Bile rose in his throat. How could he find the right words to tell her how sorry he was? How much of an epic freakin' idiot he felt for letting her walk away without chasing her? Would she even talk to him if he went to see her? Maybe he should ask Quinn.

He hadn't spoken to Sabrina's best friend since the night he followed her out of the bar, but he could. He swallowed and shook his head. He spent his life confronting challenges head on and there he was debating whether or not to go behind Sabrina's back because he was afraid she wouldn't speak to him. She deserved better.

The doorbell chimed, pulling him from his gloom. Mom's footsteps clicked across the tiles. "I'll get it!"

The door opened, muffled voices spoke, and the door closed again with a soft click.

"Wow, Natalie, this is... wow. It's amazing."

Was he going insane or was Sabrina standing in his home, talking to his mother? He peeked around the dining room door frame, taking care to stay hidden and a herd of horses charged through his chest.

Her cheeks flushed with the cold bite of the winter air, she wore a bobble beanie hat pulled low over her ears and an oversized teal sweater that fell to mid-thigh. She held three gift bags and ran her finger over their handles as she bit her lip. "I don't need to stay. I just..." Her eyes darted around the room.

Mom stepped toward her and rubbed her hands along Bre's biceps. "He's here. You don't have to see him if you don't want to. But I'm so glad you came. Jude and I made treats and a cinnamon applesauce decoration for you. I wasn't sure if we'd see you again before Christmas so we made them early."

She stepped back and bent under the tree to pick up a

large, dark purple gift bag. "I know you're not going home for the holidays... you probably don't even have a tree, but we wanted to make one for you."

Sabrina nodded and handed her bags to Mom who placed them under the tree. "How is she doing? I know I can't see her. It's not fair to her. I just... I miss her so much." Her eyes welled, and she rolled her lip between her teeth as though fighting back an avalanche of emotion.

His poor girl. It must have been hard enough for her to step back from him, but to lose Jude as well? Jude had asked for Bre a lot over the three weeks they'd been apart, and each time it hurt like she'd shot an arrow to the chest. Of course Bre had felt it too.

How had he been so short sighted? His heart swelled in his chest with pure love at how brave his girl was to come, even though she knew he'd likely be there. She'd done it anyway. How kind and selfless she was to bring a gift for his little princess even when they weren't together anymore.

"I just wanted to drop these off. I know you said I could stay and have dinner, or whatever, but..." A shaky breath came out in short puffs as her already hushed voice dropped to a whisper. "I still can't see him, Natalie. It just hurts too much."

Mom pulled her into a hug that he felt deep in his own bones. It should have been him wrapping his arms around her. Guilt hit him like a lightning bolt, leaving him breathless. "I understand, honey. I don't want to get your hopes up, but maybe I'll talk to him about Jude and me meeting you for coffee some afternoon when the semester starts up again."

Tears trickled down Sabrina's cheeks. "I'd like that a lot. But please don't get into an argument over me. I don't want to cause trouble, I just wanted to bring you guys your gifts."

"I couldn't help but notice you brought three bags."

Bre folded her arms and nodded. "I saw something for you I couldn't walk past and it felt petty getting something for

Jude and you and not for him. I had it anyway so he may as well have it. It's not much. I didn't sign my name on the bags or anything. I didn't want to make waves."

Mom pursed her lips and shook her head. "You're much too thoughtful for your own good. I don't give a shit if he's unhappy you're here or that you brought us gifts. I'm grateful. And I'm so glad you came." She hugged Sabrina again. "My invitation for Christmas still stands though. I know you say you're fine by yourself but... well, if you change your mind, there's always a seat at my table."

Bre gave a sad smile before Mom walked her out, closing the door behind her. "Well? What do you have to say for yourself, Russell Jackson Stewart?"

She only used his Sunday name when she was big mad and he was in big trouble. He didn't blame her. He'd broken his girl's heart and it was time to put it, and them, back together. "It's time to win back the girl, Mom."

CHAPTER 27
Sabrina

"Why am I in The Barn to watch the Snow Pirates, Quinn?" Sabrina slurped her Dr Pepper as unruly kangaroos punched each other in her gut making it slosh. "Why are we here so early? And why the fuck are we right at the plexi?" Her voice rose half an octave with each question.

Quinn shrugged. "It's the last game before Christmas. Maybe I'm hoping for a Christmas miracle?"

Sabrina rolled her eyes and shoved a handful of popcorn in her mouth. Maybe she could snack her way through the game and it would all be fine. Maybe he wouldn't even be playing and she was worrying for nothing.

She almost laughed at herself. Russ had been benched while his hand healed, but nothing would come between him and the last game before the holidays. People filtered down the steps and into their seats as the team took to the ice for warm ups. As soon as his skate hit the ice, her breath caught.

"You're already drooling, B." The amusement in Quinn's voice was unmistakable.

Popcorn paused mid-way to her mouth, Sabrina licked her

lips. Even in full hockey gear, with a helmet covering most of his head, under the harsh rink lighting, he was a sight to behold. And he was skating right at her.

Her heart quickened. Was he doing a warm up lap? Or was he actually headed her way? Fear, anxiety, and that mean bitch named hope glimmered in her soul. He flicked the puck he was cradling onto his blade and tossed it over the plexi to a young kid pressed up against the glass. The girl jumped up and down like she'd been handed the Stanley Cup, and Sabrina couldn't help but smile.

When she turned back to the ice, Russ was staring straight at her. He pulled something black from his pocket, pointed at her, and tossed another puck over the boards right at her. Why the hell would he give her a puck? Was it to throw at him for being such an obtuse idiot and breaking her heart?

"Are you going to stare at it like it's about to spontaneously combust, or are you going to read the note?"

Back across the ice, Russell warmed up, but he'd angled himself in such a way that he kept his smolder trained on her. Cheeks aflame, she tugged the note taped to the puck and tucked the puck into her pocket. She either wanted to treasure it forever or throw it at his beautiful idiot face, depending on what the note said.

She unfolded the paper, and Quinn scooted closer to read along with her.

Bubbles,

Thank you so much for our Christmas gifts! (And for a whole other bunch of shit I should have thanked you for while we were together, but this is supposed to be a romantic note and I just don't have space to list all the things I was a dick about.)

She didn't fight the tears as they trickled down the side of her nose.

Jude and I would love to take you to lunch tomorrow to give you our gift. I'll tell you this tomorrow to your face... I'm sorry.

Mostly for letting you walk away and believing I was okay with it. I'm not. At all.

And whether you realize it or not, I'm getting my girl back, Bre. I have a game to win first – and I hope you'll cheer for me – but I couldn't let you think for another second that I wasn't going to fight for us. Tu me manques. – R

"What does *tu me manques* mean?"

Sabrina snorted. "Keep your voice down before someone hears you butchering the French language, and we're suddenly at war. It means you are missing from me."

Quinn's dreamy sigh echoed her own. She re-read the note throughout the game, and if it wasn't for the rambunctious cheers around the rink, she'd have had no idea that the Snow Pirates even won. Her mind whirred, her heart raced, and she hoped with every fiber of her being that he was finally ready to let her in. But how much could have changed in only a matter of weeks?

As soon as she got home from the rink, carefully considering her every word, she sent him a text.

> Sabrina: Congrats on another win, and thank you for the note. I'd love to join you and Jude for lunch tomorrow to hear what you have to say. Where do you want to go?

His reply came almost instantly and her stomach dropped.

> Russell: Applebee's, noon. Wait outside. Don't be late!

He wanted to meet her where she worked? On her day off? What the hell was the boy playing at? They said romance wasn't dead, but staring at her phone, her gut curdling, she wasn't sure.

❄

Sabrina's stomach twisted as she walked from the parking lot toward the restaurant. She froze. She didn't have to wait. Russell and Jude, along with a handful of guys from the hockey team, loitered close to the door.

Jude hi-fived the players one at a time before working back up the line. Russ crouched to Jude's level and pointed at Sabrina. The little girl spun, squealed, and took off toward her like someone had fired a pistol at the start of a race.

Afraid she'd fall face-first and eat dirt, Sabrina ran to intercept the little girl, all bobbing curls and flailing arms. "Beeeeeeee!"

Spinning her around when she picked her up, Jude clung to Sabrina, arms tight around her neck. Emotion welled in her chest, choking the sob rattling in the back of her throat. "I missed you so much."

Over Jude's shoulder, Russell's face was tense, but Finn had a shit-eating grin plastered on his as he plugged his phone into a tripod about six feet in front of where the guys stood.

What the hell was going on?

Russell approached her, arms held out for Jude. "C'mon Princess. You can cuddle Bre in a minute. We have something else to do first, remember?"

With a questioning frown pinching her brows, Sabrina returned Jude to her father, mildly irritated he'd brought a bunch of his friends to lunch. Did he need an audience to tell her he was freakin' sorry? That was why they were there, right? For the kissing and making up?

Her stomach dropped. Shit. What if they weren't there for the kissing and making up?

The men had spread out a little more, Russell and Jude stood in front next to an almost giddy looking Finn. What the fuck was happening? Was this some kind of team building exercise she was about to witness? Or some post-game tradition she'd never seen before?

Her phone told her it was 11.55am. Maybe they'd all scatter when they were done with whatever was about to happen.

Finn started music from the phone in the tripod and darted back into formation. She rolled her lips between her teeth with a groan as recognition dawned. *Fancy Like* by Walker Hayes echoed around the parking lot as half a dozen grown-ass men and one adorable little princess did the Applebee's dance right outside Applebee's.

Tears gathered in her eyes as Jude copied her father, beaming up at him as they danced together. She'd heard the song forty thousand times. She'd seen people dancing in the bathrooms, in the restaurant, and outside so they could get the sign in the background.

But she hadn't seen the pure joy of a three year old dancing with the stoic man she loved with all her heart, and his friends. For a change, Russell's face was easy to read as he returned his daughter's wide smile, casting questioning glances in Sabrina's direction.

When the dance finished, Finn gave Russell such a hard bro-hug she could have sworn she heard Russell's spine pop and crack. "So fucking proud of you, man. You nailed it. And we don't even need another take. Watch this shit go viral!"

Russell's eyes hadn't left hers. Jude bolted toward Sabrina after a nod from her dad and launched herself into Bre's arms again. Anxiety licked at her skin. Was he really going to have the talk in front of a bunch of his friends?

"Singing something from The King and I would have killed you?" She shifted Jude to her hip, the little girl moved, but still held tight. Russell stood so close to her, his body heat radiated through her clothes, sending flickers of warmth into her chest.

"Not me, but we'd have had to set up a car wash to fund replacing Applebee's windows if I sang." His eyes dropped from hers to her lips, and her heart picked up speed. "If it's what it takes, I'll sing from any musical you want. Right here, right now."

Closing the distance between them, he cupped her face, running his thumbs over her cheekbones as though committing the feel of her skin to memory. "Whatever it takes." His eyes searched her face before he lowered his lips to hers, igniting a chain reaction throughout her entire body.

Blood pounding in her ears, she ached to reach out and grab him, to deepen the kiss, but rational thought demanded she protect the little girl, giggling on her hip.

There was nothing hesitant or chaste about how he claimed her mouth. He kissed her like he had every right in the world, like he was drowning and she was air, like they hadn't spent three soul-breaking weeks apart.

The hockey players whooped and cheered, Jude clapped along with them and, dizzy with emotion, Sabrina reached a palm out to brace herself against Russell's chest.

As much as she wanted him back, she needed to ground herself and not get carried away. She needed to hear him say his piece and decide whether or not she could take giving their relationship another shot.

Her lips tingled as he pulled back from their kiss. Brushing his nose across hers, he smiled. "I love you, Bubbles."

She gasped, her eyes darting to the men behind him. Everyone but Lincoln and Finn had gone, but Finn still grinned, giving her two thumbs up.

"I don't care who hears. *Je t'aime*. I know I messed up. I know I have a lot to do, but I'm not willing to let you go." He gestured at Jude. "Neither of us are. Anyway, we don't have to eat here, but Finn wanted the restaurant in the background of his soon to be viral video, and I figured it might feel like safe ground for you."

His fingers glided down the side of her face and a swoony sigh escaped her before she could stop it. "Here's fine."

Awkwardness settled over the table as soon as the trio sat down. Jude sat next to Sabrina and held her hand. Happiness bubbled in Sabrina's chest at the little girl's affection, but stubborn unease and apprehension still pricked at her skin.

They ordered drinks, then food, and as she sipped on her soda, Russell cleared his throat and took her free hand. "Did you know the French don't say I miss you?"

She nodded. They studied French together. She knew where he was headed, she'd mentioned it to Quinn at the game too, but she needed him to say it out loud.

"They say *tu me manques* – 'you are missing from me'. And you were, Bubbles. Every damn day, and I felt it right in here." He clutched the fabric over his heart. "I'm so sorry." His blue eyes held sadness and sincerity, but it wasn't enough. She needed more.

Biting her lip to stop her disloyal heart from speaking before she was ready, she nodded.

"I know that grand gesture thing sucked. Finn convinced me dancing in public was better than nothing. I just... I couldn't think of anything to convey just how..." His voice broke. "...sorry I am. I did the exact same thing I warned you about your family doing. I took your kindness for granted. You babysat my kid when we barely knew each other." He tapped his two index fingers together as though he was counting.

"You had someone take notes for both of us. You helped at

Jude's birthday party. You were patient with me when I kept you at arm's length because I was scared of being hurt or letting someone have any control over... well, anything."

The new server – Jenny, Jane, Julia – something with a J anyway, brought their food, and Jude let out a whoop of glee before tucking into her fries and nuggets with fervor.

Russell raked a hand through his hair. "You didn't flip out and lose your shit over Elise showing up – despite the fact you probably wanted to. In fact, you gave me the space I needed to get myself through it. You were there at the hospital..." His voice cracked. "I've been so caught up in myself, in making sure you don't embed yourself in my life and hurt me like she did, like my dad did, that I managed to hurt you in the process. And for that I'm so damn sorry."

Picking up her hand again, he planted a kiss on each of her knuckles. "I've spent so long thinking I had to be strong, for Mom, for Jude, for myself, that I freaked out when you kept stepping up to share my burden."

He squeezed her fingers. "None of this is an excuse, I'm just trying to explain what the hell happened with me. It's not that I didn't fall in love with you, though I admit to not recognizing what it was at first. And it's not that I didn't want to share my life with you, I did, I do..."

He loved her. Her heart squeezed. She wasn't sure he'd have the self-awareness to understand how he'd hurt her, but the more he spoke, the harder it was not to launch herself into his arms.

"I just don't really know how to do that, not healthily. But I want to learn. I know I've said it before and right now it's all just empty words from some asshole guy who hurt you and left you crying for three weeks while you overdosed on Ben and Jerry's..."

She'd kill Quinn in her sleep for telling tales about how

she'd been during their time apart. How a girl mourned a breakup was no one else's business.

His eyes darted across her face as though searching for some kind of sign, something to tell him how she felt. In truth, she didn't really even know herself. The wounds in her heart had begun knitting themselves back together when she'd read his note. And as much as she wanted to believe him, the only thing that would prove he was ready to go all-in with their relationship was time.

Hope bloomed in her stomach, taking root and dousing the anxiety and hurt which had resided there for weeks.

"Will you give me another chance, please? I'm miserable without you, and I'm pretty sure my daughter hates me for letting you go, almost as much as my own mother does. But no one hates me as much as I hate myself. The entire house is so sad without you around. I'm sad, Bubbles. I miss your smell, and I miss your laugh. I miss all the little things you do in the world that you think no one notices, like staying behind to clean up after a kid's birthday party even though you have work, or feeding a starving student chocolate covered marshmallows in the library."

Tears pricked in her eyes and coursed down her cheeks. She swiped them away with the back of her hand. Did he really see her?

He tucked her hair behind her ear. "But more than that, I love you, just as you are. And I need you to know that even though you're not confrontational like I am, it's still okay for you to have your own opinions and needs. That's why I didn't chase you when you left. You asked for space, so I respected that boundary and gave you space, but then the space became this all-consuming black hole that sucked in days and weeks and I just... Woah. I am... really rambling."

Sabrina laughed. "Usually it's me with the word vomit."

He nodded, cheeks turning pink. Their food was probably

cold, Jude had almost finished her meal, and Sabrina was yet to say more than a word or two in reply to Russell's stream of consciousness.

"Is something wrong with your food?" J-girl's frown hung low over anxious eyes.

She shook her head. "It's fine we're just chatting."

The young girl glanced at Russ, back to Sabrina, and nodded before turning away. The restaurant was getting busier and louder as the lunchtime crowd trickled in.

"Actually, can we get some to-go boxes, please? We'll just reheat this at home. It'll save us giving the little one a screen while we eat."

Russell nodded at Sabrina's suggestion. J-girl said, "Sure," and left without another word.

"Thank you. For the apology." Sabrina broke the silence hanging between them before she sipped her drink. Tears still lingered in her eyes and her heart jolted in her chest. "It means a lot to me. It's really fuc—freakin' bugged me that you never say thank you to me. Irrationally so, so I appreciate the thanks even more."

Russell reached across the table and picked up Jude's sippy cup, refilling it from his glass of water. Sabrina wiped the little girl's hands with a napkin, but the stubborn food wouldn't relent. He handed her the wipes across the table and sparks of desire raced along her skin as their fingers touched.

"My parents called last week and asked me to go to Seattle. I didn't tell them we'd... that we were... anyway. They've been trying to mend bridges since my trip. Or that's what I thought, anyway. Mom called every other morning at the butt-crack of dawn, planting little suggestions that I needed to reconsider their 'suggestion' to go home."

Sabrina finished wiping Jude's hands and face and balled up the wipes, dropping them onto the little girl's plate. "She called last week asking if I was going home for the holidays and lost her shit when I said no. She cried, asked what they'd done to deserve such an ungrateful daughter, and told me I was breaking her heart."

She sniffed, welling up at the memory. "When I asked her why her heart was breaking, whether it was because she missed me and wanted to see me, or because I wasn't going to be there to help with grandma, and the kids, and my sister and the new baby, she went quiet."

His warm fingers linked through hers. "Oh, Bubbles." The server brought boxes and the check. He handed his card to her and boxed up the food.

She nodded. "Yeah. I'm so glad I didn't book flights to see them. They don't seem to be getting it that I'm not a member of staff they can just pick up and move around to help when they need." She drank another gulp of soda. "My siblings seem to get it though. Avni even told me she was proud of me."

"So am I." His gravelly voice warmed her soul as she soaked up his praise. He stroked the back of her hand with his thumb.

"I missed that."

"What?"

"When you run your thumb along the back of my hand. Such a small gesture, but when it was gone... anyway, I missed it." She nibbled on her lip.

"What is it?"

"Can we go back to your place, reheat our lunch, and watch *Infinity War* and *Endgame*? I haven't been brave enough to watch them by myself. I hear they're real tear jerkers."

"Are you sure?"

She nodded. His eyebrows shot up, but he was already getting to his feet. "C'mon Princess, let's go see Mimi!"

CHAPTER 28
Russell

"Where's Sabrina?" Mom looked over her shoulder. "Is she in the kitchen?"

Russ shook his head. "Jude insisted Bre tell her a story before naptime. You know how that goes."

"She's asleep?"

He nodded.

"I'm guessing you talked to her?"

"As much as I could. I think a lot of the fixing will come from showing her over time, not telling her."

Mom plopped next to him on the couch. The news was on the TV, but he'd muted it since he wasn't paying much attention anyway. "And you're willing to put the work in?"

"I can't lose her again, Mom. I won't."

She patted his shoulder. "Glad to hear it. She deserves it. You both do. I wonder if she'll stay here for the holidays. She's in town anyway." She picked at a piece of lint on her pants. "If she's in town and not here, you'll be gone for some of the holidays... it makes sense if we're all together."

Russell smiled. "I'm sure we can convince her."

"I can take Jude to Target this afternoon to get a stocking

for Sabrina to match ours and some things to put in it. Do you need me to pick up something from you?"

"I've had her gift for a while."

"What aren't you telling me?"

He raised his eyebrows. She never failed to surprise him with how well she could read his expressions.

"You've got that look on your face like you're keeping a secret."

He shrugged. "I was just thinking about one of the first times I met her once you mentioned Target. Jude bolted from me while I was looking at something. I mean high-tailed it. I found Sabrina crouched next to her in the cereal aisle."

Shaking his head, he chuckled at the memory. "Jude had managed to tear open a box of cereal, pop the plastic, and was sitting in a puddle of cereal dressed as Anna from Frozen, tiara and all."

Mom laughed. "You must have been so scared."

"Yeah. I was. And so epically pissed at myself for letting it happen."

"You know these things happen to every parent, right? And they only get worse over time. Wait until she asks to go to her first solo play date. You'll shit your pants Russell."

Jude came shuffling down the hall, clutching a pink unicorn stuffy under one arm and a Captain America figure under the other.

"I'll change her diaper in my room and we can head out."

Fifteen minutes later, with the promise of some time alone, Russell stood in the doorway of Jude's room. Sabrina's splayed hair covered most of her face, and her chest rose and fell with deep and even breaths.

He crouched next to the bed and brushed her hair from her face. "Wake up, Bubbles." He spoke in hushed whispers so as not to startle her from her sleep.

"Mmm?" An arm flailed in the air, narrowly missing clobbering him in the head, and dropped over her face.

"Sabrina? I need you to wake up."

"Sleepy." She rolled away from him, tugging the quilt higher around her body.

He yanked the blanket off her. "Bre, I'd love to let you sleep, I really would. But my dick is bursting out of these pants, we're home alone, and I really don't want make up sex in my kid's bed."

Wow. Way to play it cool, Russ.

She bolted up in the bed and blinked once, then twice more, realization dawning on her face as her eyebrows curved high on her forehead. "Alone?"

He pulled his shirt off and nodded as she rubbed at her eyes and yawned before jumping off the mattress.

"Why the hell didn't you say so?" She hurried past him, and he unbuttoned his jeans as he followed her into his room.

A hiss seeped through her teeth as her eyes took in his bare chest, heat flaring in her eyes. "It should be illegal to look that good, Russell." She reached out to touch him, but pulled her hand back at the last minute.

Disappointment shivered through his chest. But when he met her gaze, the uncertainty swirling in their depths crushed him. He took her hand and placed it over his heart, stepping closer to her.

With his free hand, he cupped her trembling chin as she sucked in a breath and closed her eyes. He stroked the apple of her cheek. "Eyes open, Bubbles."

"I might cry."

"If you do, I'm here. And I'll do my very best not to think it's because of my lackluster skills between the sheets." He winked at her and was rewarded with a nervous smile.

"I don't know why I'm so anxious."

"We don't have to do anything you're not comfortable doing, Bre. You know that."

But please be okay with doing at least some things because my cock is going to cry, explode, or fall off from frustration if you say no.

Her eyes landed on his lips. Her fingers tangled themselves between his, and his heart thumped as she rolled onto the balls of her feet to close the inches between them and sweep her lips against his.

Relief unfurled in his stomach. Not at her physical touch, but that her hesitation didn't mean she was rethinking her decision to be with him. "I love you so much, Bubbles." Pressing his hand against her back, he drew her to him, tracing the seam of her closed lips with his tongue.

His dick strained against the fabric of his boxers, pressing into her stomach, and he dropped to his knees. Fingernails scraped at his scalp as she jerked his head up and shook her head. "I need you inside me, Russell. Please?"

Her chest heaved, whether from lust, or emotion surging through her he didn't know, and every cell in his body ached to give her what she needed. He kissed her like it was the first time, the last time, and every time in between, pouring every ounce of love and affection, every ounce of himself into her as he kissed.

Breathless, he backed her toward the bed, her knees buckling as they met the mattress. They stripped in a blur of desperation and fabric.

His lips painted every inch of her bare skin with a fevered spate of kisses. Between ragged, driven breaths, he nipped at her skin, kissing and licking his way across her chest, squeezing and rolling her nipples between gentle fingertips.

She held her glistening fingers up to his face and separated her fingers, demonstrating just how wet and ready she was. "I appreciate the foreplay, Hot Shot, I do. But I'm not kidding. Inside me, now."

Her hoarse and whispered plea was hot, but the demand, the need, the unadulterated lust blazing in her dark eyes almost had him coming in his boxers like a teenager. He grabbed her wrist, and sucked her fingers into his mouth, tickling them with his tongue, stripping them of her arousal.

"You taste so fucking good, Bubbles." As he rolled on top of her, she spread her legs, granting him access. He dragged the head of his cock through her soaking wet folds, a shiver of anticipation shooting up his spine.

Rolling her hips to meet him, she gasped and groped at the bedside table as he grazed his dick over her clit, grinding against her. The moan he elicited from her was intoxicating.

"Russell. Condom." She tugged at the drawer handle.

Lowering himself to kiss her, he shook his head. "You're still on the pill, right?"

She nodded.

"Then if it's okay with you, I'd rather not use anything else."

Sabrina

"W-what?" She couldn't fight the tears trickling down the side of her face. Her body was balancing on a knife edge, somewhere between an all-out emotional breakdown and being more turned on than she'd ever been before.

"I said..." He brushed his nose against hers. "I want to make love to you bare." The small movement of his hips dragged his cock along her pussy, sending sparks of a deep and pulsing need through her.

"Are you sure?" She curled her fingers into his ass cheeks.

"I am. Are you?"

She nodded. "I really don't know what to say." Her heart was bursting out of her chest. There was no way her mere skeleton could contain the love surging through her.

"I love you. I trust you. And I'm ready to build a future with you. Together."

Her only answer was to grab his head and crash her lips against his as she pulled him inside her. When he was fully seated, she clenched around him, not missing the shudder that passed through him.

"Fuck." His clenched jaw and wide eyes drove her to

repeat the tiny movement. "Sabrina, I'm going to blow my load and you're going to tell the world I'm a shit lay."

She nodded. "All part of my master plan – then no one else will want to steal you from me."

He shook his head and whistled out a slow breath as he pulled out, hesitated a moment, and sank back into her. Slow, deliberate, measured movements turned into jerking hips, thrusting as their bodies slapped together.

Her nails bit into his ass cheeks as she clutched him against her body. "Don't... stop..." Every nerve ending fizzled with pleasure as she gave herself over to the waves of pleasure.

Tensing between her legs, his pace slowed. "Gonna... come." He drove into her hard, making her cry out as he came. "Fuck, Bubbles." His sweat slicked body collapsed on top of her with a grunt. "I hope you weren't planning on going anywhere 'cause I can't move. I'm stuck here forever."

She grinned as he withdrew, cool air from his movement sending gooseflesh over her skin. Reaching across her body, he tugged a Kleenex from the box next to his bed. "Let me clean you up before you get yours."

The tenderness with which he wiped his come from the apex of her thighs made her chest ache. "You don't have to do that. Clean me up, or get me off." With every sweep of the tissue, jolts of need struck her core. Her breath stuttered.

He nipped at her earlobe as he fingered her clit. "Sure I don't. But I want to. I think it's in the rules, though. Both parties must be fully sated after makeup sex."

"Jude Natasha Stewart!"

Wild and carefree giggles were the only answer to Russell's declaration of Jude's name. Sabrina smashed her hands over her face to hide the grin and muffle her own laughter.

"It's not funny." Russell's growl sent a chill down her spine, straight to her nipples. "Jude Natasha Stewart! I've told you three times now. Stay. Away. From. The. Presents!"

Sabrina attempted to distract herself by checking her phone.

> Quinn: How goes Christmas with Russ and the fam bam?

> Sabrina: He just dad-voiced so hard I'm pretty sure I just got pregnant.

> Quinn: Dad voice: a weapon of mass insemination.

> Quinn: Severe dick-struction.

> Sabrina: Stop. Please. I can't breathe and I'm not supposed to be laughing. Jude keeps trying to open the gifts under the tree. We'll hear a tear of paper followed by the cutest giggles like she's a master criminal getting away with the heist of the century. Every time we move her, she somehow finds her way back. I think he's gonna lose it. It shouldn't be this funny.

"Aren't you going to help me out here?" The irritation in Russell's voice continued to stoke the flames flickering low in her belly.

"Me?" Her voice came out as a squeak.

"Yes. You."

"But it's not my place."

He shook his head and wagged a finger at her. "Oh hell no, you don't get to play that card. You're part of this family, and it absolutely is your place to help out with discipline and enforcing the rules. I don't get to be the sucky discipline parent all by myself."

The weight of his words slammed into her like a train.

They were going to be a family. Together. And she was absolutely there for it.

Shrugging, she forced her smile into a wide-eyed innocent look. "And Stewart rules are no gifts on Christmas Eve? Maybe Sharma rules are open everything Christmas Eve."

His frown deepened, and she sprung from her seat at the sound of another piece of paper tearing. He slapped her butt cheek, the warm sting radiating through her ass muscles.

"What's all the fuss about?" Natalie appeared carrying a tray of milk and cookies.

"Someone... I'm pointing no elbows... thinks it's hilarious to try opening Christmas gifts on Christmas Eve. Someone else – and I'm still pointing no elbows – thinks this is far less funny." Sabrina probably looked like she was doing the chicken dance, elbows pointed at both Jude and Russell, but Natalie kept a straight face.

She put the tray on the coffee table in front of Russ and waved a dismissive hand. "Leave her alone, Russell. She's happy."

Sabrina and Russ both gawped at her, eyes wide. "What? Mom, she can't tear open everyone's gifts the night before Christmas."

"You're absolutely right. She can't."

Russ's frustrated huff of breath was accompanied by a flap of both his hands toward the tree.

"She also *isn't*."

Russell stood, crossed the room, and plucked the toddler from the floor. She clutched a box in her hands and yelled "no" repeatedly until he deposited her on Natalie's knee. "She clearly is."

"She's opening gifts, sure. But your mom just so happened to learn her lesson with her own curious son when he was little. Those boxes are all empty. I've been wrapping them for weeks." She winked at Sabrina who couldn't hold back her laughter.

An hour later, cookies and milk consumed, and a fresh plate left out for Santa and Rudolph, Natalie stood with a groan, pressing her hand against her lower back. "Alright, munchkin. It's time for stories. Daddy and Bre have some important things to take care of. Say goodnight."

Bear hugs and wet kisses were given to both Russ and Sabrina before Jude toddled off, Mimi in tow.

"Where are we doing this?" Excitement coursed through Sabrina's veins at the magic she was about to help create.

"Mom's office. It's furthest away from Jude's room, and everything we need is in there. We just need to grab a drink."

"An alcoholic drink?"

"Naturally. It's Christmas Eve."

She slid her arms around his neck, dotting a kiss on his lips. "I don't suppose you have the ingredients for Cosmos?"

A sly smile crept across his face. "As a matter of fact, Mom got everything we need at the store earlier. Special request. She also picked up a salted caramel cheesecake." The way his tongue slid over his bottom lip did things to her that Santa's little helper didn't have time to get caught up in before their work was finished.

Twenty minutes later, Cosmos in hand, they walked into Natalie's office. Russell locked the door behind him. Rolls of paper and tape were lined up on the office desk next to two large pairs of scissors.

"I don't see the gifts."

Russell smiled. "That's kind of the point, Bubbles. They're in the closet so no one else can see them either."

She bopped him on the head with a roll of wrapping paper, reveling in the dull thunk it made.

Pointing a finger at her, he advanced two steps. "Don't start something you can't finish, Sabrina Sharma."

"What you gonna do about it, Sir Warm-and-Fuzzy?"

He snorted and lunged, being held at bay for only a split second by the tube of silver paper. She squealed as he attacked, tickling her until she was breathless. Warmth curled around her like a fluffy blanket. Being surrounded by the love of the Stewart family was enthralling. Her heart was happy.

She was going to have a Christmas to remember with people she loved and who loved her, just as she was. She was ready to start a new year in a relationship with the man she loved, his beautiful little girl, and figure out what the hell she was going to do next.

CHAPTER 29
Epilogue – Russell
(NINE MONTHS LATER)

Russell's leg twitched uncontrollably as he stood in the tunnel ready to take the ice. While it wasn't his first NHL game, it was his first *home* game of the new season – his first as a rookie for the Minnesota Wild. Nerves cracked in his stomach like hockey sticks battling over a puck against the boards.

"Rookie's gonna hurl."

"Swallow it down, Rookie."

The disembodied voices of his new teammates echoed around the concrete walls of the tunnel. Anxiety raked over his skin mingling with the beads of sweat trickling down the back of his neck.

"Twenty says he'll pass out."

"I'll take that bet." Hands smacked together in a hi-five.

"Keep breathing." A low voice spoke next to his ear.

Right. Keep breathing. He'd done it since the day he was born, but it was becoming more and more difficult to convince his lungs to inflate with air. Was this how everyone felt when they made it to the big leagues? Had he made a mistake? Was he not professional hockey material?

He shook his head. He'd skated since he was knee high to a grasshopper. His family and friends were in the crowd ready to cheer him on. This was his game, his team, his home, and if the hockey gods were on his side, they'd let him survive the first home game of the season without doing something stupid like falling on his face, puking on the ice, or missing an empty net.

"That's it. You're losing that tinge of green. Keep breathing."

Russell was still clueless about who stood near him. Sure, he'd watched this team play since he was little, but facing the bright white ice and the glare of the lights at the end of the tunnel, he was lucky to remember his own name. "Tell me this gets easier."

"It gets easier."

"Are you telling me that because it's what I need to hear, or because you mean it?"

Someone gave him a playful shove. Probably Austin. Nothing rattled that cool-as-a-cucumber asshole. "Guess you'll find out at the next game. How come you're worse here than you were for your first game in Dallas last weekend?"

Russell shrugged. "I guess since we weren't in our home barn I figured a way to block out the fact it was going to be a globally televised game."

The man behind him chuckled. "Alright bitches, let's fuck 'em up."

Skating onto the ice to cheers and deafening music and his heart thumping like a bucking bronco in his chest, he scanned the crowd. Maybe if he could catch a glimpse of her, she could somehow help settle his nerves before his pre-game pasta made a reappearance.

"Up in the box at your two o'clock, rookie. A quick look, then your head's in the game. You hear me?" The Minnesota Wild's captain, Cory Evans' tone was cautionary, but understanding flickered in his eyes. "You're gonna do just fine."

Russ nodded, turning his head to the box. Was she...? Holy shit, she was.

Sabrina stood with Jude on her hip. His little princess wore hot pink ear defenders and waved a Minnesota Wild pennant like it was her job, her face split into a wide grin. Bre rocked a Captain Marvel catsuit. His mouth dried up as he took in her curves. She pointed him out to Jude and they both waved before Sabrina blew him a kiss.

Three twenty-minute periods of hockey. That's all he had to survive before he could fuck her senseless in that freakin' cat suit.

With ten minutes to go in the third period, every muscle and bone in Russell's body ached. Anaheim were not taking any prisoners. They didn't give a shit that this was his first home game and he was crapping himself, they wanted the W. So did he.

Despite Anaheim's presence on the ice, by some miracle Minnesota led 2 – 1. Coach Stack was still tinkering with the roster, but for the most part Russ pulled his shifts on the third line.

The third line was generally made up of more defensively orientated forwards and grinders and played against an opponent's first or second lines in a bid to physically wear them down. Russ was fine with that, for the time being. But he had aspirations, hungering for the glory of the top line.

An elbow jabbing him in the ribs had him bolting to his feet and off the bench. Coach had switched him to the second line and he wasn't going to fuck it up.

Four minutes to go. Sweat coursed down his face, and he sent up a prayer of thanks to the hockey gods that they didn't fog up his visor. Legs like lead, he urged himself forward. Couldn't Coach have bumped him up a line when he was fresh as a daisy at the start of the game?

Three minutes to go. He slammed another Duck against the boards with a satisfying crunch and passed the puck forward to his teammate, Dylan McNally. As Russ skated toward the Ducks net, McNally sailed the puck to Tito, who passed it back to McNally, who gave it to Bents, who tucked it into Duzzi's five-hole like he wasn't even there. The goal horn sounded, the crowd went wild, and strong arms clapped him on the back.

The last two minutes of the game went slower than any game he'd ever played. Determination and sheer stubbornness not to concede any more goals had him checking the Ducks like his life depended on it.

Post-game passed by in a blur. A 3 – 1 win over a team like Anaheim was nothing to sneeze at. As proud as he was of his first home-ice performance, his very own Carol Danvers was waiting to be fucked senseless, so he changed into his suit and hauled ass like the building was on fire.

Sabrina

"Great game, Hot Shot." Those were the words she'd formed in her mouth to say. Whether or not they came out was another question entirely. She'd seen Russell post-game more times than she could count. She'd seen his shiny shoes, his perfectly tailored trousers, and his still-wet hair from his shower. But post-NHL-game Russ was an entirely different beast.

Holy shit, she was burning from the inside out. The man was a fucking delight.

Jude let go of Sabrina's hand and launched herself at the approaching man with a squeal while Sabrina squeezed her thighs together and touched her lips in case she was drooling. His wolfish grin and hungry eyes erased any lingering trace of self-consciousness over the fact she stood in a Marvel costume at a hockey game.

Natalie had raised a questioning eyebrow before they left to go to the game, but she said nothing. Russell hadn't yet said a single word, but his body language told her he was every bit as hot and ready as she was.

He picked Jude up and swung her around before kissing

her cheek and giving his mom a squeeze. "Congratulations honey. I'm so proud of you – that was a tough game."

He handed Jude to Mom before stepping toward Sabrina, arms outstretched, and pulled her into a tight hug. She fought the groan as his very erect, rock-hard cock pressed against her.

"I hope you bought a back-up costume, Bubbles, 'cause I'm gonna fuck you so hard you can't walk straight for days."

A gasp caught in her throat. While he wasn't usually shy about the things they did together, this primal, growly, dirty-mouthed man standing in front of her was hot-as-fuck and she was totally there for it.

Natalie cleared her throat. "I'm going to take Jude home. It's already past her bedtime."

Russell groaned into Sabrina's shoulder before shifting himself in his pants and turning to his mom. "Thanks, Mom. We'll see you in the morning?"

She nodded and rubbed his arm. "So proud of you, Russell." Tears glistened in her eyes.

Chewing on the inside of his cheek he shook his head. "Don't set me off, Mom. They'll never let me live it down." He jerked his head at his teammates milling around with family, friends, and fans.

She sniffed. "Don't do anything I wouldn't do." She and Jude disappeared into the already thinning crowd.

"Russell?" Bre's voice broke and she cleared her throat.

Fire flickered in his eyes. "Yeah?"

"Why are you looking at me like I'm a Big Gulp and you're dehydrated?"

"I guess hockey makes me horny?"

She laughed. "Suuuuuure, it's absolutely the hockey that makes you horny."

"I booked a hotel room. There's an overnight bag in the trunk."

Her heart raced and her tummy did a flip at his planning.

He slid his fingers between hers. "But I'm not sure I'm gonna last that long." He led her out to his car in the parking lot. "Do you have a knife?"

"A-a knife? Russ I don't generally carry a knife around, why?"

He slid his hand down her spine before turning her so she leaned against the passenger door. "Because I need to get inside you and I don't want to either a) have you ass-naked in public or b) wait." His teeth clenched as he gritted out every word like it took a behemoth effort.

She gasped as his hard cock pressed against her. "I see."

"Mmmmm." He rubbed his nose along her jaw before nipping at her earlobe. "And I don't think I can rip this thing open with my bare hands... but I'm not above trying. Maybe I need to get Mom to sew a zip down there or something."

She groaned, letting her forehead fall against his. "Can we not bring your mom up when you're trying to get in my pants please?"

"Tell me a zip for easy access wouldn't be the best thing ever to happen to your growing collection of superhero costumes."

She grabbed his hand and placed it at the apex of her thighs. His low growl suggested he felt the damp warmth seeping through the thin fabric. He dropped to his knees. "Bet you don't carry scissors with you either?"

She giggled and shook her head. "No scissors, no knives... no underwear either, so you only have one layer to break through."

He grumbled as he tugged at the fabric.

"I could just give you a blow job... or a hand job... to take the edge off till we get to the hotel."

"Do you have a pen?" He tugged again.

She couldn't help the laugh that erupted from her. "You

want to jab a pen at my crotch? That doesn't sound at all dangerous."

The grin he tossed her almost made her brain reboot. "And a knife or scissors would have been just fine." He grunted as he pulled, stretching the fabric again. The fabric gave, drawing an "Ah ha" from him as he adjusted his grip and yanked like he was The freakin' Hulk.

She'd never seen anything so hot. Desperation, lust, and an overwhelming need to be inside her drove him to quite literally tear her clothes off. A satisfying rip echoed around the parking lot, and a blast of cold air met her bare skin.

Dragging a finger through her slick folds, he chuckled as her breath hitched. "I thought I'd have to do more work to preheat the oven."

"What can I say? Watching you play in the national league, and on your knees tearing up my clothes... guess it got me a little wound up."

He stood, unzipped the fly of his dress pants, and turned her to face the car. She wasn't an exhibitionist by any means, but she cast a wary glance around to make sure no one was watching. The parking lot was almost empty.

"I'm not proud of what I'm about to do, but I promise I'll make it up to you later. I just..." He pushed the head of his dick through her wetness and hissed. "I might die if I don't fuck you right now."

Widening her stance, she turned her chin over her shoulder. "Okay drama queen. Less chit-chat, more fucking."

Fingers curled around her hips as he eased himself inside her with one long stroke. "Fuck."

She bit her lip so she didn't giggle at the feral noises he made. "Christ, Bre. So fucking hot."

Tightening herself around him, she groaned and her heart, and Russell, picked up their pace. He drilled into her from behind, her stomach slapping against the side of the car with each stroke and grunt.

His breathing grew ragged and irregular as he closed in on his orgasm, grinding against her G-spot with every thrust. He came with her name on his lips and his hands gripping her tightly.

His forehead dropped against her back as he let out a long breath.

"You okay back there?" She couldn't help but giggle. When she had dressed for the evening the last thing she'd expected was to be banged against his car while dressed as Captain Marvel.

"Yeah. Sorry. I realize that was probably no fun for you at all."

"Meh." She shrugged. "It was still a little fun."

"Just a little?" He leaned over her back, sweeping her hair from the back of her neck, sending a shiver of anticipation down her spine. "I guess I'll just have to do better in the next round."

Not finished with Russell and Sabrina? Click here for their bonus epilogue.

Link to the sound track: https://open.spotify.com/playlist/6w052aPcBBfDsPkr1BX9M9?si=5af8bc614c2946d0

Molly
(16 YEARS OLD - FOUR YEARS AGO)

"To surviving another year of high school." Molly raised the can of Fanta in her favorite 'Zero Shits Given' koozie she'd stolen from her mom, and crashed it against her best friend, Savannah's, hand.

"We survived? I feel like an extra on the Walking Dead right now." Savannah smothered a yawn with her free hand. "But don't ask me to do any walking. 'Cause, no."

The two girls were sprawled out on sun loungers in Molly's back yard next to the pool. It was the first day of summer, and their plans consisted of doing the bare minimum, working on their tans, and consuming candy faster than their parents could provide it.

Savannah slurped from her can, burped, giggled, and leaned back against the semi-reclined chair. Her waist-long blonde hair was twisted into a messy bun on top of her head. Reaching into the picnic-sized cooler next to her, Molly grabbed a handful of ice and ran it over her bare chest and neck. A sigh escaped her at the cool relief from the fierce, overhead sun.

"You kids have sun screen on?" Molly's mom peeked around the back door of the house, always the mother hen.

"Yes, Mrs. Morrison."

"Good. I'd rather not start summer vacation with sun blisters and sunstroke. Will's on his way home, Mol. We'll start lunch when he gets back."

"Sounds good, Mom."

"Wanna swim before lunch?" Savannah was already shucking her Daisy Dukes to the ground and pulling off her tank top to reveal a bright yellow bikini.

"Go ahead, I'll wait till after lunch." Molly pulled her shades from on top of her head and slipped them over her eyes before raking her long, frizzy black hair off her sweaty neck and into a high ponytail. The unusual humidity wasn't doing much for her cascading waves. She peeled her short shorts off and dropped them over her phone on the hot ground next to her chair.

"Wake up sleepy head." Savannah sprayed her with a welcome dose of cool water from the pool as she climbed out and made her way back to her chair. "Girl, you were out cold. Snoring. Drool, the lot. Pretty sure you farted in your sleep, too."

"Savvyanna we both know my farts smell like gummy bears, so that stink must be coming from you."

The gate to the back yard opened and Molly's big brother – by only ten months, but he never let her forget it – made his way into the backyard, sweat-drenched shirt clinging to his body. "Mom, do we have time for a dip before we eat?" He was already kicking off his flip flops and unbuttoning his shorts before their mom answered "ten minutes" through the open window.

Molly was only vaguely paying attention to her brother, because he'd brought a friend, a guy she'd never seen before. His strawberry blonde hair shone in the sun light. It was shaved on the sides, but longer and styled with gel on top. His faded, grey Minnesota Snow Pirates shirt stretched across broad shoulders, and had dark rings of sweat around his neck and underarms.

Will had wanted to be a Snow Pirate since he learned what hockey was. If she was a betting woman, she'd put money on him striking up a conversation with the stranger over his shirt.

Something cold against her thigh caused her to gasp and jump. "You're staring." Savannah's voice was quiet and close. She pulled her can away, tucking it back into its foam sleeve.

"You can't see where my eyes are behind these shades," Molly hissed, throwing the comment back to Savannah, but she didn't divert her gaze.

Savannah leaned closer. "Yes but your chest stopped moving so I needed to check you were still alive."

A braying laugh managed to escape Molly's mouth before she could clamp it shut. Whoever he was, was now standing in nothing but a pair of swim shorts, poised to jump in the pool. He hesitated and his eyes tracked the sound of her ridiculous laugh. He was staring right at her.

Her body temperature seemed to have shot up ten degrees. His stare was piercing, intense, and had her wishing she was already in the pool so she had an excuse to be closer to him.

"You getting in?" Will splashed his friend from below. The new guy leaped into the air, folded his body, tucked his legs against his chest, spun and landed in the pool with the precision of an Olympic diver.

Idly dragging a thumb against her bottom lip, she willed herself to look away from the boys play-wrestling in the pool. She'd never been attracted to any of her brother's friends before. From an early age, they'd set up ground rules, she wouldn't mess around with any of his friends, and he would afford her the same courtesy. With any luck this guy was only in town for the summer, maybe he could be her summer fling.

Something about him pulled her towards him. He was still staring, throwing heated looks her way when Will's attention was elsewhere. He somehow managed to suck the oxygen from the space, despite the fact they were outside.

"Lunch is ready!"

Molly didn't move at her mom's call. She was struck by an unusual barb of self-consciousness and didn't want whoever he was to see her body as she stood to put her shorts on. The boys got out of the pool, grabbed towels from the towel box, and dried off. New guy followed Will towards the house, pausing before he entered.

He cast her a wicked grin that had her girl parts reacting in ways they'd never reacted before. Body tingling from top to toe, she stood on shaking legs and pulled her shorts on. Her chest was tight, her mouth dry, and her head, light. Had she breathed at all in the last ten minutes?

She'd always been the one to ridicule all the lip biting, sighing, and furtive gazes she'd seen on TV or read about in books. That shit never happened in real life. Except her brother had just brought home the most delicious man she'd ever seen and she'd swooned so hard she'd stopped breathing.

Please let him be here just for summer.

Will's voice permeated the air as Molly and Savannah walked towards the house. "Mom, this is Finn. He moved in down the street about a month ago, we're going to be Pirates together in college."

Finn

(17 YEARS OLD - FOUR YEARS AGO)

"This watermelon salad is delicious, Mrs. Morrison. I don't even know what half of these ingredients are, but..." Finn shoveled another heaped forkful of what he'd hoped was watermelon salad into his mouth to stop his babbling and made a satisfied 'mmm' sound. With a little luck, a localized earthquake would strike right under his feet and suck him into the depths of the earth.

"It's cucumber, feta, red onion, mint, with olive oil and some balsamic vinegar." Will's sister was the one who answered. She hadn't met his eyes since she'd come into the house, her gaze had scorched him from the moment he'd arrived in the yard. Worse still, he'd been drawn to her, too. Her long, dark hair was tied high on her head, allowing the sharp edges of her high cheek bones, jaw, and nose to stand out on her pale skin. He couldn't see her eyes behind the shades, probably a blessing, if he had, he'd probably have come in Will's pool.

Finn had moved to town just over a month ago. Will had found him playing street hockey at the cul-de-sac at the end of their street and asked to join in, making small talk over Finn's

Snow Pirates shirt. Their brolationship had started almost right away. Turned out they were in the same class at school, and when they weren't in class together, they were playing hockey together.

One of the first things Will had said to Finn was that his little sister was off limits. At the time Finn had nodded his agreement. Younger sisters weren't cool, they were often clingy, needy and desperate to hang out with the cool kids. Finn had no plans to date his new bestie's little sister. Ew.

But what Will had neglected to mention, however, was she wasn't so 'little', and as Finn stood fighting every urge to reach out and stroke her collarbone, he realized he'd gotten it all wrong. She was most definitely the cool kid, he was desperate to hang out with her, and he'd already screwed himself over by giving his word he'd never touch her.

Mercifully, the girls didn't linger. They piled their plates high with food and went back outside. When the door swung closed behind her a sadness settled in his stomach. The excitement and electricity thrumming through the room left with her. He wanted to know everything there was to know about her. He wanted to make her laugh again, just so he could hear the obnoxious noise that delighted him the first time. She gave off an air of not giving a shit and he was here for it.

"That was Molly." Will scooped a mouthful of pasta salad into his mouth, chewed, and swallowed. "In case you couldn't tell."

Finn's mouth dried up, and the watermelon salad suddenly felt like grains of sand against his tongue. He swallowed hard. "She's your only sister, right?"

Please say no.

Will snorted. "Yeah. I couldn't handle another Molly. Let's take our plates outside."

He'd barely met the woman and her orbit was already dragging him into torment and temptation. Could he sit across the yard from her and eat lunch as though he didn't want to lose himself kissing her? "I..." Food lodged in his throat and he coughed. "I should probably go home."

Confusion tugged Will's brows together. "After we eat?"

Had Finn eaten something he was allergic to? His tongue was thick and heavy, and words seemed to evade him so he settled for a nod. Was this what love at first sight felt like? He shook his head. That was the thing of fairytales and Disney movies. Maybe he'd eaten too much watermelon salad and it was a case of indigestion.

"Which is it?"

"Huh?"

"You nodded, then shook your head. Going, or staying? I figured we could hang out in the pool for a while, maybe play some video games before practice."

"Sure." His traitorous legs dragged him out of the house behind Will, passing Molly and her friend on their way. He stumbled over his own feet – perhaps that was wishful thinking. Perhaps he'd tripped over the not-so-thin air that was hanging charged with secretive looks and an inability to stop looking at his friend's sister.

It was going to be a long summer.

Finn

(17 YEARS OLD – EIGHT WEEKS LATER)

The unmistakable crunch of bone on bone rang out in the field as Finn's curled up fist connected with his opponent's jaw. No one made Molly Morrison cry on his watch. Her mascara-smudged cheeks, red-rimmed, sad eyes, and quiet demeanor would be etched in his soul for as long as he lived.

Her new boyfriend had cheated on her after only a month of dating, with someone she knew from school. She'd walked into Chili's with her family for dinner and witnessed the two of them canoodling in a booth in the middle of the restaurant, not even attempting to hide their infidelity from public view. She hadn't stayed around.

Breaking up with him at full volume, spine straight, shoulders squared, she'd looked like a fierce goddess, shooting daggers from her ferocious, green eyes and spitting fire from her lips. Mrs. Morrison had sent Finn and Will after her while she placed a to-go order for dinner, and the striking gladiator deflated in front of his eyes when they caught up to her.

He wanted to swoop her into his arms and dry her tears, to tell her that asshole ex of hers didn't deserve her time. He wanted to press her against his chest, and tell her his heart beat only for her and his very being burned with need to keep her safe forever. But he couldn't. So instead, he was laying into one of his teammates under the guise of being like a big brother to her. Pretending he didn't want Will to sully his squeaky clean reputation, or get dragged into a fight he might not win, he'd thrown the first punch. With each swing he tried to convince himself it was the truth, but under it all, he was a goner for Molly Morrison and had no idea how the fuck he was going to handle it when she found herself a new man.

Pick up Two for Roughing click here. http://books2read.com/twoforroughing

To read meet cutes for the other couples in the Snow Pirates series for free click here (must subscribe to mailing list). https://dl.bookfunnel.com/gynl0v8x7p

CHAPTER 30
Molly

"Get him!"

"Hit him with the stick!"

"Kill him!"

Molly groaned into the fist she crammed into her mouth. "Fucking newbies."

"What was that? I couldn't make it out around those white knuckles you're gnawing on." Cleo's face contorted, probably in an attempt to school her face into a serious expression, but her body shook with silent giggles as she broke into a grin.

"Why doesn't he just clock him with the stick?" A group of male college students sat in the row in front of Molly and Cleo in the barn. Either the guys had taken a wrong turn on the way to the football field, or this was their first ever hockey game. From the looks of things, it might have even been their first time in public.

"Because that's assault." Molly didn't take her eyes off the play while she answered, but her voice sounded every bit as unamused as she felt.

Two of the men twisted in their seats to look at her, eyebrows raised.

"Hitting someone with a weapon? Assault. Intent to injure. Grievous bodily harm... Sure there's fighting in hockey, but they don't abandon the rule of law at the edge of the ice."

One of the guys nodded as if that made perfect sense. The Snow Pirates were ten minutes into the first period, and based on the commentary being chirped from the clueless, it was going to be a long game.

The newbies had shown up to the game without so much as a trace of Snow Pirates colors between them. One of them even dared to wear Cedar Rapids Racoon green. He either didn't know or flat out didn't care. If she didn't think it could be construed as wanting to get the man naked, she'd have demanded he remove the offending color until the game was over.

Sure, she was overreacting, every hockey fan had to start somewhere. Not everyone was born with an innate desire to watch a group of peak-performance athletes chase a three inch disk of rubber around a rink on ice skates. She should probably be kinder to those who got there eventually, even if they didn't know anything about anything and didn't give a shit who heard.

If she was being honest with herself her irritation was less to do with the guys in front of her not knowing their asses from their elbow when it came to hockey, and more to do with Finn O'Brien.

The 6ft 2 left winger crouched low in the face-off circle, still towering over his opponent. His delicious bubble butt pointed right at her. Desire coated her throat like thick honey on a spoon. She shook her head to clear the shameless thoughts.

She had no business lusting over her brother's best friend. There were lines that couldn't be crossed, and unfortunately for her, the man who held every ounce of her heart was so very, very offside. He was also the man who had promised her brother that he'd never lay a finger on her. Ever.

A finger wasn't all she wanted him to lay on her. She licked her lips.

What the hell was wrong with her? Okay, fine, it had been a couple days since she'd last gotten laid, but she'd sure as shit gotten off before she left for the game.

No matter how tired or busy she was she needed her game day O every bit as much as Finn needed to tape his stick with military precision... or Will needed his game day nap, or Austin and Seb needed their soccer kick about in the hall. It was her game day routine and game day routines weren't to be fucked with.

Maybe if she focused on Finn's opponent's ass instead, the flickering embers of need pulsing low in her belly would stop dragging her attention to Finn's butt, his thighs, or his broad shoulders. Slater Goodwin's smaller frame was less impressive, his backside, too. No matter how much she willed her eyes to stay focused on Slater's rump, it was as though Finn had magnets stuck to his butt cheeks and the corresponding magnets in her pupils couldn't fight the pull.

So what if his thighs were so thick he could probably crush a watermelon without breaking a sweat? Those thighs were not destined to be nestled between her own.

Fuck. She clenched her legs together, smacking her pen off her notebook with increasing aggression as the buzzer sounded noting an infraction on the ice.

What the hell had happened? She'd been so distracted by the idea of her legs curled around Finn's waist that she'd missed a call. She never missed calls. Shit.

"Tyler Lawson, two minutes for crosschecking."

Thank you, Mr. Announcer Man. Molly scribbled on her notebook as she watched the replay on the big screen. The

Raccoon in question did indeed crosscheck her brother against the boards.

One of the guys in the row in front elbowed the dude wearing Cedar Rapids green. "What the fuck is crosschecking?"

Green Dude shrugged. "Fuck if I know. Google it."

With an eye roll that almost sprained her retinas, Molly sighed. There was zero hope for this bunch. Crosschecking was the easiest of all the penalties to spot due to the distinctive shoving-with-the-stick action. She needed to speak up and help the poor beings before it all got too much for them.

She cleared her throat. "It's when a player uses the shaft of his stick to hit an opponent."

One of them smothered a snigger behind his hand, as the others turned to face her.

"Shaft?" It turned out that Green Dude not only had no clue about team colors, but he also had the sense of humor of a prepubescent boy.

Ignoring his bait, she nodded and jammed her pen into her ponytail. "The player holds his stick like this. One hand at the top, the other about halfway down, and does a pushing motion with it into the opposing player."

Five mouths hung open as the boys stared at her. She shook her head. "The dude in the penalty box hit the other dude with his stick. And that's no bueno, so he got sent to time out to think about what he's done."

Cleo vibrated next to her. "I think they get it."

Molly wasn't so sure. Her eyes followed the puck. Being nice to new people was one thing, missing a potential power play goal was an entirely different matter. Hockey was a turn-on-a-dime kind of sport. If you took your eye off the play for even a fraction of a second – or caught yourself daydreaming about a certain red-headed player's thighs wrapped around your body –you could come back to a different game altogether. The crowd went wild when the commentator announced the Minnesota power play.

"What's a power play?"

"Did we score?"

One of the men produced his phone from his pocket and pulled up Google, after a few clicks, he read aloud. "A power play is a situation in which a team has an advantage on the ice, while one or more players of the opposing team is serving a penalty."

"So they're all cheering 'cause we have one more dude on the ice than the other team for two minutes?"

Points for Green Dude. In his defense, he seemed as though he was genuinely interested in the game and trying to understand how it worked.

On the ice, defenseman Lincoln Scott sailed the puck to Finn, who grinned and passed it forward to Will. Her stomach flipped. This particular combination of players were proving to be unstoppable. Finn and Will had played together since they met as teenagers. They knew each other's strengths, weaknesses, and habits. Molly had always wanted to try blindfolding the pair to see if it made an impact on their game – she doubted it would. If Will was on the ice, Finn had a way of finding him.

From the moment they'd met, they'd all but imprinted on each other like some kind of fated bromance. She often joked they were like *parabatai* – warriors who fought together as lifelong partners, bound together by oath. Being hockey players and having roughed each other up playing street hockey as much as the two men had, they were probably bound together by blood as well.

She had no doubt they'd willingly lay down their lives for one another. She shook her head. While they didn't have matching rune tattoos or even understood the Shadowhunters reference, the guys were tight AF. Bros before hoes was a common phrase tossed about by guys, but bros before sisters was an even stricter moral code.

Will passed the puck to Finn, who sailed it back to Will. Molly leaned forward in her seat, a chill of anticipation running up her spine. She'd seen this play a thousand times before, and while Cedar Rapids had a solid wall of goaltender, the combined speed, agility, and sheer determination of Minnesota's top line was impressive.

"Glove side." Her announcement came a split second before Will shot the puck at the goalie's glove side and the netminder grabbed at it just a fraction too late. She grinned and wrote the goal in her notebook, taking great care not to write something about how delectable Finn's ass looked as he assisted.

"How'd you know?" Cleo shivered, rubbing her biceps with her palms.

It was her best friend's first hockey game and Molly couldn't help but smile. "It ain't my first rodeo."

Three heads turned to face her from the row in front. "Do you play?" Green Dude pursed his lips.

She snorted. "No. I write for the school paper. I just watch a lot of hockey. And number 82 is my brother. I know his playbook."

Green Dude's eyebrow arched and he nodded. "Wanna come down here..." He patted his thigh. "And help me learn the rules?" His eyes sparkled with mischief.

"Nice try, Green Dude. But you couldn't handle me." She picked up her soda, took a big slurp, and put it back on the floor next to her feet.

He flicked his gaze to his shirt and smirked. "Max. And don't be so quick to judge, Pretty Girl. We might be a match made in heaven."

"Oooh, Max. I judged you the second you wore Cedar Rapids green in my barn."

One of the other guys snickered.

"You're not my type."

"What is your type?"

Finn O'Brien.

Max's friend eyed her as though he was thinking about throwing his hat in the ring.

"Nope." She shook her head.

"Ouch. Want some ice for that burn, Hardy?" Random man no.3 rubbed his knuckles on his friend's scalp.

"You realize there's a game happening down there, right?" Molly pointed to the ice with a cursory glance at the five amigos. "We're actually a pretty good team."

"It's too fast. I can't keep up." Random man no.4's grumble was almost inaudible over the wave of boos rippling around the arena.

Molly was on her feet, flailing a hand at the ice. "Hey Ref! Maybe if you sucked a little less on the whistle, you'd blow it right!" She plopped onto her seat. "Fucking Iowa."

"Okay, Iowa's like the least offensive state in the continental United States. That doesn't work. Fucking Florida? That works. Fucking Alabama? Also acceptable. But Iowa? What has Iowa ever done to you other than give you beans and corn?" Max was quickly falling out of favor.

Molly narrowed her eyes. Cleo grabbed her hand and squeezed. "Murder is bad, Mol."

Another ripple of boos erupted around the rink as the Raccoons bagged a power play goal of their own. "Mother fuck."

"She knows it's only the first quarter, right?" Max spoke to Cleo but jerked a thumb in Molly's direction.

Molly rolled her lips between her teeth but still managed to speak before Cleo opened her mouth. "It's a period, not a quarter. And yes, I'm aware we're still in the first *period*, but this is dumb as shit."

One of the guys brayed out a laugh. Was he seriously laughing at the word *period*? She couldn't fathom a grown-ass man still snickering, but so many people cringed at the word *moist*, she supposed anything was possible.

Moist. Her absolute favorite word in the entire dictionary.

Used to describe that feeling between your thighs when you think about Finn fucking O'Brien.

She shook her head. But it did little to dislodge the thought since Finn threw his leg over the bench to take to the ice.

What I wouldn't give to have him throw his leg over—

"C'mon, Obi!" A fan screaming at Finn jolted her out of her lady boner stupor.

Finn hurtled toward the net on a breakaway. Molly scooted forward in her chair, holding her breath. For such a big dude, he moved on the ice with all the elegance and grace of a dancer – and when he'd had a few beers, he shook his money maker off the ice as well. She'd seen him dancing on the bar with his shirt off more times than she cared to remember.

Except the memories were burned into her mind. Finn. Shirtless. Her mouth dried up. Probably because every ounce of moisture in her body was rushing to pool between her thighs.

Fucking pay attention.

Finn lined up the shot, swung, and... clink. The bright chime of a puck hitting the crossbar sent a collective groan around the arena and her stomach to the floor.

It was going to be a long game.

❇

"Where's the goalie going?" The panic in Max's voice at the absence of a goaltender tugged Molly's lips into a grin despite the nail-biting status of the game.

"Why's he leaving the court?" The guy next to Max let out a gush of air as he elbowed his ribs.

"It's not a court." His arrogant, "are you a fucking dumbass?" tone made her giggle.

"I don't give a shit what it is. Where's he going?"

Four out of the five guys turned to face her. With a sigh she tracked the extra skater leaving the bench and making his way onto the ice. "Coach pulled the goalie so we can have an extra attacker on the ice. With only a couple minutes to go and the game tied, some coaches remove the goaltender from play, to try to get the W."

"But... surely..." Max's head turned between the action on the ice and Molly. "If one of the Raccoons gets the puck, a goal is a dead cert, right?"

She nodded. "Almost always. Especially at this level. Even from the opposite end of the ice. These guys could basically score from anywhere."

Max snickered. She ignored it.

"So why risk it?" Throughout the game, Max's questions had gotten progressively more intuitive. She'd even go so far as to say he was becoming a fan.

"There's no rule that says one of your six players must be a goalie. And when you want the win badly enough... sometimes it's worth the risk. Especially if your D-line is solid."

"And..." He squinted. "Stewart and..." He squinted again. "Morgan? They're both... solid?"

She nodded, gnawing on her lip. "Austin has already been drafted by the Wild. They're just waiting for him to finish out his senior year before he joins the team."

"Is that good?"

"Drafted by a major league team before you leave college is a pretty good thing, yeah."

Finn took a hit against the boards and crumpled onto the ice like an empty potato chip packet.

"Fuck!" Molly was on her feet, Cleo too. Molly's stomach clenched. "Get up, Finnegan. Get the fuck on your feet."

With a shake of his head, Finn lumbered to his feet, dusted himself off, and got back to the play.

"No, no, no! Don't let him have it." Max yelled at Will with some serious aggression. "I can't watch." He turned his head so his chin rested against his friend's shoulder, peeking over the fabric back to the ice. "And yet I can't not watch. Shit. Pretty Girl you're clearly a masochist. How do your nerves cope with this insanity?"

Despite the knots in her shoulders, Molly smiled. Her jaw ached from clenching as she urged Russell to pass the puck forward to Finn, or Will... hell, anyone in an ice-blue shirt would be great as long as it wasn't in their own zone. "Get. It. The. Fuck. Out!"

Cleo's fingers dug into Molly's forearm as the entire arena watched with bated breath. Russell collected the puck from just behind their blue line and passed to Austin, who cruised forward, sending it back to Russ. Molly's notebook was forgotten as she clutched Cleo's hand like it was game seven of the Stanley Cup playoff finals.

Russ passed to Will. Then Will to Finn. They advanced on the opposition like soldiers riding into battle. A skirmish at center ice almost lost control of the puck for the pirates, but Finn threw a last minute open-ice hip-check that made her knees weak and her eyes roll back in her head.

Nothing stoked her fire more than a well-executed, open ice hip check. If they weren't seconds from the end of the game and trying to send the Raccoons home with their tails between their legs, she'd have swooned right there in the stands... or hauled ass to the bathrooms to release a little pressure building up between her legs.

Finn sailed the puck to Will, who passed it to Johnny. She cringed as though she'd bitten into a lemon. Why did that asshole glory hunter have to be so damn good at hockey?

He circled behind the net, pausing as though he wasn't racing against the clock. Faking out the defender, he passed right instead of left, straight to the blade of Finn's stick. Finn one-timed it into the bottom corner of the net, the lamp lit, and a roar engulfed the arena.

The five guys in front of her double hi-fived and hugged each other. Max hopped over his seat, picked Molly up off her feet and spun her around. "You're the least patient teacher I've ever had, Pretty Girl. But I'm buying tickets and coming back next week." He put her back on firm ground.

She patted his chest. "Stalking's illegal in Minnesota, Max."

"It's for the protection of potential newbies. If I'm sitting here, I'm saving someone else from your ire. Not everyone could stomach your caustic wit and muttered threats of bodily harm and murder." He winked.

"See you next week, Pretty Girl, maybe I can convince you to come sit on Maximillian's lap while we watch the game together." With a wave, he jumped back over his seat and filtered out of the row behind his friends.

"That was... wow." Cleo remained in her seat, staring at the ice. "Does it always feel like this?"

"The adrenaline? Yeah, it's a doozy. Feels pretty good, right? Know what's good for post-game adrenaline?"

Her friend narrowed her eyes and pursed her lips. "What's that?"

Molly grinned. "Sex."

Continue reading Molly and Finn's story in book 3, Two for Roughing here.

To read meet cutes for the other couples in the Snow Pirates series for free click here (must subscribe to mailing list). https://dl.bookfunnel.com/gynl0v8x7p

Also by Lasairiona McMaster

Two for Interference - Minnesota Snow Pirates book 1

Freezing the Puck - Cedar Rapids Raccoons book 1

Two for Tacos - A Snow Pirates Novella

www.Lasairiona.com

Author Note

If this is the first book of mine you've read, you might need a lil heads up. I don't write the picture perfect daily lives of my heroed and heroines. I shamelessly write the warts-and-all, bumps-and-bruises kind of love: the farts, the giggles in bed, the deep-seated insecurities of imperfect people, and the societal taboos that are far more commonplace than we're led or allowed to believe.

As a parent, and someone who struggles to maintain a good relationship with her own family, Sabrina and Russell were another close-to-my-heart couple that resonated with me on various levels.

The juxtaposition of Russell and Sabrina drew me in. My stoic, strong, confident, decisive straight talker. The protector, the father, the introvert, with Sabrina, my empathetic, sincere, self-sacrificing sentimentalist. The helper, the friend, the martyr was something that intrigued me. The complexity of their characters mixing together in a relationship was certainly fun.

If I'm honest with myself, I wasn't sure what to expect from this couple at all. With Cleo and Linc for book one, I knew their dynamic, I knew how they gelled before I put pen to paper. But with Russ and Sabrina, I found myself adapting my outline and changing my notes more than once. They surprised me (and bossed me around) more than I was prepared for, but I was totally there for it.

In book one, Russell was the steadfast, smart, and wise best friend; I admit it tickled my sadistic author bone to watch him flounder in this book a bit until he found his way. I tried to make sure Russell's daughter Jude was an important character to the storyline, too. I read a review for another book, and the person said she disliked reading single parent tropes where the child is just trailed out every now and then when it worked as a plot device. When I really thought about it and what I wanted from this book, I felt the same way so I wanted to make sure that Sabrina, that all of us really, fell in love with Jude as much as we did with Russell.

For those of you who loved Gregg, the inspiration for his character came to me via TikTok. I know that elements of this book will instantly be dated by the mention of the TikTok dance and even the app itself, but when it came together in my brain, I loved it too much to care about pop culture references.

Gregg is based on the TikToker: @Gregisms. Greg's TikTok videos helped me get through lockdowns 1 through 4 by making me laugh till my stomach ached. If you haven't checked him out, you should. He's everything good in the world and I am here for it.

Up next is book three, Molly and Finn, in my first brother's best friend romance. I know so many of you are excited for Molly's story, and while part of me is a lil nervous about doing her justice, I am so freakin' excited about where her story is going.

Acknowledgments

Nothing great ever happens inside your comfort zone. I said that earlier in the Coronapocalypse and put it on a Post-It next to my face where I work. I say it to my friends every time they tell me they're struggling with something hard. It serves as a constant reminder to me to just do the scary thing.

But doing the scary thing is, well, scary. And I find that I often need a nudge, a kick, or an outright push off the ledge to do the thing I'm scared to do. And that's where my people come in.

With this book, I changed up my process. I needed eyes on it fast, so I could get it turned around in the window of time I had. So I used an alpha team.

Let me tell you, having four pairs of eyes reading your every word almost daily? Fuck that's nerve-wracking. My friend LeeAnn writes in real time, her team has access to her words as she writes and to be honest, that scares the crap out of me. With *Two for Holding*, I dropped a chapter at a time into a Google doc and let them read at their own pace. It was still pretty anxiety inducing.

That said, they helped me whip this book into shape in no time. So to my crack team of Alpha eyeballs, Savannah, Robynne, Erika and Sarah, for helping me with everything from developmental points and consistencies to typos. And for believing in me and encouraging me when I thought this was a steaming pile of shite? Thank you!! Suss wouldn't be what it is without your real-time feedback and for that, I think we **all** thank you.

To my amazing son, Lewis, thank you for forcing me to acknowledge when I work too much and need to step back. Thank you for telling me I need a day off, and thank you for asking me to spend it with you. Watching Marvel movies snuggled up in bed fighting for the M&M's in our popcorn is one of my very favorite things to do. I love you 3000.

Clare – Wifey dearest, there's not much new to say. With each book, my thanks bloom, the list of things to attribute to you grows, and your superpowers become clearer. There aren't enough thank yous to convey how grateful I am that you made fun of me in that bar in March 2020, but bloody hell am I ever glad you did.

Kate Farlow at Y'all That Graphic for this shamazeballs cover. Working with you is as easy as pie and I am forever grateful.

Tracie Delaney – You've become a kind of mentor over the past few months, a big sister I never had and it would be remiss of me not to mention you here. Thank you for your kindness and encouragement. Some days it's really gotten me through.

Lavanya Lakshminarayan – Thank you for your cultural insight, and for making sure I didn't start an accidental war with India for saying something stupid. I enjoyed my time in your country more than I thought I would and I'd love to return someday.

To my Beta readers Micky, Sharon, Heather and Corinne, my ARC readers, my reader group, friends, and everyone who has picked up Russ and Sabrina's story, a million thank yous. Without you, I wouldn't get to do the thing I love, every single day. And that's pretty fucking epic.

About the Author

Lasairiona McMaster writes sassy, classy and badassy women and strong, yet vulnerable men. She challenges reader's expectations by openly dealing with mental health issues, often exploring tough-to-handle topics and 'taboos' and books with a whole lotta heart.

She can either be found enjoying a gin and lemonade by the Irish sea, or baking sweet treats in her kitchen while singing at the top of her lungs. When she's 'home' in Texas, and isn't eating fresh-popped popcorn while buying things she has absolutely no need for in Target, she can be found at Chuys eating her body weight in chips and queso and washing it down with a margarita swirl. She loves to make friends out of strangers.

facebook.com/queenoffirelas
instagram.com/queenoffirelas

www.ingramcontent.com/pod-product-compliance
Lightning Source LLC
Chambersburg PA
CBHW020134130526
44590CB00039B/162